Mum,

Happy birthday.

with much love from

Jai

27. 8. 84

AMONG FRIENDS

AMONG FRIENDS

AN AUTOBIOGRAPHY

Alastair Dunnett

CENTURY PUBLISHING

LONDON

Cover photograph of the author
by Yerbury

Copyright © Alastair Dunnett, 1984

First published in Great Britain in 1984
by Century Publishing Co. Ltd,
Portland House,
12-13 Greek Street, London W1V 5LE

British Library Cataloguing in Publication Data
Dunnett, Alastair
Among friends.
1. Dunnett, Alastair   2. Journalists—
Scotland—Biography
I. Title
070'.92'4   PN5136.D8

ISBN 0 7126 0932 6

Typeset by Columns of Reading
Printed and bound in Great Britain
by Butler & Tanner Ltd, Frome, Somerset

Contents

CHAPTER ONE
Settlers' Effects

I should have been born in Denver, Colorado, for the adequate reason that my mother was there when I was due to arrive. But she got us all back to Scotland in time, and I was born in the genteel little burgh of Kilmacolm in Renfrewshire, a few miles inland from the Clyde river where the boat from New York had come in. It was a poverty-stricken arrival, on the day after Christmas 1908, the thin morning light being eked out by two candles stuck in empty bottles, since the electricity had been cut off, maybe because the bill had not been paid.

Long after, when I began to realise the story it was to perceive that the bleak events of the previous months had been a triumph won by my mother out of an onslaught of hardship. Earlier that year my parents had emigrated to America to make their fortunes. My father's elder brother Willie had gone there years before, married, and was about to set himself up in the hotel business in Denver, a boom town. He had the premises and the capital, it was said, and all he needed were the chef and bakery skills of my father and the housekeeping energies of my mother. We would be set for a great future in the land of opportunity. They had been married three years earlier. My brother George was already aged two. They sold their small possessions, and took emigrants' passages out of the Clyde. All my life I remember a large wooden crate in some corner of our homes, labelled 'Settlers' Effects'. Except for a small hamper of baby clothes and travelling gear, this was all they had. It was a steerage trip, of course, lasting many days at sea. When, at the age of eight, I sat with George one night in our kitchen in Yorkhill, Glasgow, and heard them both tell the story from start to finish, there were some elements which they still found hard even to recount. They took a three-day-long train journey to Denver, sitting on a hard bench with the little boy between them, while opposite were two large Lithuanians, drinking and snoring all the way, each with a leg stretched to rest on the outside of our parents' bench.

Whatever Denver turned out to be, it was not the end of the rainbow. Uncle Willie had been exaggerating. There was no hotel and little money apart from my parents' savings. Once the hotel got started, if ever, my father was intended to be the sole kitchen staff, and mother the

1

maid of all work. My father set out to find work, and got nothing more than occasional day jobs. He got addresses from employment offices, paying a dollar a time, and when he arrived to make his application, often found that there was no such address, nor tenant. Denver was a frontier town, and settlers were fair game to the earlier arrivals. He wrote for jobs, rarely getting an answer.

Neither was there any clan feeling about the household, which later they seemed to recall as a shiftless scene, waiting for something to turn up. In the midst of these sorrows my father declined in spirits and at length fell very seriously ill. Nursing him, my mother, ever buoyant in spirit, could not get him to overcome his despair. In the end she felt sure that if they stayed there he would die. She decided to take him back to Scotland, selling up some of their possessions, which, added to the rest of the savings, were enough to get them back on to that train and then the endless boat journey. I was nearly due, but she got everyone through the reverse trek. There was this meagre accommodation to let in Kilmacolm, and talk of a job in a local bakery. That was where they went. I just missed being born on Christmas Day. Late at night, the kind local doctor allowed himself to be summoned, in memorable dress clothes, from an important dinner party, Kilmacolm being the location of many large villas inhabited by the merchant princes of Glasgow. It was not time; my mother and I struggled all through the night. The doctor came back twice again, bringing me home late in the morning. My mother said, all the rest of her life, that I was a cheerful baby, grinning and chuckling perhaps far too soon, an excess which I have tried in vain to eradicate on and off during my own time.

My father was still an invalid. He ran through a series of extra ailments such as pleurisy and pneumonia, but his main affliction was that he had been injured in the Ibrox Disaster of 1901. At an international football match between Scotland and England at Ibrox, a wooden stand had collapsed, throwing layers of men forward so that those in the lower rows were crushed and killed. My father, being tall, had his head and shoulders clear, but could not breathe. The youth who had gone with him, Danny Mowat, later his brother-in-law, was thrown clear, and ran up and down to look for my father who shouted 'Danny' with his last gasp. Mowat seized him by the collar and dragged him out. He suffered from crushing of the heart valves, taking this impairment with him through a long life.

In the early days at Kilmacolm, in that almost empty room and kitchen tenement top flat, they had no goods or furnishings. It was then my mother decided, in cold-blooded courage, to borrow £40 from some relative, which she spent in buying a fine new bedroom suite. This was installed, and no questions answered. Apparently my father brightened up at once, working his way to recovery. Two years later they started to pay back the debt, somehow finding a golden sovereign a month, until they were debt free.

2

Mother took in a young man lodger, giving him bed and breakfast. Once I found the small penny notebook in which she had kept costings of the breakfasts, with entries like:

egg . . .	penny
bacon . . .	4d
brown loaf . . .	2d — and so on.

At that rate he was doing better than the rest of us. Later he asked her to cut out the bacon and egg, as it was proving too costly, so was on a par. She was old when she told me this, and had remained sorry for him all that time. When she died, my father once said to me, 'More than anything else, I wish you could have known her when things were really bad.'

There was suddenly a piece of good fortune. In the small bakery business in Kilmacolm there was a man employed called James Burnett. He had been an apprentice baker in Skinner's of Glasgow at the same time as my father, and they were close friends. As my father recovered, he came to him one day and said, 'Davy, I've spoken to Ewing [the bakery owner] and you can have my job. I'm going back to Banchory. There's a job there for me.'

He went away with little more said. There was no job waiting for him in Banchory. He found work in Dublin, but did at last go to his native Banchory, where he prospered exceedingly as a baker, owning several businesses, as well as becoming provost of Banchory for almost twenty years, with many other public appointments. He taught Sir Harry Lauder to fish for salmon and hosted him and many another celebrity in the great rivers of Aberdeenshire and Kincardine. The Burnetts were immense figures for all my young life, and although James would fend off expressions of gratitude, my parents remained convinced that he had left his job, with few prospects, because his friend David Dunnett had met so much misfortune. Perhaps also because Bel Dunnett had shown so much valour.

We stayed in Kilmacolm for less than a year, then moved for two years to Wick in Caithness, my father's native country. Dunnett is a territorial name native to Caithness, where a number of places are so named, including the majestic Dunnet Head, the most northerly point of the British mainland. An incidental oddity arises here, in that the Dunnetts, like the Smiths and the Beechams, have a notion to spell their names in different ways. Every now and again the argument breaks out in correspondence in the Caithness county paper, the *John o' Groat Journal*, which I once bought. I do not mean I just bought a copy of the journal, which had been amongst my first reading. I bought the paper itself, putting it into the Thomson stable of papers, and although it has changed hands again, it remains to me the most familiar and the most reliable. The Dunnetts carry this spelling feud to unique lengths, with unheated disagreements even in the same family; my father's spinster sister, Aunt Charlotte, spelt her name Dunnet, even on the brass nameplate on her door which was for a time close to the door on which we had Dunnett.

We came back to Glasgow about the time I was three years old, to remain there for all of my schooling and education and early working life. I have one or two flashes of memory about Caithness; one has me in a pony-trap going somewhere with my mother and friends. Another finds me playing on the floor of my Aunt Min's bedroom, and that enormous bulk of a woman leaning forward among her pillows and asking me to hand her the *People's Friend*, which had slipped to the floor. This was my first contact with the press.

When I learned to read, I was soon finishing every word of that paper, except some of the grown-up love stories. There was a fascinating small feature called 'Love Knots Untied', with readers' problems answered by The Wizard. These were mostly sad little dilemmas posed by young ladies who saw nice boys every morning at the tram stops, and wanted to know how they could get to know them without being forward or unladylike. The Wizard, doubtless ahead of his time, was up to such situations, if repetitive, with his 'Seek the friendly assistance of an older person . . .', or at times a dashing 'There can be no harm in an honest smile and a harmless remark, perhaps about the weather'. Things have moved on, to judge by the advice to sixteen-year-olds that today's 'Wizards' are handing out, but not, I notice, in the *People's Friend*.

My youthful memories seem pallid compared with the claims of Monty Mackenzie (Sir Compton), who lived until past the age of ninety, and used to tell me of remote recalls. As he grew older, he proffered reminiscences from farther and farther back, until it became usual for him to describe incidents that had happened before he reached the age of one. Competitors dropped out whenever the subject came up.

My first clear memory of my mother is of her winning the Married Ladies' race at some picnic in a crowded field. She was wearing a white blouse, a long black skirt, with a narrow-waisted black belt, and a huge picture hat. I was three. We were often at these picnics, travelling to the country by special train, the children with tin mugs hung round their necks by ribbon, and you got milk or tea, and sandwiches and cakes that weren't made by your mother. There was great cheering when she came skipping up the straight but I thought it was nothing out of the ordinary, since I knew she could do everything. Her prize was a sewing outfit in a yellow velvet case with embroidered flowers. This was such a treasure it was never used, but she would sometimes take it out and show it to me as a special treat.

Because I remember most of all some of the difficulties there were when she was old, it is pleasant to think back on her amazing agility. George came home once from school — he would have been about eight — claiming that a girl in his class, at playtime, had 'stotted' (bounced) a ball a hundred times. 'A hundred times!' mother exclaimed. 'That's nothing. Get me a ball!' We handed it over, and she stotted it two hundred times, which was more than I could count at the time. Of course there simply couldn't be anybody else's mother who could do this. Or who would even try.

Her great feat, however, was swinging the can full of water. We had this can, a receptacle of chipped blue enamel, which was used when we were sent for extra milk. When she was in the mood she could readily be persuaded to swing it round her head, half full of water, without spilling a drop. Then we would cry 'More water'. She would fill it three-quarters full, and swing away with centrifugal violence. The excitement was intense, as by this time the fevers of performance were in the air, and 'More still' we would demand. 'Make it full.' So, with the old jug brimming, she would set off again, while we watched the miracle. It is a sure winner with children, but if you try it, practise first, making sure that there is nothing in the way like children's heads, and testing that the handle won't come off. The main problem is the slowing down and bringing the receptacle to a stop. I can tell you, there were giantesses in those days.

But mother was small. She was a dancer of renown, and a truly wonderful singer. She sang and was recorded in Gaelic, Scots and English. She knew every Jacobite song, and so, still, do I. And all the others. Not long ago I went through my volume of Burns and counted that I knew the words and music of forty of his songs. She was able to remember old songs and music, most of which I think had never been written down. If there was nothing more than that, it was not a bad inheritance.

Neighbours looked on her as one who could cope, who could deal with troubles and horrors. We lived for a time on the ground floor of a tenement flat in Esmond Street in Glasgow. There was an uncultivated patch of grass before the front windows, surrounded by high spiked railings. One day when some of the older boys were playing on the pavement, the ball went into that patch, and a boy from up the road climbed to jump in to the grass. As he stood erect to jump his foot slipped, and falling forward he impaled himself with a spike through his leg half way above the knee. And he hung there screaming, with the blood spouting. My mother was out in a second. Ian Lang, one of the biggest boys, lifted him off the spike and let him fall to the grass. My mother, tiny thing as she was, got the boy over the railings, and carried him into our house. She stopped the blood flow until the doctor came and sewed the lad up, and later that night, when it was dark, my father carried him home in one of our blankets.

Her father, after whom I am called, was a master mariner from Loch Fyne called Alexander MacTavish. He had of course been christened in Gaelic, Alastair being the version of his first name. But to his chagrin, all his life his Clyde river friends had called him Sandy. There was to be no such familiarity with me. He was on his deathbed when they told him about my birth and that I was to be called after him. He sat up and spelled it out, demanding there should never be nicknames or shortened versions, however affectionate.

As a young boy, people often told me in Argyll, that sardonic place, that I seemed to be like my MacTavish grandfather in temperament and style. I should like to think so, although there was never very much to go on. He was of middle height, and he loved songs and ploys. For most of his life he was master of one of the Clyde Trustees' sludge boats, carrying cargoes of effluent down the river to be dumped in the open sea. On these trips he often took bands of riverside boys, larking about the clean decks, and — with great joy — getting ready for the moment when, after the dramatic discharge, he would sluice out his hold by some sleight of the giant valves and fill the ship with clean estuary water, into which they dived whooping.

My MacTavish grandmother was Christina MacNicol, daughter of a Minard man who raised a large family. On their birth certificates he is described as a fish curer, but he also ran a small fleet of cargo smacks plying to the far outer isles and the ports of the west coast. Returning from one of these trading voyages he tied up at Lochgilphead on the way up Loch Fyne to Minard, and paid the proceeds, £90 in gold, into the branch of the City of Glasgow bank where he had his account.

The manager — at that time he was called the agent — came in front of the counter to speak to him. 'Are you paying in or drawing out, Mr MacNicol,' he asked. 'I'm paying in, of course,' my great-grandfather told him. 'What for would I be drawing out at this time of year?'

They took the money. The bank did not open the next day, nor did any other of the City of Glasgow bank's offices. It was the greatest failure in the history of Scottish banking, and many thousands of people were ruined, including the MacNicols of Minard. Shortly afterwards my great-grandfather had a stroke, and took to his bed, where he took many years to die.

In his active days he was a fierce and bitter disciplinarian, devoted to the self-imposed Calvinistic doctrine which many of the Scottish Presbyterians imposed on themselves in the absence of royal or political leadership of their own. On Sunday mornings the small church in Minard had a two-hour service in Gaelic, followed immediately by a two-hour service in English. In the summer months my mother and her brothers and sisters sat in a row with him in the middle through the four hours. He would tie a penny in the corner of a handkerchief, and flick woundingly at the knees of any child who wriggled. My mother once told me how her younger brother Duncan was heard mildly whistling a tune on a Sunday. 'I'll thrash you for that tomorrow, boy', said his grandfather, Sunday being too sacred a day for this essential office. At five o'clock the next morning the old man rose, dragged the boy from his bed, and thrashed him unpityingly. I never met Uncle Duncan. He went to South Africa before he was eighteen, and never came back. He used to write long letters to me, sending books like *Jock of the Bushveldt* and *The Outspan*, and pieces of gold quartz.

6

Apart from spending the summer months in the MacNicol home in Minard, which I was to do in my turn, the MacTavishes grew up in Glasgow. When she left school my mother trained as a dressmaker. But her great outlet was the church of Finnieston, where she sang in the choir and taught Sunday school. When the Fisk Jubilee singers from Nashville came to Glasgow on their world tours, there was a wave of fan worship for negro spirituals, my mother becoming part of a quartet which toured the other churches and working men's homes, and other captive audiences. So we were brought up knowing all the spirituals from Louden's original edition, not only such well-worn items as 'Steal Away' and 'Coming for to Carry Me Home', but more advanced items like 'Bright Sparkles in the Churchyard' and 'Turn Back Pharaoh's Army'. In due course she was elected president of the Young Women's Christian Association branch in the church, where in the way of official business she met the president of the Young Men's Christian Association, whose name was David Sinclair Dunnett.

Our eventual father had come to Finnieston Church by a long detour from Caithness. He was the son of a farm labourer who had been condemned to such work by his wealthy and revengeful father-in-law. Sinclair Laird farmed the whole of the beautiful island of Stroma in the Pentland Firth, and there my grandmother grew up in comfort, being taught her lessons by a tutor, imported from the mainland. George Dunnett, originally a fisherman, arrived to work on the farm. My grandmother was eighteen, and George Dunnett more than twice her age, when they married. Unless there is an unnoticed error of the registrar, the records show that their first child was born hardly two months after the wedding, which must have been a shotgun ceremony, otherwise Sinclair Laird would never have allowed it. The most he ever did for them was to grant his son-in-law a humble job on his farms. When the Crofters' Acts were passed in the 1880s, Sinclair Laird was bought out of Stroma and came to Canisbay and West Canisbay farms on the mainland, near the Castle of Mey, and there the couple brought up a large family, of which my father was the Benjamin. He was so much younger than most of the rest that he had three sisters married with families before he was born. So that we of the next generation were brought up knowing a number of elderly women, older than our parents, who were our full cousins. It was thought too familiar to call these matrons by their Christian names, so they became Cousin Nellie, Cousin Meg and Cousin Bel. But this was a long way ahead.

My father's parents made several attempts to break away and possibly better themselves. For some years they kept one of the toll-houses on the outskirts of Wick. My father once told me of the swell of anger he used to feel to see his mother run to open the gate for some gentleman to come riding through, and how she would have to scrabble in the mud for the penny he would throw down, being too important to hand it to her. He was working in a grocery store by the time he was twelve, schooling over. But he remembered the silent joy with which he would sit with his father, fishing from the slabby rocks of the Caithness coast. It was one of my old aunts who told me that her father, old by now, got stuck when climbing one of these terrible sea cliffs, and how the boy had worked him up to the top, handhold by handhold, foothold by foothold. My father never mentioned this incident to me, but he often said that, to the end of his life, his nightmares were always of being rigid, unable to move, on a cliff face sloping inwards with the sea boiling below.

When he was fifteen they decided to emigrate to Glasgow, where my father might have a chance of entering a trade, and where some of the family were already working. In a few months he had become the main breadwinner in the family, serving a long underpaid apprenticeship as a baker, at which he seemed to become adept. Later he qualified as a confectioner, decorating cakes. He was to make his own wedding cake. He then advanced to the status of a junior chef, serving for several summers in one of the great hotels in Oban, at times when the whole bay would be crowded with steam yachts, white ships with yellow funnels and large crews of paid hands who walked the beach road wearing new jerseys with the yacht's name embroidered in red. The head chef was a muscular Swiss who taught him to swim and dive with style. In the winter he worked most nights at debating classes, advanced bakery courses, and the intensive reading of books which he had missed in his early boyhood. After he died I found the notebook where he had listed the title and author of every book he ever read since the age of fourteen. No observations were added, but he could remember them all, and he bought many of them. In that list, in due course, I was moved to see listed two or three books of my own.

The injury he got in the Ibrox disaster began to force him to look outside the intense long night work of baking. It was probably this search for more air that made him decide to take the family to America. For years after that failure and the humiliating homecoming he may have been burdened with a sense of inadequacy. Months after they came home, when he was still poorly, there followed and found him a letter posted some time back in America. He had answered an advertisement from a man describing himself as a writer, who sought a literary and social personal secretary to organise his household and his research. The headquarters was a ranch in the farther west country, with a separate house, horses and school near by and an enchanting new life of wind and sun. My father must have composed and sent his letter of application with an eager poetic spirit, for the writer's reply was a firm offer of a job and a request to advise him at once when he could be there and start. It was too late. He had given up America, and his spirit was laid low. He could not bear even to keep the letter. He laid it in the flames of the small fire in the Kilmacolm kitchen and watched it burn to ashes. The writer's name was Zane Grey.

By the time I was getting to know my father he had put aside any continuance of that old bitterness, and he bought all the Zane Grey books as they came out, so that my first full-length books were such titles as *Riders of the Purple Sage, The Light of Western Stars, The Lone Star Ranger* and many another. The first editions of the Neil Munro novels were already at home too; and I well remember the day when my father read out to us the very first Para Handy story from the *Glasgow Evening News,* of which Munro was editor. He had written the story as a filler for the Saturday paper, whose earlier editions few people bought, as the West of Scotland preferred to wait for the final edition with all the football results and reports. I must have been about eight when my father took me through the shelves of his bookcases, finding out how many of the books I had read already, and mildly telling me about some of the ones I should tackle soon. I had read half of Dickens before I was ten. When we got Sunday school or day school prizes the authorities asked us to nominate the books we wanted, and we would hand in requests some distance removed from boys' adventure stories.

By this time my father was well restored. There had been that two-year interval in Wick, where he had gone to take up an insurance agency which had fallen vacant. He set to, with passion, to sell insurance to his cool fellow northerners, fighting back his own diffidence. Once he sold a life policy to a man who at the time was sitting on a WC. Also, the evenings were taken with engaging in the brisk debating competitions between clubs which ran all round that county, and he apparently found few able to take him on. He became a telling public speaker, one of the best extempore speakers, perhaps *the* best, that I have ever heard. He had the great gift of picking up cues from previous speakers, rising to the occasion, as when he more than once spoke to gatherings in such places as the Mansion House in London. He had also a fast wit, not always kindly. I remember a night in our kitchen — I could not have been older than six — when George, my older brother, and I were both trying to get my father's attention. George was declaiming a poem which he had learned by heart, and I was hoping to get a word of praise for some animal I had modelled in plasticine. My father at last said to George: 'Will you shut up for a minute, Henry Irving, and give Michael Angelo a chance.'

Most of my remembered childhood ran with the years of World War I. We were in Glasgow by then, my young sister Doris not yet born, and George and I at Overnewton Public School. That was its full name, and more than one ex-pupil, being interviewed for jobs in the City of London, declared this seat of learning when asked where he had been educated. 'Damn good school', one southern interviewer said, believing that public schools everywhere were up to his own meaning of the word. It was what must be called a working-class school. In the summer months more than half of the boys came to school barefoot. We begged vainly to make my mother allow us the privilege, but she always refused, and it was years before I realised the pride that had made her refuse. We were badly off, but in the matter of food and shelter I do not remember any sense of hardship.

Our street, which had no through traffic, was full of boys, the pavements were firm and only mildly hilly, and it was an ideal nursery-ground for the manipulation of the tennis-ball sized object with which we played football. I became perhaps one of the experts in this game; at least when I got to the socially much superior school, Hillhead, there were always about half a dozen of us who had come from similar nursery slopes, and in the huge playgrounds, concreted and even, we could play and win against the rest of the class, hulking clumsy fellows, as it seemed, who had no footwork at all.

We played card games and board games at home in the winter evenings, and practised standing long jumps, my father competing, on the kitchen floor. And once in a while, when the daft mood took him, my father would suddenly inaugurate what he called 'the hot five minutes' which consisted of the three males throwing a ball also on the kitchen floor and kicking it wildly in all directions. Occasionally, while my mother cowered in the lobby, we knocked a dish off the shelves, but the main victim was generally the gas mantle, which would douse from its brilliance to a blue flame as the shreds fell to the floor, whereupon we would suspend the workout for the night while my father went through the fascinating ritual of installing a new one.

My father's health forbade his calling-up, but for all the time of World War I he served in the Volunteers, the contemporary Home Guard. He turned out to be a crack shot, and found himself a musketry instructor, even called in to help with the training of the regular army. Perhaps because his confectionery craft had made him nimble-fingered, he was unbeatable in the assembly and dismantling of the sectional Hotchkiss machine gun. He used to practise for hours with it on that suffering kitchen floor, with my mother timing him in seconds with the gold watch which she had saved up to give him.

There was also the nightly ceremony of what he called 'rowing' up the clock, consisting of pulling up by their chains the weights of the ancient treasured wag-at-the-wa' clock which thundered its pendulum in the same kitchen, the common room for all of us. This would be followed by the winding up of the gold watch, and it all signalled bedtime for the boys. He marked the seasons invariably by the annual observation, shortly after the start of January, that 'the days are stretching out'. The verb changed for the other solstice, when not later than the end of July we would hear, 'the nights are creeping in'.

It would be easy and perhaps also entertaining to follow the familiar nostalgic pattern in describing the happy carefree days of boyhood. They weren't so, and they were to mark brother George and me for long. A terrible thread of ambition, and a dark one of fear of ill fortune, pervaded our house until I was into my teens. It took George and me many years even to understand this, and he never recovered from it.

A fierce discipline was the keynote of all that happened, running for me from the age of about four or five. It came to be assumed that we must bear with us at all times the necessity 'to do well at school' so that

10

'we would get on'. After a year or two into my scholastic career I was already getting home lessons, with the requirement to memorise passages of poetry and the Bible, and to do sums for correction by the teacher the next day. One or other of my parents 'hearkened' us (listened to) the literary exercises, and clouted us savagely if we went wrong. There was also such an accountancy device as Bills of Parcels, where we were supposed, I think, to be grocers' assistants, and make up the sum required for payment for a number of items. When these sums were finished and checked, with wrath doled out as thought proper, my father would set us a new series of problems, with longer verses to learn by heart, while his Bills of Parcels were perfectly fiendish, with such warehousing predicaments as:

500 ounces of apples @ 1/6d a stone . . .
17 feet 4½ inches of rope at 1/11½d a perch . . .
A gallon jar of paraffin, one-third full, @ 1½d for 1/3 pint . . .

and so on into other endless horrors. I used to sit in my corner, suddenly blinded by the tears of my inadequacy, while my father — the most adept deployer of sarcasm I ever encountered, with my mother a close second — would move about the kitchen voicing such a commentary as: 'Well, indeed, this is a happy home tonight. What a pleasure it is for the likes of me to come home to this bright fireside after a hard day's work . . .'

But there were other and darker occasions. Both parents hammered and pounded us frequently with hands and fists and belts. This never seemed to be for grave sins like cheek or disobedience. It was unknown for us to attempt such defiance. We were punished for mistakes and accidents. Looking back on those distant episodes of torture, I realised how so much of my young life was spent in a mental posture of timidity and fear. I had a double dose of all this, it seemed, for George, who suffered no less than I did, would occasionally turn upon me and pummel me by way of personal relief. He was once engaged in this in the street, and I was clinging crouched to the railings of the new Sick Children's Hospital, yelling, when the attack all at once eased. My father, arriving home from work, had caught him at it, and pounced, knocking and punching him all over the pavement. He knocked me as well away from the railings with a blow on the head. '*You* must have been doing something', he judged.

Doris was spared most of these assaults, which had largely ceased, as they did suddenly, by the time she was of the age when we had been reckoned as able to benefit by the treatment. It was she, long after, indeed after George had died, who explained placidly what had induced this spirit of revenge for small sins. It was the absolute necessity for us to escape, by toil and application, from the set-backs of life. My father and mother had seen and remembered the worst of it, and any means by which they could persuade their family to secure goals simply had to

11

be taken. I think I know now something of the motives that forced us all into this fearsome chapter. It was years before I set to and rid myself of the terrors of these times, and came to terms with a life that could be challenged in some other way. George never recovered from it. He qualified handsomely, setting aside long years of illness, while at university he made a notable breakthrough into a full understanding of mathematics and numeracy — his despair previously — and went on to become an economist and one of the first international civil servants.

There were holidays. We took a small house for a month or two every year in Cove on the Firth of Clyde. I have often found myself lying reminiscently about the happy days at Cove in those summers. They, too, were clouded by disciplines and expectations. My father went to work every morning by one of the innumerable steamers which raced each other to the countless piers up and down the waterside suburbs of Glasgow. After the evening meal we would set off for the jetty below Inverclyde, where we would be forced to jump off and into the water, however high the billows. Neither of we boys could swim, but we had to thrash out with my father's hand under our chins. He would remove the hand suddenly and we would at once sink into head-high water to his repeated anger.

A jealous God was worshipped in our household. The family connections ran deep into the Scottish Church, requiring undemanding obedience to the rules and the utter acceptance of the word of God. We had family worship every Sunday night, after we had been to a morning service and an evening service, with Sunday school for the children in the afternoon. We sang a hymn or a psalm or two, read a chapter, verse about, round the circle, and knelt to pray, my father speaking to the Lord with wary hope, after which we would all join in the Lord's Prayer. I was taught the Lord's Prayer by the wife of Danny Mowat the hero of the Ibrox disaster, for they lived above our flat in Esmond Street, and they had no children. Danny's brother had married my father's sister, Aunt Georgie.

Part of the macabre accompaniment of the religious scene was our required attendance at funerals. Not only the ceremony, but the ghastly view of the corpse. Before I was nine I had seen several of the dead, in particular my father's mother, and then old Auntie. We would gather round the coffin in the parlour, where the lid was laid aside. A service was held by the minister, who would repeat it all soon at the cemetery. Then the nearest relatives would kiss the corpse farewell, and retire weeping to a corner, when the undertaker's men came forward and screwed down the lid. We boys took turn about of going on to the cemetery, for this involved a spectacular perk, the ride in one of the horse cabs which followed the hearse. In our best suits we would join in the slow route through half of Glasgow, with men raising their hats and women inclining the head, and making us feel important although not stricken with grief. My cousin George Mowat and I drew the chance to make the trip to the cemetery with Granny Dunnett, and he was, as ever, a congenial companion.

Old Auntie I had known all my life. Towards the end she was taken in to live and be looked after by my Granny MacTavish (whom we called wee Granny, the other one, my father's mother, being big Granny) because she had no near people of her own. They were cousins. At the age of nine, Auntie had gathered with a crowd of mainly older girls in the square at Lochgilphead in the hope of being selected to go and work in the Paisley mills. Knowing that the foreman would pick out the biggest and strongest-looking girls, Auntie brought up a flat stone from the shore and stood on it. She was picked, and shipped to Paisley, not seeing her people again for four years, although some of her seafaring uncles sometimes sought her out on their home voyages to the Clyde. She came home in her late teens, married a fisherman called McEwan and bore him a son. The husband was drowned before she was twenty-one, and she was a widow for sixty-seven years. Most of that time she worked, but she was frail at last. She used to take me for short walks to the fruit shop at the corner of Argyle Street and Church Street, where we bought a few strawberries in the season. On one of these walks — I must have been five, for I could just read — we passed a blind beggar man to whom she gave a ha'penny. He wore a card saying 'Blind from Birth' and I remember my pity and wonder that he had been blind for all of my life. All the things I had ever seen and could remember, and he had been blind all that time!

Great numbers of friends were always visiting us, and even staying. Somehow they all got tucked away into the houses we lived in, however tiny these seem to look back on. At that time people just dropped in. There was no phone call in advance to see if it was suitable. None of us had a telephone. They came and sat round talking, and then tea was made, with sometimes two kinds of scones and two kinds of jam, and even at times a cake or two. The talk was fast and witty. We children were never expected to say anything, nor did we, but we learned a lot about conversation and the world.

It is essential for someone who became a newspaper man from modest beginnings, to say that he started off by delivering newspapers. I have not that claim. It was milk that I delivered. Starting at eight years old, for two years I rose each morning except Sundays at half-past five, reported at six o'clock, along with George, to the St George's Co-operative Society's dairy in Dumbarton Road, and along with about sixteen other boys set off on my rounds, or 'rake'. We had a fixed round of customers, and in preparation for the servicing of these customers, we delivery boys, the night before, prepared a list of their names and addresses on a length of paper, half cut into strips. These were stuck on the lids of the hand milk cans by simple adhesion with the plentifully spilled contents, and we went off into the winter darkness. The cans were of tin, lidded and with long looping wire handles. Knocking at the doors, we became often the morning alarm systems, and in time there would come a padding as the woman of the household, immense in long nightgown and bare feet, would slap across the linoleum of the lobby, open the door, thrust out a huge hand and retire, as the milk was poured from the can into the jug which would be standing ready in the kitchen, probably on top of the coal bunker. Then the great feet would come back, the door would be opened, and the empty can would be thrust out. No words passed as a rule, but my mother insisted that we must say 'Thank you' on each occasion. Sometimes in the summer, or at Easter, we would be given a penny; once I was given threepence, and I spent it on the way home in another dairy, to buy a giant slab of chocolate for my mother — knowing, I suppose, that I should get my share in time.

It was bad in the winters, though, for the cold was fierce and the wire handles were bitter to grasp. The stairways of the tenements were ill-lit and often the doors had no names on them, so it was frequently the case that we knocked up the wrong house only to be hounded down the stone stairs in the terror of having to try again. Once I finished my rake and came back cockily early to the dairy, only to be handed another boy's rake to deliver, for he had not turned up for duty. Nor had he handed in the grubby strips of paper identifying his customers. The woman supervisor had done this in a cursory way, and in a grown-up hand which I could scarcely read. I toiled for a long time round closes and alleyways getting rid of three of my cans of milk, but got stuck at last. George, coming round a corner blithely with his empty cans, found me crying under a gas lamp-post. I told him my troubles, and as he was to do so often, with an ill grace but inevitably coping, he thrust his empty cans on me and snatched my remaining ones, setting off into the dreary dawn to deliver them himself.

I have an unusual souvenir of these early ventures into working practices. For our six-day morning week we got paid two shillings a week. My parents decided that I should learn to save, so a sixpence was set aside each week for the purchase of a War Savings stamp. After thirty-one prudent weeks of this I was able to buy a whole War Savings Certificate, the precursor of the National Savings Certificates. I still have two of these dated from 1917 or so. They are never to be cashed in my time.

I was fairly happy at Overnewton School, which still stands, and it is touching somehow to pass it now, and see the playground where we mustered to be drilled through the doors and up the stairs to the classroom. I occasionally sat at the top of the class, along with Jimmy MacKenzie, who became a power in the carpet industry, still a close friend, who lived nearby in Blantyre Street. There were some lively cards in that class, which hung together for years between the ages of four to nine. One particular name which springs to mind is that of George MacTurk. We joined school on the same day and I was able to tell my mother when I got home that I had not cried, but he had. He

14

became one of the most adept at the football games in the playground. A spirited lad, he never knew manhood. At the age of twelve, climbing along the glass roof of the Partick Cross Subway Station, he fell through it and was killed on the line. One or two of the boys 'got into trouble'. One stole a pick from a road repair site, and broke for some reason into a tenement stair WC, where an older boy was engaged on his legitimate business. Another boy, often at the top of the class with us, was birched for some later offence. Others were sent to the training ship, a hulk of correction which used to sit at anchor on the Clyde as a sort of floating Borstal. Such things were talked of in our home in hushed voices, but I had reservations about this exile as a form of punishment, for it was well known that these bad boys had football teams with real jerseys, and could play music in bands, as well as learn to row and sail boats, privileges which were deferred for many years for the conformists. There were ways also for the girls to get into trouble. It was a great grief to me to learn, some time after I had left Overnewton, that the beautiful girl who was the star of our class, with golden hair and blue eyes, had borne a babe to some fellow who was clearly far too good for her, but obviously luckier than the rest of us.

I have lost sight of most of the boys with whom I played then. But I remember all their names. One stands out as a junior Bob Hope, a child of the same age as me, called Jackie Graham, who purveyed a unique and sardonic series of funny stories which he may well have invented, for the like never came from anyone else. They remain in my mind as classics; and more than that, because he may have been one of the geniuses who invent the great jokes. Ever after I have heard, on great occasions, at banquets, the House of Commons, receptions in Washington and elsewhere, stories told with éclat which I swear I first experienced springing new-made from the inventive mind of Jackie Graham.

It was about this time that I remember the onset of the mild (I suppose) migraine which has been with me ever since. I should not have been surprised. My mother had frequent bouts of headache, and the time came when George suffered acutely from this curse, to the extent that he had to quit school for a year and go to the country, to Minard. Even at the age of eight I often dared to have the feeling that certain food was causing my ailment. Food was an ordeal anyway in our home. My mother was one of those who believed that if a male ate his dinner heartily he would be all right, so that we boys had to finish everything that was served up; or if it was impossible, it was put before us at the next meal. This was the thing that wrecked my digestion. One of the greatest blessings I enjoy now is to be able to stop eating as soon as I want to.

I see that into the modern theories there has lately crept the speculation that some causes of migraine may arise out of certain foodstuffs. I could have told them that sixty-five years ago. There was one after-dinner dish which I came to christen 'sore-head pudding' and

15

forced my way through this dish while the inevitable blinder came on. My mother thought this was hilarious. Headaches, it seemed to her, were for grown-ups, and my resistance could only be attributed to some form of childish defiance.

My sister Doris was born in 1916. She and I were to be very close for all the years until she died, having had a life of sore misfortune but always a heart above her troubles. When she was a baby we boys used to take her out in her pram and race her up and down the safe pavements of our neighbourhood. We lived next to the Yorkhill Barracks, crammed with young soldiers in training, and many of these young men would make much of her, cut off as they were from their own families and about to be sent into the war. The front, we called it. There was a pipe band at this barracks, and it was from them in the middle of World War I that I heard, insistently and every day, the now famous tune 'Scotland the Brave' to which Cliff Hanley, a brilliant member of the *Daily Record* team in the days of my editorship, was to put words nearly forty years later.

All this time my father, now well so far as we could see, was pursuing his dogged task of learning and studying. As well as the demanding role he had undertaken in the provision of spare-time classes for students of the bakery trade in the Glasgow Royal Technical College — now the University of Strathclyde — he enrolled incessantly in evening classes, and having left school at the age of twelve, he attended extra classes until he was well over sixty. He took them all — languages, philosophy, archaeology, history, everything. In church he used to follow the read lessons from a French bible. One of the last classes he took was one in logic, a source of much amusement to my mother, who, when they disagreed, used to repeat his assertions and query, 'Is that what you call logic?'

My mother died suddenly in his presence, at the age of seventy-six. He went two years later, lingering for a long time and nursed patiently without complaint by Doris. Near the end, I sat one day at his bed and said to him, 'How is it with you?'

He told me, 'I'll really be quite glad to go, Alastair. With your mother away, there is not much for me here now, a sick man and old. I have done nearly everything I ever thought I would manage to do. I got the church out of debt and I think it will stay that way for a while. I have seen you two boys make your way in the world. I have been very lucky in my family and friends.'

In his later years I got to know him better than I ever thought I would. I should like to have been closer to him. The fears and harshness of the early days could not easily be taken away. People talk often and lightly of youthful disciplines. I think they lie. I have never been able to forget much of that time. Only once have I had a chance to say something about my father in public, when I had to answer for the honorary graduates, including myself, at a ceremony in the University of Strathclyde, where his mighty extra-mural work had been done. I told them:

16

... As one whose entire schooling was started and finished in Glasgow I have some knowledge of the old Tech's place in this neighbourhood, and the door it opened on the wide world of opportunity. While rejoicing with you in the new and splendid prowess of the University of Strathclyde, in which it may be I can now claim some involvement, or even responsibility, I find myself deeply drawn to the thought of all these generations of men — men from nowhere — who came to this place over the years, to pitch themselves, with no backing but that of talent, among the forces of purpose and precision in the new world that was forming, and to do it mostly at the end of the day's work.

I think now particularly of one of these men, born a hundred years ago on the shores of the Pentland Firth, who because of a family disaster had to leave school at the age of twelve and go out to earn his living. Two or three years later, in his early teens, he came to Glasgow and was apprenticed to a baker, qualifying in the departments here in an extra-mural way. Many developments came to him professionally, but his great contribution was to take a lead in the setting up and running, for nearly fifty years, of a voluntary association of bakery students who used to meet here nearly every Saturday night — their only free night of the week — pay a small fee and see and hear demonstrations by master craftsmen. Not only demonstrators from this country, although there are no higher bakery standards, but by confectioners of genius from Rome, Paris, Vienna, and further afield. Hundreds of these young part-time students used to cram each week into the old Tech bakeries, paying for it, finding the time . . . And I hope it still goes on, or something like it.

This man had two sons, and because times were hard it was possible to send the elder son to the university, but not the second one, who went out and took a distasteful job somewhere. But things improved, and one day the man said to the second son, who was twenty then, 'I have been looking at the budget, and I can see a way of getting you to the university too.' And I — because he was my father and I was the second son — I never thought as much of him as I did then. But I said, 'Well, thank you, but no. I can see the way ahead.' And indeed, I felt I could — but not as far as this.

It may be reckoned perhaps one of the minor glories of our education, and of our expectations too, that such a story should be commonplace.

CHAPTER TWO
It's an Education

I can never get away from the fact that it was newspapers that shaped me and made me what I am, whatever that is. I was forty years in the trade, and ten years before that hack writing and trying to get in. After I made it I suppose I had a run of unusually good fortune, but it meant that for the most part I was in the forefront of decision-taking, which is where the responsibility rests. Yet, looking back, especially to my earlier years, there were other influences that had a part in the formation. I have gone through life burdened with the preoccupation of what I was given by church and school; and in another degree, however ill it fits into this group, sport.

We were a church family. From the youngest ages we walked every Sunday more than a mile to the church, George and I in front and my parents behind, with my father carrying our infant sister, Doris, until she was able to make the distance. George and I had to hold hands in the earliest years, a procedure we disliked for we were in a state of permanent hostility; and every time the hymn 'Jesus Loves above all Others' was announced, George and I standing in our pew would grin at each other when we came to the line, 'His is love beyond a brother's'. We went three times to the church every Sunday for the morning and then the evening service as well as Sunday school in the middle of the day. For Sunday school we had to learn a verse of the Bible, a verse of a psalm, a question and answer from the Shorter Catechism, and to read the chapter of the Bible from which the Sunday school lesson was to come. To ensure that the Lord would not be affronted by us, my father used to hear our lessons before we set out and he used also to grill us about the content of the Bible chapter.

We belonged to an Evangelical Church, Finnieston United Free at Kelvingrove, which in 1929 joined the Church of Scotland, although my mother swithered for a long time as to the desirability of her joining some branch of the United Free Continuing. Our church had sent out many missionaries to the foreign fields, as we always called them, and they came home looking very prosperous for a furlough of six months or so and went round ours and other churches, and the Bible classes and Sunday schools, telling how the work of God was prospering in their parts. In the Sunday school we used to collect our pennies (ha'pennies really) for such notables as Dr and Mrs Mayhew of Darjeeling, Miss Jeannie Anderson of the China Inland Mission, Dr Laws of Livingstonia, Mr and Mrs Angus Ross of Calabar. The Rosses were remote cousins of mine and Miss Jeannie Anderson was a childhood friend of my mother and a courtesy aunt. She used to come often to our house, bringing presents of Bible texts which we hung up on the wall. She was good fun and once brought me a model of a Chinese porter's barrow where a passenger could sit beside the wheel. When I was about seven she told me, 'Alastair, when you're a grown-up man you'll laugh at this.' And she sketched out the characters. 'The word for "peace" in Chinese is a woman under a roof; the word for "strife" or "war" is two women under a roof.'

These missionaries never came on leave or holiday, but always on furlough, a word probably selected to denote that good works were still afoot. I remember an elderly spinster who talked to us about her work in darkest Africa, saying, '. . . and oh, dear boys and girls, the boys and girls in our village are just like you — full of laughter, full of fun — but, oh, full of sin!'

Our church was a large cavernous place where the minister for many years in earlier times had been the hymn writer Dr Andrew Bonar, a memorable name which I purloined later to foist on Cliff Hanley as one of his pseudonyms in the *Daily Record*. The services were of a routine character, sometimes comforting in their mere repetitiveness. At some point we always repeated the Lord's Prayer all together and as boys it was a common ploy for us to stop our loud responses to listen to the continuing feud between the 'debtors' and the 'trespassers'. We were a 'debtors' church for the most part, but there was a dogged minority of 'trespassers' who always stole the show when they came to the line 'As we forgive those that trespass against us'. The sibilance of the second part of the line, spoken through ill-fitting false teeth, lingered as susurrant echoes for many seconds in the vaults of the roof. We seemed to be enterprising, however, in the many unusual characters we attracted to our midst, particularly the performers. I never quite recovered in my meagre muscial training from hearing the singing of a Fisk quartet of negroes. I remember the sermons preached by Sahdu Sundar Singh, an Indian converted to Christianity, and also one by an admiral in the Royal Navy who spent his leaves (no furloughs here) touring churches which would take his message. He had been a late convert and he told us that his nickname aboard the battleship which he ran on Christian principles, was 'Ring the Bell for Prayers'. There was also the Reverend John McNeill, a native of Greenock, very famous on Fifth Avenue, and memorably superior to Billy Graham, whom I heard much later. And there were evangelists of a less adroit order who would be permitted to run a week of evening services which one was expected to attend and who generally opened up, faces beaming with forced bonhomie, with 'Now I want every one of you to give the right hand of fellowship to the person sitting next to you and as you shake hands say "Bless you brother or sister" ' — a self-conscious procedure, because handshaking was a gesture we rarely resorted to, and the person sitting next to you was generally your mother.

There was more fun to be had in a mission our church ran in a slum called Grace Street, long since swept away by the Finnieston Bridge. Here the dwellers came on a certain week night and were issued with tea and buns, after which they had to listen to pip-squeaks like us reciting poems to them, dressed in our Sunday suits and new boots. Sometimes accordian players would come and lead the gathering in rousing revival hymns, and there was an occasional gospel entertainer who would tell them the story of the water changing into wine, showing this happening before their eyes. A sure winner for people who had never heard of permanganate of potash.

When I was about ten or eleven the fever of evangelic religion seemed to die out in my family. The Sunday night family worship stopped, and although we were expected to go to church and take an interest there was some scepticism expressed in the privacy of the home. My mother was the more outspoken. 'Alastair, you can't believe some of the promises, like "Seek ye first the Kingdom of Heaven and its Righteousness and all these things will be added unto ye". It's just not true.' And she would refer to some godly but stricken and impoverished person in trouble. She was no doubt helping with some burden, although my mother would never claim this. My father was less blunt. He turned to the organisation of the church's business affairs rather than to the theology of his youth. On one occasion there visited us several times at our home a contemporary of my father's called Willie McLellan. They had been lads together in the church and when Willie's mother had died he had gone away alone to America where he had done well. He was many times a millionaire, and my father persuaded him to install a costly pipe organ in our church in memory of the dead mother.

We all had voluntary jobs about the church. My cousin, George Mowat, and I for years marked the attendance cards of the children who came to the morning service. One small, kilted boy presented his card with brisk regularity. He was Max McAuslane who grew up to be made news editor of the *Daily Record* by me, as well as editor of the *Edinburgh Evening News*. My father gave himself the task of counting the church collections immediately the service started and getting it all ready for handing into the bank on Monday morning. This permitted him to walk silently into the church and take his place when the sermon was about to begin. Like the rest of us he remained a believer all his life.

Some spirit of Christianity hovered over me at that time during my early school days. When I was nine I went to Hillhead School and finished my formal education there after six years, for the last five of which I paid my own fees through winning bursaries. Every morning Miss Stratton took a combined class — I was in the half taken by a man teacher for the rest of the lessons — for what was called 'Bible'. This was a memorable ritual. Miss Stratton would stride up to the desk and say, 'Class stand, hands clasped, eyes closed, Our Father', and we would all repeat the Lord's Prayer together. None of the 'trespassers' minority there. The rest of the lesson consisted of reading passages of the Bible, verse about round the class from top to bottom and sometimes round again. Miss Stratton was a severe person who could wield a belt as well as any of the men teachers, but she had a kink which she was apparently allowed to gratify freely and we were too young and inexperienced even to question it. It often happened that the selected Bible passages contained some of the notorious 'dirty bits' which we'd already discovered for ourselves and sometimes her choice revealed new treasures which we had not come across so far. Our eyes would coast ahead to discover what sexual or cloacal relevation was in store and we became expert at calculating which victim the dirty verse would fall to, so that furtive and gleeful hands were pointed from all over the class, behind other backs. The victim would invariably be red in the face and sweating by the time he got to his feet and read his horrid script.

I was not particularly happy at Hillhead High School. I think that my early upbringing and my father's expectations had developed in me a spirit of diffidence and shyness — frankly, timidity — which clouded those days. I was good at the miniature football games we played in the cement playgrounds but didn't make much of field sports. Much later, toward the end of my teens, I took this sense of apprehension in hand and, I think, overcame it. The canoe trip and other ventures were part of this exercise. To be sure I have often been anxious and frightened since but I think I have been able to hide it.

Until I was almost fourteen those wretched schooldays were almost entirely redeemed by two superb teachers who stand out like shining stars, the like of which I had never experienced before that time, nor have since. One was John Lapsley, who taught maths up to that intermediate stage; a man full of wit and understanding with an amazing motivating style. He became a headmaster somewhere later on and I lost touch with him. He had two sons, Alastair, who became the Scottish champion at pole-vaulting and javelin-throwing and field sports; and a younger, non-athletic son, full of gallantry and spirit, who never came back from the Burmese jungle. He also had a nephew called Graeme Lapsley, whom I never knew until I went to Orkney in the early 1970s to talk about oil and discovered him as chief executive of the then County Council, now the Orkney Islands Council. For what he has done there he deserves well of Scotland.

The other teacher was George Menary, who opened the doors to me of English literature and writing and story-telling; all this with unforced encouragement and some mysterious input of confidence. This is a quality which owes much to some power beyond ability and even beyond the sense of simple leadership. He gained a PhD for a treatise,

21

published in book form, about Forbes of Culloden, which turned out to be a heavy going and not very distinguished piece of writing. By this time he had become one of HM Inspectors of Schools, where for reasons I never discovered he had become so angular and difficult a character, at least to the civil servants superior to him, that they were amazed when I talked to some of them about George Menary and the doors he had opened permanently for me and, I have no doubt, many others. He became a great friend as well, stirring in me a great desire to write — to be a journalist.

Everything after that was useless in a school which I now realised was badly run. The few of us remaining to go on to the Higher Leaving Certificate were taught our English, German, French, History and Mathematics by the school's heads of departments in these fields. There were four of them. Two were blatant neurotics. One was an outrageous bully, much mutilated in World War I, and the other was an ineffective and foolish teacher. There could have been no dutiful respect for any of them. I was glad to leave Hillhead.

I was bitterly disappointed, though, that I could not go into journalism, and had to sit an exam and take a job in the Commercial Bank of Scotland. This turned out to be the only job in my life for which I have applied. Every other job I have had since then was offered to me and I was invited to take it. I suppose this gives one a certain strength and even leverage, but when I look back to my bank years, during which I qualified as a Member of the Institute of Bankers, coming out top of my bank entrance in my final year, I fret at what appears to me still to have been a waste of time. And yet even as a bank apprentice in West George Street in Glasgow I met a surprising number of interesting people. There were two customers whose business I transacted because they could not speak English and my French was good enough. There was another man importing steel from Germany and I did a great deal of his business. In fact, I could easily have done the thing myself and set up as a teenage tycoon, for it consisted of writing to Germany and arranging for a shipment of steel, picking up the bills of lading, taking off the invoices and attaching a new set of invoices with the bills of lading to be delivered to the new buyer, while the dealer sat back and received the difference between his buying price and the sales price; and never saw the steel at all. This seemed to me a simple procedure and I was the one who did the things with bills of lading, and presumably the only one who knew how it was done, apart from the principal who never even gave me a kind word.

There were much more interesting people to meet. We had the account of Alexander Reid and Son, who had an art shop almost next door to us. Alexander Reid was the Scottish art dealer who discovered Whistler and promoted him to such an extent that he had his own son christened Alexander James McNeill Reid. I knew them all quite well although they probably never remembered me; and I also knew Tom Honeyman, a pugnacious, merry, all-rounder, who became a partner in that organisation. He was a qualified medical doctor in Glasgow who went into the world of dealing with pictures and became an expert at it but was called home at the very outbreak of World War II to be the director of the Glasgow Art Galleries.

Once my bank exams were finished I made an intensive study of commercial French and German, believing that Scottish banks should venture abroad. No executive in the bank that I ever discovered was interested in these modest qualifications but what carried me into the élite of the bank's head office in Edinburgh was my winning a prize in the Institute of Bankers Annual Essay Competition on the subject 'The Art of Investment' (a trifling triumph which I mentioned jocularly not long ago to a lordly partner in the firm of Cazenove in London, who fell silent with what might have been disbelief or even respect, but which brought the joke to an end). I stayed there for hardly a year, and then my friend, Seumas Adam, and I started a weekly magazine for boys, the *Claymore*, and I was into the cold winds which have braced me ever since.

With the banking transfer to Edinburgh my mother was certain that I had made it to the big time and she used to try to encourage me in the most inappropriate ways, in the manner in which mothers invariably fail to read the signs. She was certain that what I needed was a safe steady job with a pension, and when she and my father made sorties into the country, he to return with some comic account of triumphs on the bowling green or at the annual dinner at which he had been speaking, my mother would make an opportunity of telling me how they had met '. . . the banker. He's the manager of the bank there. He's got a very nice wife and they've a lovely house and he's not much older than you.' Since this banker who had made it was probably at least forty-two and showing it, I was in no mood to settle for this prospect although I did nothing to offend her expectations. It was an amazing thing for me to be told years later by an old bank colleague from those Edinburgh head office days that he had often thought about me in the context that: 'I often wondered what it would have been like if you had become general manager. What fun we would have had and we'd have gone places.'

Our general manager then was a youngish man in his middle thirties called John M. Erskine. I never formally met him until the day I left the bank, when he called me into his room, heard with great interest about the *Claymore* magazine we were founding and very generously offered to take advertising space for the bank in the pages to help us with the revenue. We never felt that we wanted him to do this but he remained a close friend until he died. He was to become Lord Erskine of Rerrick and many a colloquy we had about what might be counted our mutual interests. He used to introduce me to people, when I was editor of *The Scotsman*, as 'one of my most promising boys in the bank'. He moved from eminence to eminence, being a man of some professional as well as social ambition, and he was the last Governor of Northern Ireland, although that turned out to be a disaster because the shooting started at that time and showed no sign of stopping. Before he took the job he knew that I was fairly familiar with Ireland through my travels, but in fact I wasn't able to help him very much. It was the real Ireland I knew, the one where Dublin is the capital, and from what I already had learned about the Belfast complex it seemed to me to be a wicked and repressive regime. I always remembered how I had come across in Galway a lively young group of people who were running a Gaelic theatre. They had wanted to take one or two plays into the Six Counties but had been refused. I tried to warn Jack Erskine of the long history of hostility that lay there seething, but I honestly thought he might well be a reconciling influence. As it turned out, it was all too late.

I should like to be able to say that even in a modest way I left my mark on the Scottish banking scene. The time was to come when I was able to persuade them, but only with real difficulty, to set up oil departments and get in on the North Sea oil boom. But at my time there wasn't very much enterprise of any kind going. I was no accountant, although I was so reckoned, but before I left I had invented a speedy way of calculating the amount of deposit interest on any income tax year, running back to about a dozen years, which estate lawyers require to know, often for death duty purposes. Up until then it was necessary to slog through all the withdrawals and find out which fiscal year they fell into, and I had often had to do this. When I found a way of pinning it down to single years from the registers then in use, I explained all this in great detail to our then chief accountant, Peter Irving, who looked at it with interest and said that he had already thought of such a system. I never discovered if my system — or his if it existed — went into operation. No doubt it is all done by computer now.

My last ever games of rugby and association football were played in scratch teams for the bank. Nowadays I am happy to watch most forms of active sport and athletics. I never did anything on the track, but as a young teenager in Minard I spent a whole summer practising the pole-vault and throwing the hammer, and often wished there were lightweight competitions in hammer and the caber, since in those days I could take on most people of my weight in these pursuits. By the time I was fourteen I had discovered that it was football, and international football at that, which focused a feeling and sense of Scotland for me. About that time my father took me to some of the great international games at Hampden Park. It was a day-long adventure, because I used to call at his office for him on Saturday. We would have a businessman's lunch in the town and go by train to Mount Florida. There were amazing preliminaries in the music of the Glasgow Police Pipe Band and Brass Band who used to walk round the track playing all together such masterpieces as 'The Barren Rocks of Aden' and 'Jeannie's Black E'e', the great chords of the brasses soaring among the spectators and mingling with the sounds of the pipes, outdoing anything that has been done in that field since. The bands were directed by Pipe Major Willie Gray, from whose book of bagpipe instructions I used to learn elementary simple tunes, and Drum Major John Seton, who introduced syncopated beats to the great band tunes and whose masterly drum score for such a piece as 'The March to the Battlefield' was a model of simple perfection.

Then would come the almost unbearable moment when the teams came on to the field, with the dark shirts of the Scottish team worn by players so famous that I listened with awe while people all around referred to them by their Christian names. It was a common habit for the members of the Scottish team, who had probably been miners and shipyard riveters before becoming full-time professionals, earning unheard-of sums of money like £10 a week and £20 for appearance in an international team, to indicate their coolness as they took the field by blowing their noses nonchalantly as they stepped across the track by the simple method of pressing one nostril shut with a forefinger and voiding the other one on to what was universally known as the sacred turf. I was there at the game against England which looked like ending in a draw until Alex Cheyne of Aberdeen playing on the wing, scored a goal direct from a corner kick. George Allison, then the self-important boss of Arsenal Football Club who was doing the radio commentary in his normal long-winded fashion, had announced that the game was virtually over and was talking it out when his attention was drawn to the fact that the ball was in the English net. Undismayed, this Barnum of the early large-scale football days changed key and proceeded, 'While I've been speaking it appears that a goal has been scored by Scotland at the other end of the field . . .'

I remember, in 1924, when at the famous Rangers Football Club sports day practically the whole American Olympic team appeared and gave stunning displays of javelin-throwing and field events, so that the weeks of my summer holiday were spent in trying with a makeshift javelin to get the implement to climb the sky. They had with them their Olympic champion high jumper H.M. Osborne, who set up a new British all-comers record of 6ft 6in, an unheard-of height among us. Running a close second on the field that day was an amazing little French high jumper called P. Lewden of Stade Français, who was still with Harry Osborne long after the others had dropped out. He was so small that, tying his handkerchief to the middle of the bar as a guide to his eye, he had to stand on tiptoe and stretch his arms high above his head. Eric Liddell ran a quarter-mile race that day, his wispy hair flowing behind, his head held far back and his singlet so loose that another runner could have got in along with him. Liddell came to our school a few weeks later and gave a talk on Christianity. It was not a memorable performance and he was no preacher of any style but a likeable man, a great hero to us, and I got his autograph. There were probably 60,000 or 70,000 people at that sports day at Ibrox Park, but this was nothing in Glasgow because the international football game at

Hampden against England used to get 130,000 or 140,000 people and I was there on the day that all records were broken and it was said that 155,000 people had been in the ground.

One of the characters of football in my youth was Tommy McInally, a Celtic player who appeared many times for Scotland but was particularly fierce in the international games against England. Once at Hampden, the game had hardly gone for four minutes when he fouled most desperately an English attacker. The referee blew his whistle for a free kick and said in passing to Tommy, 'Watch your behaviour, McInally. There's Royalty present.' And Tommy, spitting and rolling up his sleeves, snarled back, 'F . . . Royalty! I'm playing for Scotland.' Even when he had become old and fat, he remained as game as ever. I once saw him on the top of a tram-car watching two little boys, who had not brought enough money for their fares, being harassed by the conductor who was going to put them off the tram. Tommy leaned over and paid the money, saying to the boys, 'When you go hame tell your faither that Tommy McInally peyed your fare.' The boys stared at this stranger run to seed, and they had obviously never heard of Tommy McInally. Apart from the big football games a feature of the great athletic meetings held was the five-a-side football between teams from the senior clubs in Scotland, and I was there the day that Tommy McInally held up one of these games merely by sitting on the ball in the middle of the park and refusing to get on with the game until the defence of the opponents came out to make him move.

Tommy was a regular visitor to the *Daily Record*, where I had my first job as a daily newspaper executive and where I became editor in 1946. The paper had a formidable history of sports coverage with page after page of gossip to such an extent that a relatively minor player could hardly buy a new pair of bootlaces without this being recorded in our pages. The magical name of the chief sports writer was Waverley. This character had been developed as a pen-name by John Dunlop, whose writing style was incapable of imitation, but for most of my time there it was Willie Gallacher who was Waverley. He had been a police court reporter and had covered the boxing stories before he became full-time Waverley. He was enormously well-informed about every aspect of football. I once asked him how he read so accurately the games that I had often seen with him, and how he was able to assess the performance of each player. He explained to me that for many years he had seen the greatest players in the world in these particular positions and he assessed every player he ever saw against what he knew to be 100 per cent perfection in the position; so he was not easily carried away by suddenly rising stars. It was a man called John Allan who was editor of the *Daily Record* in the early 1930s when Seumas Adam and I were submitting articles on an extensive canoe trip we made in the West Highlands. Allan greatly grudged giving us any money at all for the many stories we had sent from that desperate voyage, eventually producing a pitifully small total representing a payment for a cut-down lineage fee. John McCall, himself a writer of great charm, who became editor of the *Sunday Mail*, told me once of how he had been in charge of the *Daily Record* on the night when the news broke about King Edward VIII and Mrs Wallis Simpson. He had rushed in with it to John Allan's room, where the editor was sitting with his cronies, drinking and talking about football. Allan interrupted his discourse to look at the story and hear John McCall saying, 'This is very important, Mr Allan. It must be front page.' Allan looked over the pages briefly, puffed his pipe and handed the pages back saying, 'Aye. Two columns down the page', and turned to his visitors with '. . . as I was saying, Davie Meiklejohn is always at his best when he's in defence . . .' This was a man who knew little in life except football and he was a rabid Rangers supporter, which did not do the paper any good at all.

In my time as editor of *The Scotsman* I was able to get John Rafferty to cover football and boxing and Norman Mair to cover rugby for us. Norman Mair had gained a few international caps at forward for Scotland's rugby team, falling out, I think, with the Scottish Rugby Union, a body compared with which the Tories 1922 Committee is positively *avant-garde*. John Rafferty had been the trainer of Jackie Paterson when that little Glasgow flyweight became world champion. I once myself did a story about Jackie Paterson when he was preparing for a world title defence and in Collin's gym, where he trained, I saw him tear an overhead punchball out of its moorings and send it across the floor of the gym with a high left hook. Outside of the ring Jackie was as vulnerable as most of the rest of his kind. He failed in trying to start a few businesses, and even a jazz band, went to South Africa and was killed there in a bottle fight.

Of all our *Scotsman* sports reporters the star turn was Frank Moran. When I got to the paper he had been the golf correspondent for fifty years, the first full-time golf correspondent in the world. Everybody knew him through the whole golf scene, and to celebrate his renown I set up the Frank Moran Trophy as a memorial to him in his active lifetime. This still goes annually to the golfer who is a Scot or of Scottish origin, anywhere in the world, who has done most that year for the cause of golf. I got Bobby Jones — R.T. Jones — to give us a spot at his great annual tournament in Atlanta one year so that Frank could hand over his own memorial trophy to Tommy Armour, and I had letters from Bobby Jones telling of his pleasure about this event. Bobby was by this time far through but he managed bravely to sign the letters in a trembling hand.

It was through Frank Moran that a site was found for the annual Royal Highland Agricultural Show on the outskirts of Edinburgh. For many years it had been a travelling show going round five or six centres, changing every year. We campaigned in *The Scotsman* for them to settle down and get some permanent buildings up and they narked back at us saying, 'Well, you find a suitable place. *We* can't.' We talked about this in the office with Bob Urquhart, the sturdy agricultural

27

editor who always wore the kilt but was slightly impaired in his gait through having been shot down twice in bombers during World War II, both times having had to be fished out from the sea. Frank said, 'I think they could buy Ingliston', which was a golf course that had already been encroached on by the extension of a runway at Edinburgh airport and had become less than a standard-sized course. We made all the arrangements for the people of the Royal Highland to meet the Ingliston people concerned and they made a deal. I promised that if the deal went through *The Scotsman* would build the first building and headquarters. This was duly done.

But in newspaper life there are always a great number of things which never come off, however good the ideas seem. I got Frank Moran very enthusiastic about my idea that every few years there should be a great international golf match between the United States of America and Scotland with well over 1,000 players a side. The idea was that the various golf clubs would be paired off into suitable partnerings, an American course with the Scottish one of roughly the same standard, and that on a certain day the club champion of each club would play a round under strict scoring rules. No travelling, just letters and phone calls of goodwill across the Atlantic and an eventual score. We would give trophies and prizes. Frank was very keen about this but he died before we could get it going, and it doesn't seem to have been taken up since.

People look to newspapers for the presentation of trophies, and certainly in the *Daily Record* and later in *The Scotsman* we had a large number of these things, some of which had become obsolete. It was quite common for someone who asked for a cup for, say, the West Lothian Darts League, to be given one dug out of the cellars which had originally been for the Fife Quoiting League; the original engraving could be handily buffed off and the cup fettled up for the new proud owner and winner. As a young journalist I promised myself that if I had some day the right to decide these matters I would not have any kind of silver mug at all, but would get some good young artists to design trophies particularly apt to the recipients and their cause. At last I was able to do this and there are a number of these items about, carved in wood or shaped in glass or metal by some young craftsman happy to do the job.

Happy, I think, are the people to whom sport is a matter of indifference. I never see a Scottish team engaging in any kind of international contest, no matter what the sport, without agonising over the result. We have so few medals to display that it seems important, perhaps beyond all reason, that we should have victories. We are far from being a lucky country in sport although we invented many of the modern events which have become Olympic and world championship classes. Rugby and association football and perhaps also athletics have fallen on evil days, being run by people too restricted and unimaginative to make the best of the substantial talent available and capable of being developed. Perhaps our size and way of thinking is against us. John Rafferty used to say (and it must apply to many things apart from sport), 'Scotland is too wee to be big and too big to be wee.'

I should have been greatly content, perhaps beyond my meagre pretensions, to have been able to include a fine range of music among the influences which have helped to shape me and my outlook. I have no claim to do this. I spent more than the first half of my life with my mind and imagination dirling with nothing more profound than the whole body of Scottish folk-song, stirring ballads, and our great treasury of six-eight pipe band marches and drum beats. I could make nothing of the great classical music of opera and symphony, for the most part hearing simply nothing there. And it was not until Dorothy got me a recording of Beethoven's Seventh Symphony that, playing it over and over again, I came to see the beauty of it in growing fragments. In this way, year after year, all of Beethoven, and other masters of his time, became revealed to me but I can still make nothing of important modern music and it does not seem that I ever shall. Intimate friends, whose judgement I value, invite me to listen to some masterpiece and it sounds to me like the movement of a rusty gate. I say this out of affectionate envy of them for in that dimension from which I am barred they get such pleasure which is beyond me. I keep trying, but I do not waste my time in pining. There are only two conclusions. One is that there may well indeed be much music in the sound of a rusty gate on its hinges; more likely is it that there is no real basis of music in me. It must be that in the human ear there is something akin to colourblindness in the eye; an inability to discern subtleties of tone and sound that infinite nature reveals to those who can truly hear.

It is a deprivation, but it did not entirely debar me from making some contribution. Scottish Opera was founded in my home. One Friday night in a winter of the 1960s I had a phone call from old friend, Dick Telfer, whom I had known for many years. He is an astonishing musical all-rounder who finished up his working life as chief music master in George Watson's school, Edinburgh, but I had first met him when he was a cinema organist at one or two of the big picture houses. Before that he had made a living showing tourists round the treasures of the Louvre in Paris. Later he was a cinema manager. There is almost nothing about the world of music that he does not know. For years he found promising young musicians to perform for our guests at the huge Edinburgh Festival parties Dorothy and I held in our home, but this time he was on another tack. He said on the telephone that he wanted to bring Alex Gibson to see me that night. Alex was another friend who was conducting the Friday night concert of the Scottish National Orchestra in the Usher Hall. The two conspirators turned up late when the concert finished and we sat until the small hours with the two of them telling me that they thought it would be feasible to found a

Scottish Opera Company which might develop an annual repertory and could even tour. They were convinced of the talent and enthusiasm available, and of course I became fired with the idea because, if it worked, it was big with prestige for Scotland. I don't think any of us realised then that the idea had in itself the seeds of success and acceptance on a world scale which would see Scottish Opera with its own Opera House and rehearsal rooms. Money was needed to get the idea off the ground, and within a few days, after a meeting or two and some confident phone calls I had persuaded Noel Stevenson, then managing director of Scottish Television, to put up £1,000 for the part finance of a first opera and the promise of television broadcasting of at least extracts. Nowadays Scottish Opera has to talk in terms of fairly substantial sums of money as happens to all opera ventures. But this was the beginning.

There was also a modest contribution, by way of committee work, to the beginnings of Scottish National Ballet where again we had a few talented dancers scattered about the world's ballet companies but had never been able to bring them together. Ballet was an art in which I had no passionate conviction, but any newspaper I was ever responsibly concerned with was dedicated to the idea of cherishing this elusive art, for the aficionados are so devoted and entranced that it is brutal to deprive them. Off-stage, so to speak, my interest tended in earlier days to take a more practical turn, as when I once insisted to Anton Dolin that he tell me how high he could jump if he were an athlete in competition at a sports meeting. He was a man who seemed to be able to cross the stage in immensely high leaps, but I was disappointed when he told me he had once competed in the high jump somewhere, and had been obliged to drop out when the bar was not much higher than 5ft 6in.

Another friend, himself a dancer, who helped me to further my inability to grasp the visual delights of Western ballet was the Indian, Ram Gopal, who once in my *Scotsman* boardroom launched into so descriptive a gentle denunciation of Western ballet that I asked him to demonstrate what he meant. And he got up and moved across the carpet, performing with only slight exaggeration that terrible penguin-like waddle with which the male dancers come upstage, flat-footed, with toes pointing outwards. The great hazard about being able to enjoy the company of the great performers, in the professions or politics or the arts, is that you can be taught, or untaught, by the masters, and you are not likely to forget it.

CHAPTER THREE
Media

Minard is a small village on Loch Fyne in Argyll, where from the ages of nine to fifteen I spent ten or twelve weeks every year with my old Aunt Maggie. She was the last of the MacNicols of our family, to whom my mother's mother, my 'wee' Granny had belonged before she became a MacTavish. It should have been a great place for a boy and I got much out of it. I learned to play shinty and rove the hills, fish for trout and row boats, and catch sea fish and speak some Gaelic. Sixty years ago it was a Gaelic-speaking area. Now, I think, there is little Gaelic spoken there. Nobody tried to teach me the language, and indeed my elderly relatives discouraged me because it was held to be a handicap to people who were expected to 'get on'.

Before my middle teens I had learnt a great deal about working on a farm because there was one next door to us. The boys of the village worked there as a matter of course, in some cases because their parents were being rewarded annually with, say, two drills of potatoes or the loan of a reaper to cut their crofter hay. I used to fancy myself as pretty good at working the 'Tumbling Tam', a horse-drawn wooden rake which gathered up hay from its coils in the meadows and brought it to near where the tramps or stacks were being erected, at which point the driver would heave up the handles so that the points of the rake caught in the ground and turned over, leaving the gathered hay behind. The mare, Jean, and I swept up many a meadow in this way.

But there were days of immense boredom with nothing to read, especially the endless, inevitable rain-sodden days of July and August which come to the West Highlands. My brother George and I were set annually some task by my father to complete in these school holidays. We had to write an essay, learn a full chapter of the Bible by heart, make a drawing of some scene, and write a poem. Most years for about two weeks my father and mother would come to Aunt Maggie's house for the Glasgow Fair holiday, and the great feature of that event was the delivery each day of the *Glasgow Herald*. This is more complicated than it sounds. My father was by way of being an expert in logistics, and it would have appeared much too simple for him to have the paper sent by mail and delivered to us by Sam, the postman. Instead he had an arrangement by which the paper was wrapped by the *Glasgow Herald* distribution office in Buchanan Street, addressed to him, delivered to the train which ran from Glasgow Central to Gourock and there put aboard the turbine steamer, *Queen Alexandra*, which called at all the piers in the Firth of Clyde and the Kyles of Bute. George and I had the task of walking the two miles from our house to Crarae Pier to await the arrival of the *Queen Alexandra*. The deck was manned by Glasgow University students, tricked out in reefer jackets with brass buttons and wearing white-topped, skipped caps. They exchanged badinage with the village girls who came to look them over at every pier between Gourock and Inveraray. But one of them generally had time to flick the wrapped paper ashore over the rails to be caught by George and me, and we would then walk the two miles home. My father would settle down to an hour and a half of solemnity over the news of the day.

The *Glasgow Herald* had a daily feature called 'The Casual Column' consisting of a series of gossipy and informative paragraphs, headed often by a poem, some of the poems being translations from the Gaelic by my mother's cousin, Duncan MacTavish, who was to become the joint county clerk of Argyll. I used to read these with interest, and once in the rainstorms, 'on a day of days', as the old tales begin, I wrote an item intended for The Casual Column about an ancient quern which lay at Aunt Maggie's door. It had been discovered by her younger brother many years before in the bed of a burn and it now lies in my own garden. To my astonishment they published the item and sent me a postal order for four-and-sixpence, so that I became hooked on journalism for life.

It was the best part of ten years before I got my first break on the payroll of a newspaper. In the meantime I slogged through life in the bank and I kept writing, getting paragraphs and short items in here and there, keeping it up until, in fact, I had a newspaper of my own, when I was really too busy to freelance. Most of the proceeds went into my small savings which were eventually to be swallowed up almost overnight in the *Claymore* venture, but however small the postal order, I always kept a shilling or two to buy a book. I can go through my thousands of books now and point to those that I got as a result of this hack writing, some of them being bought from barrows for as little as fourpence.

I was hardly out of my teens when I had the presumption to think that I might be able to write for broadcasting. A friend from the Scouts, Jim MacDougall, and I, on one of our trips in the Highlands, once came out of the north into Fort Augustus and from there set off to cross the Corriearick to the south. On the lower slopes we encountered a middle-aged man, accompanied by a young girl, descending from a large black limousine which had taken them as far as the road went, and they were about to venture another hundred yards or so on to the old track. They had obviously never been there before, and we passed the time of day with them, pointing out the route and the hills on our maps and telling them of some of the gallant sorties that had been made on that same track where much history was made as well. We thought nothing more about that until we were listening together a week or so later to a radio series being given by a man called S.P.B. Mais, when we heard to our astonishment of his encounter with our two selves on the Corriearick and his rendering, in an accent of the home counties, of our efforts to enthuse him. This was subsequently published by *The Listener*, and I was moved to write something of a modest fan letter to Mr S.P.B. Mais. He did not reply, but obviously passed the letter to his publisher, since I duly received, in an unsealed envelope, a publicity pamphlet inviting me to purchase his forthcoming book. I resisted this, but it struck me that if he could do it, I could do it.

I sketched out an idea which would make some sort of a feature programme with singers, to be called *Scottish Road Songs*, indicating where the songs would be sung and my contribution to the text. I phoned the BBC office in Glasgow, was dealt with courteously and was put through to a man who turned out to be Andrew Stewart, then the programme director although he wasn't much older than I was. This was to be the start of a great friendship and, on my side, a hero worship, for he smothered me with encouragement, as a result of which I completed the script and in no time at all we were doing half-hour productions with singers in Gaelic and English, some of them even singing my own songs, while I did the linking passages. I did many another programme with Andrew and came so much to admire his style, that great virtue, and his expectations of what a scriptwriter should aim for, that he conditioned my quality of production for many a day, even for things I was not writing for him.

On an unforgettable day in 1936 the national network of the BBC broadcast a play I had written called *Steam*, to celebrate the bi-centenary of James Watt. We had an enormous cast and high drama, but nothing in the drama compared with what we were dealing with behind the scenes. The play ran from 8 to 9 pm one evening and we had been told as we were about to begin that it might be interrupted and brought to an end with the announcement that King George V was dying. We got through it safely, and immediately Stuart Hibbard came on the air with the announcement 'the King's life is moving peacefully towards its close'. *Steam* was the last item on the air in Britain in the reign of King George V.

I was also trying film scripts and especially documentaries. I did a whole series of treatments about Scotland but couldn't get anyone to venture upon it. I came to know John Grierson and all his documentary team — Basil Wright, Harry Watt and the others — and Grierson offered me a job with him at thirty shillings a week, which I ached to take in the very early 1930s, but could not see a way of keeping myself in London at that price and there were no family resources to see me by. I kept going with broadcasting, however, and did many talks, especially under the direction of James Fergusson, a remarkable character, historian and scholar, who succeeded to the Baronetcy of Kilkerran, became the Scottish Keeper of the Records and at one time, Lord High Commissioner of the General Assembly of the Church of Scotland. He took a Whiggish view of the Scottish story, and I always felt sure that I liked him rather more than he liked me. In the early days of World War II I wrote a play, produced by Howard Lockhart, called *The Long Reveille*, about an assortment of Scots in a prisoner-of-war camp in Germany. One of the cast was a young teenage actor called Gordon Jackson.

All through the war I was broadcasting, especially on the overseas wavelength, accounts of what was going on at home, eventually reaching so familiar a basis of relationship with the Corporation that I was able to walk through the doors of the studios in Queen Street in Edinburgh, go downstairs to my studio, switch on the lights and the microphone, call up somebody in London, give my spiel, switch off and walk out, not having seen anybody except to nod to the commissionaire at the door.

Soon after the war there turned up in my life a young Highlander called Finlay McDonald, and when he became a producer I wrote a play for him called *The Original John McKay* which had as its theme the old tale about the difficulty the Scot seems to find in making confident success in his own country. This created some interest, and the Glasgow Citizens' Theatre ran the play for a fortnight in their repertory. They assembled a wonderful cast of young actors like Andrew Keir, Fulton McKay, Walter Carr, Norah Laidlaw (gallant girl, she played the young, female lead with great spirit, although she was five months pregnant) with stalwarts like Molly Urquart and James Gibson taking up the mature roles.

Our family had never been a theatre-going one. As children we were not even ever taken to the pantomime, although my father and mother went frequently, my mother coming home to regale us with vigorous renderings of the songs and the patter of the comics. I was fourteen when I was first inside a theatre, to see a performance of *Julius Caesar* by the Baynton Company, and the only reason I got to go for a one-and-threepenny seat in the upper circle of the Theatre Royal was on the pretext that we were supposed to attend as an adjunct to our school studies. I can recall every scene and subtlety of that amazing experience, right from the sacramental mystery of that curtain rising. Nowadays Dorothy and I sit almost in the very same seats to watch the first nights of Scottish Opera.

Glasgow was a great music-hall city, with memorable variety bills interspersed with trial runs of plays destined for the West End. Many of the plays were bad and never made it, and Glasgow audiences, and I dare say audiences elsewhere in the so-called provinces, grew tired of paying their money for what were no better than dress rehearsals of indifferent material. Much the same thing happened in variety shows. Some good resident shows ran for whole summers in Glasgow, but some of the visiting bills were paltry and badly rehearsed. We were expected to laugh at jokes we had heard twenty times before and much better told by our own contemporaries, for nothing. Some of the English comics used to chide us from the stage for our obtuseness. I remember one fellow who came on and told us a joke or two on the lines of 'Why does a chicken cross the road?' When we did not roll obediently in the aisles he came forward on the stage and said to us tolerantly, 'I see — I'm too fast for you. Well, try this one.' And he told the next bit of tedium at half speed.

I was in the theatre the night in the 1930s when Max Miller's company died a death. Ever after he went round the trade warning them that Glasgow was the worst place to play, but I don't think anyone told him what went wrong that night. It was an indifferent string of variety acts with a compère who came before the curtain to start the show. He gave us a few patronising remarks, told a story and introduced the next act before leaving us. The story he told was the one about the inmates of the asylum diving into the swimming pool which had no water in it. The first act, duly introduced, was a stand-up comic, and he started off by telling the very same joke. It was a public demonstration that they hadn't rehearsed a bit of the whole show. The audience rose with hostility, grudging their money and their time. After another act or two Miller himself, 'The Cheekie Chappie', came in front of the curtain, out of his turn, and told us, 'They're saying behind here that you're a bad audience. I think you're a good audience. Let's see how we get on.' He gave us, bravely enough, some straining patter. I was sitting with Jock Lang, an old scouting buddie, later to be fairly well known as Stevenson Lang, the actor, and we started some applause, feeling always as we did that the stage is a hard life and those who try should get something out of it. The audience responded to some extent and the show went on. But that kind of theatre died, not only in Glasgow but elsewhere, and it deserved to. They weren't working at it hard enough.

But the great ones went on until at least the wartime. In Scotland we had our own indomitable comics, with Harry Lauder and Tommy Lorne being succeeded by Tommy Morgan, Harry Gordon, Dave Willis and Jack Anthony in hard-working weekly shows with a change of programme and, for the most part, packed houses.

I remember an unforgivable show toured round by Jack Hylton in about 1936. It was based on the idea that the great aim of every British variety act of that day was to appear in the London Palladium, and Hylton's theme was that he was sorry for those who had never made it and he longed to give them a break, so he had gathered a great collection of second- and third-rate acts and put them on stage two or three at a time, jugglers among acrobats and dancers with violinists, with a final parade round the stage and, as I recall, up the aisles of the stalls and down again. It seemed to me a humiliating exploitation of failure, and even at the time, I liked to hope that there were somewhere, still working the second- and third-rate halls, acts who had been proud enough to refuse to be the captives in Hylton's triumph.

As a feature reporter for the *Glasgow Weekly Herald* I wrote the life story of Tommy Morgan. For weeks I chased him round Scotland as he travelled with his own mobile show, sitting in his dressing-room a precarious day or two only away from press time. I had greatly looked forward to this excitement. Much later I came to know Tommy very well, but these were early days for me and he was already renowned. C.B. Cochrane once said to him, 'You are the funniest man I have ever seen'; and he drew great crowds wherever he went, with people laughing themselves into hysteria.

He turned out to be a disaster off-stage, able only to talk lugubriously about his personal troubles, and his funny jokes were long and tedious, often without much point. Was this the man who could keep a thousand women shrieking, choking, clutching their stomachs, begging him to stop for just a moment or they would die. I took lengthy notes for hours during the first session as he plunged in and out of the dressing-room, making up for some other scenes. When I came to assemble this raw material I found I had to rewrite all the jokes, slip in one or two new ones and point up pretty nearly every statement he had made. When I joined him, in Dundee I think, to gather the second instalment, I asked, 'What did you think of last week's, Tommy?' There will be many who still remember his way of speaking, a blurting, explosive, lisp. He told me amiably, 'Oh, it wis aw right — aw right. But lithen, thun [listen, son] . . . Ye bugger't wan o' the gags.' Since any gags in the piece had been mine I felt this was praise, and we set to the next labour.

I was doing slightly more original work elsewhere. I wrote songs for Billy Carroll, who along with his wife, Hilda Mundy, ran triumphant summer shows for many years in Glasgow. All this time during the 1930s the variety music-hall was dying, but occasional acts of originality and merit turned up, like Will Mahoney, an Irish-American clog dancing comedian, the climax of whose act was to have a giant xylophone wheeled on to the stage. He would dance up and down it to a tune hammered out by his own clogs. In the company was his wife, Evie Hayes, who sang 'Blue Moon' so memorably that I have never wanted to hear it sung again by anyone else. There were the three Wiere Brothers from Denmark, a comedy team; and Eddie Peabody, the banjo man, whose travelling manager, Graham Thompson, was a Dundonian who later turned to press photography and was finally a cinema newsreel operator covering wartime landings.

A great post-war event of the Scottish stage was the founding of the Glasgow Citizens' Theatre. The mainspring was the playwright, James Bridie, who was otherwise a Glasgow doctor called Oswald Mavor, with a strange gift for play writing which sent his products regularly into the West End of London's theatreland. He wrote occasionally for me in the *Daily Record*, but had few aggressive views which he was prepared to thrust upon the public. I came to know his son, Ronald Mavor, 'Bingo' to everybody. He was also a doctor and a tuberculosis specialist in charge of a hospital on Deeside. When the vague, but experienced, Charles Graves (he had covered the Shakespeare season at Stratford-upon-Avon for fifty years on end) decided to leave the job of drama critic in *The Scotsman*, I asked Bingo Mavor if he would come and do the job.

He said, 'You couldn't have asked me at a better time. I have no future.' What had happened was that tuberculosis had been almost defeated and there were no promotions in the next thirty or forty years for a young TB specialist. 'So all I have to look forward to professionally is sticking needles into people for the rest of my life.'

'That,' I told him, 'is precisely what I want you to do on *The Scotsman*.'

He joined me at the time the British theatre was undergoing its explosive entry into the new trend. Osborne, Pinter and Beckett were surging on to the stages with great portentousness and profitable controversy, although few people knew how to deal with them. Bingo swam into this torrent with great effectiveness for years. He is now a professor in Saskatoon.

After about three years on *The Scotsman* I developed a little spare time, and following the rule that one ought to write on what one knows about, I decided to write a play about a newspaper takeover and the turmoil that happens to the people involved. I had just finished it when Peter Saunders called one day to see me. Peter Saunders, the 'Mouse-trap Man', had been a young reporter on the *Daily Express* in Glasgow, but the call of the theatre had been too much and he fought his way into the West End of London as a producer. He took my play away with him and wrote to me in a few days saying he would contract me to let him produce it. The London Players put it on at the Lyric Theatre in Shaftesbury Avenue one Sunday and it seemed to go well before a professional audience. I was particularly taken with the work of Charles Leno in the role of the news editor and the actor who played Archie Pander-Brown, the front man of the takeover mob. There was a long delay since no available theatre was in sight, but we spoke with a succession of directors, the first two of whom, although offered the job and accepting, fell ill and had to be counted out. Finally we got Norman Marshall, who had written books about theatrical direction and whose productions of the Gate Revue I had much admired years before. Charles Leno was offered the part he had played in the Lyric one-night stand, but Peter Saunders felt we needed a very prominent name to play the lead. I had rewritten some of the scenes and we were now calling the play *Fit to Print*. It was a play anticipating many matters that are familiar in the popular press nowadays, including the use of full-page nudes. As is well known, there is no profit in being ten years ahead of one's time.

One day Peter Saunders telephoned me at my office in *The Scotsman* to tell me that he could get Sir Donald Wolfit to play the lead and would I agree. I leapt at this. Wolfit was one of my theatrical heroes. I had admired his 'Lear' and other Shakespearean roles which he had toured bravely for so many years in his own company and management. However, he turned out to be in no way a crowd-puller, and after an opening week in Nottingham, we did not run for many weeks in the Duke of York's Theatre in London. The audiences were thin. At that time, 1963, one still required the Lord Chamberlain's sanction to put on a play. One day when we were at rehearsal, Peter Saunders came walking down the centre aisle of the theatre, fresh from his encounter with the Lord Chamberlain, announcing, 'We've got to get rid of two "sods" and a "bugger".'

The kind of character I had created for the leading role was a smooth, ingratiating, soft-spoken, menacing figure and I first thought of Donald Pleasence to play the part. Peter tried him and sure enough Donald read the play, but felt he didn't want to take it on amongst his other commitments. To my grief, Wolfit was a great disappointment as a player. He was severe and even unfair on younger members of the cast; also he could not remember his lines and used to rant in a bullying extemporisation in only the general meaning of the speech, whereas the character required a cool, precise, meticulous, threatening rendering of the stock of clichés, 'full of bogus reassurance', with which I was so familiar and had reproduced for the role of Pander-Brown. Some of the other players were very good, and it made a star of Frances Whyte, who went on to more West End success and is notable in some of the big historical television plays. I was sorry it did not seem possible to get the play to run longer because I thought we should have come through. I had worked out a number of adaptations and would have kept the script up-to-date with that day's or week's topicality in Fleet Street. For example, there appeared on stage from time to time posters typical of the stories in the new-style production our newspaper had become, which read, 'Chelsea's Street of Shame' and 'Hampstead's Street of Shame', and so on, a device which I see appears regularly in *Private Eye*. It was sad to see a good team disperse, for they had worked hard and they all liked the play. One solace came from Peter Saunders, who told me that he had been saying to his impresario friends that our play with its three acts had two of the best curtains in the West End of that year.

In everything to do with this play I was greatly helped by Michael Powell, as I have been in so many things before and since. To bring in his name at this time opens another and admiring chapter of my friendships. I had met him in the wartime, but he had an interesting contact with my paper, *The Scotsman*, long before that. In the middle of the 1930s as a young film director he had written a script about the evacuation of St Kilda, but had been refused permission to film on that island and had spent a long time searching for some other remote island with the same conditions. It was in *The Scotsman* office where he was researching files and old records under the auspices of my old colleague, Forsyth Hardy, that someone suggested the island of Foula which lies near the Shetland coast. He had gone there and filmed *The Edge of the World*, now as great a classic of the fiction documentary as Grierson's *Drifters* is in its own field. By the time I knew him he was in the middle of that great series which traced the history of Britain at war with *The Spy in Black, One of our Aircraft is Missing, 49th Parallel, The Life and Death of Colonel Blimp, A Matter of Life and Death*, and all the rest. He had the idea of making a film of human values in wartime and this became *I Know Where I'm Going* with Roger Livesey and Wendy Hiller. In the Scottish Office, headquarters of the Secretary of State for Scotland, we got him the necessary official permissions to film this on Mull and Colonsay and on an impulse I took a week of leave and went to join them in Mull, where I got to know something of his mind and his work. I never made it into films even as a crowd extra, but in the scene where Wendy Hiller embarks for the dangerous crossing to her island and is caught up in a motor boat in the maelstrom of Corrievreckan, she is wearing my yellow oilskin instead of the black one the wardrobe department had issued, because mine showed up better. It was snatched off my back by George Busby, the location manager, and I had to cower in a shed out of the rain until they got me a replacement.

All this was no hardship, and for years into the 1940s and 1950s Michael and I, often with Bill Paton, went climbing every year into the hills of Scotland which Michael knew so well and loved, like me. Bill Paton was generally there with a small stove and a kettle in his rucksack and he would brew up tea for us and put out sandwiches. He had been a journeyman baker in Lerwick in Shetland, had teamed up with Michael's company to cook for the squad on Foula, and had remained in the film industry ever since. Once the three of us, stopping for a midday lunch on the hills high above Loch Broom, were regaled by a fabulous cold roast duck which had been cooked by Frankie, Michael's Irish wife from Dublin. Michael has two sons, like me, both called after Irish saints — Kevin and Columba. My two are called after two Scottish saints — Ninian and Mungo.

I cannot now name all the hills and islands I went to with Micky Powell, and he seemed to give a blessing to all of them. I used to visit him while he was shooting in studios with budgets somewhat larger than he had had in those earlier days. Some of his later films made immediate success like *Red Shoes* and *Battle of the River Plate*; others have still to find their full acceptance but are coming back by way of the specialist film societies to take their place, you may be sure. Not long ago he turned up in the Red Square in Moscow outside of the Kremlin walls wearing a bowler hat and arranging for the production of a film on Pavlova. A great spirit, still at it and always looking for new frontiers.

CHAPTER FOUR
That Young Girl Halliday

Five weeks before I started work in the Scottish Office, where all the home-based Scottish government departments are found, a sixteen-year-old girl called Dorothy Halliday had been taken on to the staff. It would have been a great surprise to both of us if we had known she was to marry me. When it came to pass it was also to astound our fellow workers, and of course it astonished and surprised my mother.

Dorothy had applied to enter the Civil Service after a bright scholastic career at James Gillespie's School in Edinburgh, which she had gone through four or five years later than Muriel Spark. She had been the school's junior dux, and had been the leading soprano in their latest annual Gilbert and Sullivan operatic prduction, for which she had also designed the posters. She should have gone to university. But neither of her parents knew a thing about universities, and there was no apparent advice about careers to be had in her school. There was a war on, and civilian jobs were assumed to require some direct connection with the effort. She was put to filing, and to learning to peck out a message on the typewriter, and to running down the road to buy cigarettes for the men. At home, her mother, Dorothy Evelyn, started to teach her shorthand.

Her parents had met in the last war, when, as a young wounded rifleman, Alick Halliday found himself in some wartime hospital, occupying a bed alongside a Londoner called Charlie Tye. They became friends during the long days. Among the letters which Charlie received from home was one regular bulging envelope which he seized upon eagerly, to lie and laugh out loud as he read. To Alick this appeared most unusual, inured as he was to the 'Hoping this finds you as it leaves us' communications which arrived from his devoted but succinct relatives in Fife, and he asked presently:

'There's one letter you get that makes you laugh a lot. What's it about?'

'Oh, that's from a young niece of mine — a school kid — she writes the funniest letters . . . Listen to this . . .'

Presently the young niece's letters became a weekly entertainment, to be read out as soon as they arrived, to the utter enchantment of Alick.

One day he found himself saying:

'Do you think she would write me a letter?'

Suddenly Alick was moved to a convalescent hospital in Lanark, but not before he had prudently equipped himself with the girl's name and address. The first she knew about all this was when, out of the blue, she received an admiring letter from a grown man, who was not only a soldier but a Scot, a species she had not yet encountered.

She still has that first letter. She replied. They wrote to each other every day of the years that passed before they were married.

She has rarely ever been back in England. They had thirty-three years of marvellously happy marriage, and she has had about the same time of brisk and uncomplaining widowhood. Dorothy was their only child. I lost a very good friend when Alick Halliday died. He should have had a son of his own. A mining engineer by training, later a technical expert who installed boilers in mines, factories and power-stations, he spoke almost exclusively of boilers in his own home, never questioning that what absorbed him would fail to grip the attention of his wife and daughter. They listened with the rapt and absent deviousness which women offer to men who have but one idea, so that it was not until her late teens that Dorothy came to understand that the phrase 'boiler mountings' did not denote a range of hills.

We were not much in touch in the early years. I was away a good deal in attendance on the Regional Commissioner for Civil Defence, the post Tom Johnston held in the first year of the war, and also on the then Secretary of State, who was Ernest Brown. I was in St Andrew's House on the first day that Dorothy wore lipstick, and this milestone was duly noted and boisterously drawn attention to by big John MacPerson, who ran the public meetings for the Ministry of Information. He later became HM Inspector of Schools when our extraordinary team dispersed after the war. We met him occasionally, especially in Arran. Once we had a hang-dog meeting with him, a year or two after our marriage, on the top deck of a Glasgow tramcar. It was crowded, and he was crushing his way off, carrying a small child in his arms, as we were struggling on. As we greeted and squeezed past him — for he was a bulky man — he held forward his child and queried, in an amiable Glasgow bellow that cocked all ears, 'Have ye produced any o' these?' We must have given some sheepish indication of our inadequacy, for he turned to the stairs well content, pronouncing, 'Aye — ye're no' proving very fertile, ur ye?' The small child, Fiona, now plays the viola in the BBC Scottish Orchestra, and teaches the instrument.

There was a recreation room in the basement of St Andrew's House, since many of the staff had overnight duties and many slept in, on stand-by. There were made-up beds in most of the private executive rooms. I used to encounter Dorothy at night, being taught table tennis by George Mowat. I sometimes took a hand in this tuition, and I also taught her snooker.

41

At that time I was far sundered from my close friends. Jim MacDougall was dead, Seumas Adam was in the army somewhere, Robbie MacLean was doing a security job in the north of Scotland, and Johnnie Burt was in the RAF, doing something technical for which his apprenticeship in the instrument-makers Barr & Stroud had qualified him, and would doubtless keep Johnnie in some inferior rank (just as journalists, having to reveal on interview that they had shorthand and touch typewriting, found themselves posted as secretaries to some commander for the duration). Willie Ballantine was good value, but we were much together already, and I was often warmly received in his hospitable home. All these heroes turn up later in this narrative. The civil servants were a new breed, worth knowing, and glutted with academic wisdom and urbanity, but I was never in their homes. Never, that is, until long after wartime.

I found myself, though, becoming interested in the companionship of that young girl Halliday. When you spoke to her, she had a view. She could make deductions within the context of the modest clerical jobs we gave her, and could follow through. She knew little about Scotland, but was anxious to learn. (The anthem of her school, sung fervently at assemblies, was the one about building Jerusalem in England's green and pleasant land). She knew about music, she could read books, went to the theatre, and I discovered she was the author of some of the witty verses that turned up at the staff parties, pointed at distinguished figures. But she knew nothing of the hills, nor of course the seas, and I thought it was about time.

Our first jaunt together was to climb Arthur's Seat, a modest eminence of 823 feet which is a part of one of Edinburgh's inner parks. We met at the Abbey Strand near Holyroodhouse, and I well remember her jaunty stride as she came down the hill of the High Street towards me, wearing her office coat and a little black-and-white fez which I later cannibalised for a personal smoking cap in our first house. That tiresomely correct old pedant Baden-Powell tells in *Scouting for Boys* how he fell in love with the stranger who he was determined should become his wife when he saw her walking, and indeed it isn't a bad test, one way or the other. Anyway, we went up the hill, and down again, and we have climbed many a hill since. We took to the Pentlands then, and the cinema, and for two summers we had bikes and rode them into the fine country around Edinburgh which she should have known already and I had never had much chance to. I visited her home once or twice, hearing about boilers, and she sometimes came to my flat, generally in the company of office colleagues. These opportunities developed and enlarged, and I was at the stage of knowing that there had never been anyone in whose company, in a degree, I was more pleased to be.

Sometimes we sat on hillsides, as at Balquhidder, and sang suitable songs, generally of the Scots kind. She had a marvellous voice for the folk-songs, with that slight nasal drift which gives such poignancy, and she was also able to remember some of the ones that I knew. Later she went to singing classes of a superior sort, and they seemed to train most of the tune out of her, leaving, for the most part, a fine big and accurate voice but seeming to leave out what I most loved, and what is the most precious of the singing virtues, 'the hert'. In our early married days she tried for a singing LRAM twice, on both occasions sweeping triumphantly through the theoretical elements. But the singing tests, at that academy in London, did not come off. The first time she had a sore throat and cold, and should not have travelled. The second time I was with her, and sat in the dusty cubicle where she was allowed to practise for half an hour. She panted for a drink of water, but there was no such luxury available, and I scoured feverishly through the streets of Bayswater until I came upon a small bottle of still lemonade in a seedy Italian café, but this was not enough to see her through. She deserved to make it. If it had succeeded she would no doubt by this time be doing her own programmes somewhere, words and music and all. But she had to turn to other arts. She writes her books to recordings of the great music, and sings as she moves about the house.

But we have not come to that stage yet. The war finished, and in 1946 I was asked by my old paper in Glasgow, the *Daily Record*, to come back and edit it. This seemed altogether more apt than anything that stretched ahead in the Civil Service, which had, however, not seemed moved to make me an offer.

We became engaged when I told Dorothy I would not want to go to Glasgow without her. The day before our official announcement, I took out to dinner, to help me celebrate, my two most senior colleagues in our department, Willie Ballantine and Forsyth Hardy. They were stricken into silence by the news, as if they knew something I ought myself to have known. Easing my way through this painful situation, I came to realise they were merely staging a reaction of aghast ignorance. Neither of them had the slightest idea that a move of this character was in the air. They knew me all right, but it seemed that they had scarcely ever noticed Dorothy.

The preliminaries of most marriages teem with comic anecdotes. This is because situations arise of a laughable character, and do not much require the exaggerations of later years. In our case, Dorothy wanted a private wedding. So much so that she was much put out when I told her that even a registry office ceremony required the presence of another two people as statutory witnesses. However, by the time her mother and aunts had worked on her it became clear that the Usher Hall was not going to be able to accommodate the throng that must be present. So many elderly relatives from Fife and elsewhere were going to be mortally offended if left out of this event that the list grew to an army. The Halliday parents, who were paying for it all anyway, started in with red pencils and cut the muster down to something like reason, although the turn-out was in the end a fair gathering of the clans.

Dorothy designed her own wedding dress, and on an August evening, sitting on the top of Calton Hill, she sketched it out for me. It was Scottish in style, with a suggestion of a white silk plaid across the shoulder. Getting a trousseau together was to be much more of a problem, for there was clothes rationing, and no kind of selection in the shops. Her girl friends gathered up a quantity of their own personal clothing coupons for her, women always seeming to be movingly loyal to each other at such a time.

We were married in Corstorphine Old Parish Church, near where she had been brought up and had spent most of her girlhood. It is a beautiful building, standing there for centuries on the far outskirts of Edinburgh, with the underlying meadows so treacherously marshy that the tower of the church had anciently had a permanently lit lamp in the belfry to steer travellers across. We helped to keep the lamp alight when they revived it and set it burning again, although the marshes are nowadays inhabited mostly by council houses. As a concession to Dorothy's repugnance of personal ceremonial, we had no bridesmaid, and no best man, and at the reception later there were no speeches of any kind, although my father and Sir Alex King, the cinema-owning tycoon, would dearly have wanted to orate, and Derick Whitfield, an old friend of the hills and the banking scene, was ready with a poem of the kind he normally composed for matrimonial occasions among our small sodality. He had done a memorable one for Johnnie Burt's wedding. Johnnie, one of the inner five of the *Claymore* group, had developed a good connection as a commercial traveller for a firm of confectionery manufacturers, and Derick's unforgettable opening couplet read:

Frae Glasgow up to Aberdeen
He travels with the jelly bean . . .

Our insistence upon the utmost formality had deprived us of such a beatitude, but there were other diversions; music had to be an accompaniment. Dorothy and her parents had taken a light lunch every Tuesday in Patrick Thomson's — a store now defunct — where even during wartime a gallant small chamber orchestra had performed, and this group was hired to play background music. Dorothy had given them a suggestion of two or three suitable melodies to be included, prominent among them being 'Morning Papers'. All through the arrival of the guests, the reception, the preliminary drinks, the lunch, and the reading of the telegrams (no speeches) the band played bravely on, sticking, however, to the shortish list the bride had supplied, so that 'Morning Papers' and the others turned up about every four and a half minutes (thus perhaps anticipating the practices of later discos and pop performances, where repetition is regarded as *de rigueur*). I have always remembered with a pang the sheer niceness of our friends, their happiness, and their understanding of our start to the voyage.

We extricated ourselves at last from these scenes of gaiety, to be driven by a large black limousine to Dorothy's suburban home, where we had laid up the baggage and impedimenta for the next stage. Aside from the clothes we would require, I had added to the stash an adequate selection of claret and muscadet bottles, as well as more than ample supplies of whisky and gin. Dorothy had been brought up in a teetotal — indeed a Rechabite — household, but I do not recall that anything was said to me about these clinking crates which had been delivered to their house the night before, to accompany their daughter on some prolonged and nameless debauch in the company of a man fifteen years her senior.

All this was transferred to another car and a driver, which were waiting for us. We changed too, and set off for the West. Our honeymoon was to be spent on an island in Loch Lomond. The man who owned it was a good friend, Malcolm Irvine, an engineer who had taken to the making of small film documentaries. In addition he ought to have been the most wealthy man in the whole world-wide film industry, for he had invented a cheap and effective way of recording speech on to film, and should have had a huge royalty from every talking film ever made. But someone else had invented another system, much more expensive, perhaps marginally more effective, or so Hollywood claimed, and Malcolm's system never got much of a show except in his own productions. Still, he had done well enough, and had been able to buy the island of Inchcruin, and build there a blockhouse of a bungalow, which I tried to rent from him and which he handed over for the duration. It was a blessed spot, near the south end of the loch where the crowded islands are so abundant in variety and charm that one could spend enchanted weeks exploring the unsurpassed richness of only three square miles.

The second driver took us to Balmaha, where at the slipway was the new boat of Alex MacFarlane, himself splendid in a reefer and skipper's bonnet. Alex's people had been ferrymen on Loch Lomond for generations, and he was also the postman and the census man and some kind of a registrar, and so long rooted in the elements of the place that he was inclined to think that the Colquhouns and the Buchanans and the Grahams were newcomers. With many a pawky double entendre he swept us up the loch to Inchcruin, where Malcolm and his daughter were waiting to welcome us. They helped us ashore with our plentiful supplies, showed us the rudiments of the cosy interior, (the WC cisterns had to be filled by hand from a pail of water — no hardship and no shortage of water) and soon they were waving themselves away in Alex's boat, leaving the house to us. It was a still night, with the ben in the last of the golden sun, and the near islands glowing remotely and then taking the dark. 'Strange blessings, never in Paradise', fell upon us like a balm.

We came ashore at last, and set ourselves up in the house I had rented in Glasgow at 10 Grosvenor Terrace, or rather, a floor and a half of it. In later years Reo Stakis, the purposeful and friendly property man, developed numbers 1 to 9 into the Grosvenor Hotel. This hostelry burned down completely one night, long after we had gone away and were in Edinburgh, but our old number 10 escaped the holocaust. Reo lost no time in rebuilding 1 to 9, reproducing the fine Venetian frontage as it had been, so that when we stay there overnight, we feel near neighbours to our younger selves.

Dorothy wasn't one to waste time. In the early months she got herself a job with the Board of Trade, and before long had become one of the statistical experts on the internal Scottish industry situation. Her official handbook — she was the one who produced and researched it for several editions — stands as a definitive account of the post-war attempts to get back to a trading norm, and see the way ahead. It seems that they gave up its production after she went to Edinburgh. We had a piano where she practised her scales, and she got some book illustration commissions. One set is a household treasure. A not very reliable book publisher commissioned her to illustrate some Highland folk-tales, which she did superbly. Some of these are breathtaking in draughts-manship and observation. The publisher then abandoned the scheme, as he had done for other projects, on the grounds that he had been unable to raise the money to finance it. So we have kept the drawings, and they remain a contemporary wonder.

Our housekeeping was of a haphazard character. Dorothy knew nothing whatever about cooking, and I taught her what I knew, which did not take long. I knew, for example, nothing about roasting or baking, but we hashed our way through meals, with frequent blow-outs in the reviving restaurants. Once a well-intentioned friend, about Christmas time, gave us a plucked but raw chicken, and we leered at it wastefully for long enough to be sure that it had gone beyond redemption. Then I wrapped it loosely in a paper, and stole down the street to thrust it unseen into a hanging waste basket attached to a lamp-post. There it remained until the collection some time later, with myself passing it several times a day and aware uneasily of its resemblance to a dead baby.

Accordingly, we ate mostly in town, the indoor meals being of an elementary character, mostly of boiled eggs, and it was in this context that there was revealed another shameful secret of her semi-English upbringing. Nothing demonstrates the essential differences between our two notable nations than the fact that when eating boiled eggs, the English beat in the tops to get at the meat, while the Scots, as ever like civilised folk, cut off the top.

In a vain and lifelong effort to bring civilisation into our small household, I used, when serving the boiled eggs, to write legends upon the top of Dorothy's, like 'Mind ma heid' or 'Hey, that's sair!' or even 'Hit somebody your own size'. She would read these injunctions with surprise, and then take up her spoon, crying aloud in defiance, and beat the hell out of the top of her egg. Education is a long and slow process.

Still, we considered nothing beyond our powers, and on a memorable day we invited both sets of parents to a Sunday meal and gave them a fourteen-course dinner. This was made partly possible because, when Dorothy decided to cook, she followed the instructions in the cookery book to the letter, measuring everything meticulously. The meal took long in the planning, but it was worth it. The guests each got a printed menu, on an embossed stand, and at each place also there was a different small glass animal, with an appropriate verse printed on the sign-pole to which the beasts were tethered. My mother's animal was an elephant, a subtle filial allusion to her latter-day weight, and hers is the only verse I remember:

She's big and braw, but there's nae herm
To see you like this pachyderm.
The hert that all God's creatures have
Is XOS with Bel MacTav.

Dorothy had been up three times during each of the two nights before the event, anointing with a cream concoction of her own a batch of small cakes from which the fondants were running like lava. They stuck, eventually. But, in spite of the early days and weeks of devotion, the meal took more than four hours from start to finish, and not a minute wasted, not a fragment rejected. It was a feverish joint effort off-stage, leaving the elders plenty of time for neighbourly talk. We had to wash and replace the knives and forks several times, and at one point I was in our cramped kitchen, tending course four, the clear soup, and standing astride Dorothy, who was kneeling on the floor, the only available working surface, covering with pastry the tenth course, a chicken pie, which had still to do an hour and three-quarters in the oven. We never did all this again, nor anything like; and I doubt if anyone else will either.

It was time, however, to inaugurate Dorothy into the rigours of the outdoors, otherwise I might have found myself bound annually for Scarborough. It had to be sailing, of course. I had never any intention of buying a boat for ourselves. Boats, like horses, have a trick of possessing you, needing so much devotion and emotional input that your spare time becomes engaged in cleaning them, and mucking them out, and other tasks of maintenance. There is a zest in the mere travelling, be it riding the waves or moors, but the arriving is often much more rewarding than the travelling hopefully. Anyway, for a start, the problem was get the girl afloat in conditions of reasonable comfort and privacy, and find how she would respond to the scenes and places on which I doted so unbearably. Once, perhaps years before we married, we had been talking on some hillside, skimming near to the topic of human affection, and of what it was that made people attach themselves for life to places and even to other people. At one point I said, 'Look! I'll show you a picture of my sweetheart.' And I produced and held forward a small map of Scotland. I suppose any woman would look on this as an unpardonable affront to the one I was bent on marrying; but it was better to get it over with.

In the years immediately after the war there were few yachts about, and you never heard of one available for charter. Every owner was afloat in his pre-war craft. But I did find a man who had a boat laid up in Tarbert on Loch Fyne, and he was willing to let us have it for two weeks on condition that he came along as skipper-cook. This was ideal. He lived in the North of England, with some tenuous family business attachment, but he knew the West well and was mad about the sea and sailing. We met in Glasgow and made an arrangement.

Frances Louise was the name of the boat, a Morecambe Bay prawner whose hull he had bought new before the war, finishing off the interior to his own fancy. She was adequate if on the rough side, but good at sea, as he was. He liked to be called Skipper Woodman, and it was not difficult to gratify this inoffensive request. He turned out also to be a good plain cook, with our modest help at times, especially at the cleaning up, for he did not much care to get his hands wet.

We drove to Ardrishaig with our gear, and picked up boat and man in the Crinan basin at the beginning of the canal. The first evening and night we spent aboard and getting to know each other. He had many quirks to the point of eccentricity, and a canal character with whom I exchanged a few greetings aside had time to confide that our skipper was well known locally as Tammy Troot, which seemed at least to indicate that he might be safely regarded as harmless, if odd. He had frequent bursts of nautical impulsiveness, as on the next morning early, after breakfast and with the dishes unwashed — indeed, everything unwashed — he noticed that the first lock gate was opening for the start of somebody's overland passage, and he decided, 'We'll go too'. He started the engine, flipped the mooring ropes aboard, thrust the tiller into Dorothy's hand, saying 'You take her through'. And we were away.

Dorothy had never seen a tiller. I had time to say 'You push it this way to turn that way — and this way to turn that way . . . Got it? This way — that way. And this way — that way . . .' I also had time to rush overside with the stern check rope as we surged our way into the lock, then to get my back to the lock gates. Happily the steering turned out to be logical, and we bumped and barged our way with fair precision to Bellanoch, where we made a first halt.

Dorothy liked it well from the beginning, and we might have been happy to think of the many years ahead of unequalled sailing. That time, the tensions were soon gone, the joys remaining. From the high grounds around Dunardary we saw, beyond the falling of the land, the loom of the western sea and the peaks of Jura and the islands, and because she was so happy, my own heart filled up to see it all again. I had stolen a far look at this prospect once or twice in the wartime, but never with a small boat to take me, and she with me, and I realised again the terrible ache of the sundered folk. In Loch Crinan we stopped to freshen the bilges, and to hoist all the sails, including the effective tiny gaff, white against the tan spread of the other canvas. And then we were away.

We started on a good wind, seeing the remembered small islands that meet you once past the Dorus Mor. They were all there, as ever. People all over the world ask you about them with longing, thinking that they may have mysteriously changed, lacking the exile's regular pilgrimage. And you have to tell them that, yes, they are still there, not adding that it is they, the departed people, who have changed with the years.

The wind died that evening, as it generally does in these parts, while we floated north. Skipper Woodman had meant to get into the anchorage of Puilldobhran, where I had never been, but as the late hour came we were a mile or two away and the moonless sky had darkened, so that he could not make out the entrance among the scattered and fanged rocks of the Sound of Lorne. We had some fortune here, for as I hung over the charts with him I was able to anglicise the descriptive Gaelic name of one of the outlying islands and was able to tell what it meant. Then I found I could pick its outline out from the black skylines as we took it close aboard, and we swung into the channel of the anchorage, searching our way in past the near small cliffs fringed with seaweed to the wider but still small bay where we put down our hook and swung quietly at last. No one else was there, and with drinks, food and a long sleep we had a perfect night of it — but if you were to go there now in almost any of the summer months you might have to shoulder your way through the many others who have found this spot. It is always like this in sailing; if you need to be free, you need to seek farther and find the newer and unknown places. As on the hills, I always hoped to induce other like-minded people to go where I thought I had found solitude. But if they took the advice and followed, I little liked to find them there, and had the need to push on and away.

And so on to the remembered places north and west — Aline, Ardtornish, Tobermory, Canna, Eigg, Skye — it was a fair beginning. This strange skipper was a seamanlike and sailorlike fellow, for all his oddities, and before he was finished with me I knew every sail and rigging and cordage of his boat, and how she responded sweetly to the helm under all winds. Among other marginal tricks, he taught me some of the skills of sheering, which I had never encountered then, nor have since, in the West of Scotland. To do it you have to trail astern of a yacht doing a few knots, you in the dinghy and at the end of a long towline. You kneel well forward in the bow, and lean inward, tilting your small craft to starboard She goes with an unbelievable rush forward to the port side of the mother ship, the line straining, until you find yourself alongside the ship and at right angles to her. You can take photographs of her from there, for she is side on and a rope's length away; or you can simply sit there and rejoice in her loveliness as she takes the stream, as the old shellbacks used to do in the square-riggers, sitting out in the far end of the bowsprit in the off watches, to see their ship come along.

49

I have mentioned that our skipper disliked having his hands wet. He went further. He could not bear having his hands wet with paraffin. And since the engine was a little unsteady (we seldom used it) he was wont to dismantle the whole thing of an evening in some anchorage to find if there might be a drop of water clinging to the jet, or somewhere. This was an operation requiring the participation of the whole ship's company.

Dorothy did a memorable drawing of him, surreptitiously, showing the owner leaning back from the dismantled engine in an attitude of terrible distaste, holding his fingers helplessly forward waiting for her administrations, which involved handing him hot cloths from a basin of water so that he could wipe his suffering hands, if only temporarily. This took place in the cramped cabin most evenings, and largely eliminated the hopes we had had of perusing some improving literature, of which I had made a selection so that Dorothy might, after her somewhat Anglified childhood, catch up on the inheritance she was not likely now to escape.

There was, however, another and more wretched predicament to which Skipper Woodman proved to be prone. Dorothy and I slept on the facing settees of the cabin, while he went forward to the forecastle, where there was a folding bunk. Also installed there was a sanitary bucket, requiring much manipulation before and after, since he was one of those thoroughbreds who do not like having a hull bored through for any kind of plumbing and other fancies. He often talked and chuckled to himself, but each night, after we had retired, we could hear him making boisterous use of the utensil. It seemed necessary for him to perform here with cries and groans, and as these mounted nightly during the first few days it was clear that his rituals were producing, not cries of satisfaction nor accomplishment, but of pain. In due course I made *sotto voce* enquiries, whereupon he confessed to me that he suffered severely from periodic attacks of acute haemorrhoids, and that one of these onsets was about to reach a climax. His diagnosis was correct. In a short time our nightly peace at anchor was highlighted by the drill where I rowed him ashore to the adjacent beach. There he would divest himself of his trousers, and wade by torchlight into the chilling water up to his calves, and then, crying distressingly, lower his agonised rectum into the tide, where he performed some screaming manipulations by hand, aided by a tube of shaving cream by way of lubricant. The whole performance was not one to which I, nor anyone I knew, would readily expose his new bride. I enquired as to his need to resort to surgery, perhaps a little less expert then than now, but he felt able to cope with his handicap.

I did succeed in getting him to call for relief upon the lady doctor on the island of Eigg and I went with him to make sure he would parade. She received us at a time when she was obviously in the midst of some household duties, but she said, 'Will you just come in and sit down for a few minutes.'

He answered stoically, and indeed with style, 'Madam, that is exactly what I am trying to avoid doing.'

We caught fish in Eigg, and ate them so fresh you could not recognise them as the creatures you knew from city shops. A small boat with two muffled men came alongside once, and we had them aboard for a dram. One of them was a lobster fisherman, and the other was a young and handsome priest, Father MacLean, his dog collar muffled under a MacLean tartan scarf. He was the one who showed us how to cook and eat mackerel. You lay the fat fish on the gunwale, slice off the rich steak on one side, skimming clear of the bones; then lay it on the other side and take the other steak. You throw all the rest away, frying the two steaks, thus pleasing man and beast, for the gulls and the cannibal fish below get their share too. (I should say that as a Presbyterian, I know, or I once knew, pretty nearly every Roman Catholic priest in the Hebrides. Well, you never know!) Poor Father MacLean had to do a wee penance for the dinner, because the skipper insisted on his coming below to the very timbers, and had him tapping and thumping there, agreeing to the boat's unequalled condition, while they crawled alongside below our feet with a torch, the skipper exclaiming, 'Sound as a bell o' brass'.

One task which Dorothy set herself on this voyage was to knit me a mighty woollen sweater, an undertaking which turned out with her usual success, although she has never performed the same operation since. It involved the use of many hanks of wool, and these she had wrapped in paper so that the whole affair, in mid-knit, was a dangling congeries of small parcels like an octopus in hair curlers. At one point she ran out of a certain coloured wool, and introduced another colour cunningly at the shoulders, to produce an effect like that achieved by latter-day SAS men. This garment wowed the yachting establishment later at that year's Clyde Fortnight. 'My wife made it for me', I would say nonchalantly.

We got back to Crinan at last, and tied up *Frances Louise* there in the Ardrishaig basin. I picked up the car from a nearby garage, to discover that the skipper had decided to travel back with us at least as far as Glasgow, so that we had to postpone our cries of laughter and relief. He did more. He came home with us and waited while we scrambled together some sort of meal, spending the waiting time crawling under the large sturdy oak table which was part of our rented furnishings, tapping the baulks of wood and joints, and pronouncing 'Sound as a bell o' brass'. Eventually I was able to entice him back to the car and drove him to the Central Station in Glasgow, where I got him aboard a train which was bound to some such place as Liverpool. I reached home again in time to share a few enfeebled laughs with Dorothy.

We had an altogether more efficient time the next year when we chartered the fine little sloop *Jane*, with twenty-year-old Arthur Houston, long since a good friend, coming in the handy role of skipper-cook. His lawyer father had lately died, and Arthur, having completed a

51

law course at Glasgow University, was head of the house and engaged in putting the family's assets to use. This trip was an unalloyed success, with great June nights of fishing in the Sounds of Harris and of Iona, and long wind runs the whole length of the Outer Hebrides, with the inevitable two or three cronies coming abroad, dog collars or not, at such places as Eriskay and Castlebay and Skiport. We all flourished in this congenial mix, with many a song and story, and we had no hitches, except that we lost Dorothy for some hours on the island of Staffa, where Fingal's Cave is. Arthur and I twice searched the whole shoreline of the island, and were planning the next serious move of a mainland search party when we found her at the base of some cliffs, absorbed in the marine life of some tidal pools and quite heedless of the passing of time.

For the first week or so it was necessary for Arthur to seek anchorages from which he could telephone home nightly, to enquire if his university results had come through and how he had fared. This led to one or more additions to the leg-pulling mnemonics we had devised, to add to the crude rhyming couplets which young sailor cadets learn by heart to help with navigations. The apposite one went:

When the wind begins to blaw,
Nip ashore and phone yer maw.

He came whooping back one night to say that the result had been posted and he was now a qualified lawyer with a degree. This we celebrated in some style, as we noted also his twenty-first birthday a few days later. All this seemed worth recording, so that I wrote the log and Dorothy illustrated it with drawings. The book was entered in Arthur's name for the annual competitions of the Clyde Cruising Club, where we won the Ogg Cup for the best cruise of the year, with his name inscribed upon it still — the youngest winner ever. In that same club, of which we are all members, he is now entering Commodore rank.

There were many other voyages, including a preposterous trip in a large twin-screw diesel yacht with a professional skipper, whose mother sadly died at home in the Moray area while we were away, so that he left us at anchor in Stornoway harbour for an enchanting ten days. We took with us on that trip a sixteen-year-old lad called Eric Luke, who has since been making a living around the world running his own public relations business. There was also the sweet *Eileanach*, a small motor cruiser owned by a friend of Dorothy's father, which was based in Ullapool and which he asked us to sail to the Clyde, making a holiday of it on the way. I am handless with engines, and unlucky with them too, but the owner wrote page after page of instructions, for that sea is no place to be caught with a broken engine in the prevailing south-westerlies. But we got most of the way, after some glorious days swimming and pottering around the Summer Isles, and skipping on the blue and white water round the great headlands towards Skye and the narrow firths. Badachro was a great discovery, visited many times since, a charming anchorage with a Cornish-style pub, unusual even in coastal Scotland, which rises on stone steps from the sea itself. We got caught by an engine failure coming out of the South Rona anchorage, and were lucky to get started only a few feet from the lee rocks. On we went, and there was a long and secure if unpleasant passage round Ardnamurchan to Tobermory, where we laid up and visited friends for a day or two.

Fate caught up with us south of Kerrara Island after we had cleared the Sound of Mull. A twenty-four-hour summer southerly gale hit us suddenly, although we could see it coming, and after an hour of wild and tossing headway at half power we were taken by a steep wave, thrown on the gunwale; the heavy unfastened lid of the engine casing bounced off, and the engine stopped. Nor could it be started again. We jilled there for an hour or more, pressed always towards the southern reefs of Kerrara, while I got the anchor ready in the hope of stopping us in the shallows, and also feverishly consulting the long since discarded handwritten sheets of instructions. The trouble with me is that I don't even know the principles of machinery. But it was one of those engines which starts on paraffin and runs on petrol — or it may have been the other way about — and it occurred to me that if the main engine power would not come on, it might be possible to get the thing started on whatever it was, and keep it going that way, if it would go, until we were in shelter. After a few trials it made the starting sounds, the screw turned, and we eased off from the shore and into the Sound of Kerrara. There we crawled slowly through the posh waterside suburbs of Oban, waiting for the thing to switch off. It didn't, and we put away some mighty drams seconds after we had seized one of the old naval moorings on the seaward side of Oban Bay. That was the end of *Eileanach* for us. Granny Spence, the boat-hirer, took us ashore the next morning with our gear and we got the train to Glasgow. The owner came, fixed the engine and took her the rest of the way. The trouble was only some water in the engine. Only! What are they thinking about, the people who make engines?

We had interludes of horse riding, and golf and Abroad, but we came back to boats when our son Ninian was four. I chartered *Ron Mhor*, a Tarbert skiff hull with some kind of yacht-like fit-ups inside. Sight unseen. The owner, a school teacher, had largely semi-finished it himself, and he came along as skipper with a girl to cook. This time we took Granny Halliday, for I wanted her and Ninian to have a taste of these seas and islands of which they had both already heard so much. We joined the boat at Mallaig, after the long train journey, to board this far-from-luxury cruising yacht. She was festooned inside with dangling electric wires, paint daubed inside and out, with anchor chains that swung and battered in any sea. Dorothy wanted to leave at Portree and take the best road home; but we stuck it out. There are, of course, great benefits in having your own boat, for you can get to love her. The alternative is the charter, where you get rid of the thing as you tie up for

53

the last time. But there isn't much choice. Still, we went there and back with *Ron Mhor*, knew the old enchantments, and simply had to put up with the irritating times when the owner would rise at first light and up anchor, setting out for some place which he wanted to visit, but which we had made clear the previous evening we didn't want to call at.

There were minor upsets, none of them dangerous. We came to anchor in the shallows near the head of Kinlochhourn, and soon we were aground, listing to the dried gunwale so steeply that a jelly which the cook had left to set, stiffened on the tilt and was eaten in spoonfuls from a shape that looked like a horizon experiment with a primitive sextant. The other thing about this skipper was that he believed himself to be a healer, and this may have been reasonably true. Strolling ashore, in the long sunset that night, leaving our stranded ship on her side, we came upon a doctor and his wife camped among the meadows of the river delta. The doctor turned out to be suffering acutely from a wretchedly painful back disability, for which camping was no doubt about the worst treatment. Our nautical mentor modestly proffered himself as skilled in the arts of massage, and they retired to the tent, the doctor certainly believing that nothing worse could befall him. When they emerged the doctor looked much relieved and even supple, and we left in a cascade of physicianly gratitude. As has probably been often said, none but abnormal people go sailing regularly.

Our Hebridean sailing reached its peak with the chartering of *Gay Pandora* from Dougie and Puff Lindsay. Dougie was a really skilled sailor fellow, the son of my old friend the architect Ian Lindsay, who did such handsome schemes as the redesigning and restoration of Inveraray and many other projects of beauty. Puff had cooked for us at home for a year or two before they were married, so that department was to be supreme. We had the two boys with us this time, and Granny Halliday again — always on for a ploy — and it was the greatest pleasure to take Willie Mackinlay, head of his own family paint firm and a yachtsman of renown, who had so often taken me in his various boats. He joined us some days late, and I picked him up at the airport in South Uist when we were tied up in Loch Skiport. This time there were always new anchorages, and fine fresh sailing, a steady boat well handled, and the finest comfort. You wrap up and sit in the cockpit and the day seems endless, looking to those far and familiar blue-veiled skylines, with each wave to be met and dealt with and greeted.

Horses! Ah, yes! Here too there was to be no escape for Dorothy. I arranged lessons for her at a riding school near where we lived, and she became, of course, very good at it, with a splendid and compassionate instinct for horses. She learned to jump too, with Glasgow citizens lining the rails of the rather public circuit and applauding as she went over. However, this was all much too decorative for the ordeals which lay ahead. We had already taken part with Jock Kerr Hunter, the outdoor sports pioneer, in the setting up for the hotel-keeper Ewen Cameron of the first pony-trekking school at Newtonmore on Speyside, and we had gone with the Perth Drag Hunt, set up by an eccentric called Captain Milton whom I had had dealings with in the wartime. The time had come to take to the road — and to the moor.

Our first substantial expedition was to be a sortie into the far west of Scotland, riding the narrow valleys during the long June days and sleeping at nights in some small hotel or bed and breakfast place to which a suitable enclosed field for the horses might be attached. We picked up our hired horses on Speyside where they had been consigned by horse-box, and took the road. For the weeks we were to be away we needed a few changes of clothing, night things, personal gear, and a supply of hard feed to keep the horses going. For weeks before, when we were preparing, we were constantly assured by Milton that he would supply us with suitable saddle-bags and other strapping-on containers which would make us self-sufficient, and it was only on the day before the expedition set out that I found he had no such apparatus at hand. When I pressed him he produced a leather receptacle which I thought might be intended to receive a folded telescope, showed me how it could strap on to the front of the saddle, and said, 'There! That would hold a pair of shoes.'

There was no point in being irritated. I sped back to Glasgow, did some shopping in the Army surplus stores, and overnight produced two pairs of saddle-bags made from old webbing Army backpacks. They saw us through. It was one of the many lessons about never trusting anybody. So equipped, and without a hint of how to manage the affair, we went with that equipment through Atholl and Badenoch, Lochaber, and away over the long hills to Cluanie and the western sea, and beyond Lochinver in far Sutherland. And then back by the eastern sea to the other side of Ross-shire, where we meant to train the horses back from about Inverness. One of them split a hoof near Muir of Ord, and we led him to the smithy in the village there — the smith lived in the red sandstone cottage called Vulcan's Forge — and he fettled him up and shod him again. Then at the station they had a horse-box, and a book of instructions telling railway men — then still so dedicated — how to manage the carriage of horses. The whole staff and a lot of retired old railway lags turned out while we got them aboard, with old oak buckets for sawdust, of which they had a supply, and a battle of hay. We had corn for them. There was an end carriage with a single seat facing the box, and a lifting window partition which we could raise to talk to them, and fill their manger with feed, while we trundled south. At Inverness we were hitched up at the very front, behind the engine itself, to the south-bound express, and we travelled like a triumph, with the passengers and their children getting out at every station to run up to our exclusive carriage to see how we were all faring, and to say 'Hullo' to the horses, who were getting very blasé with all this attention.

55

I doubt if it would be possible to do all this again. The north-west glens of Scotland are high and narrow, and by the time the main road and the river, and sometimes the railway, have squeezed through, there is not much room left for old-fashioned traffic, and the average motorist knows little about the consideration needed when passing horses who are used to wider scenes. I had hoped to use some of the old Wade roads and the drove tracks higher up the hillsides, but we found them all bogged up, overrun and squelching with burns foaming off the steeps, so that they were quagmires where we sank, and the horses were likely to lose shoes. We could make no progress there. There were one or two spells of bad weather too, although you do not notice bad weather much when riding until you get cold and tired late in the day. Enthusiastic motorists would draw up alongside, wind down their windows for a moment in the gale, and shout admiringly, 'It's a fine way to see the country.' In fact, on hard roads, and with traffic, you don't get much chance to see the country. But they meant well.

Another category of folk encountered was to be passed leaning over farm and croft gates where they had long since switched to tractors, but had retained some horse lore. They would step on to the road in front of us and, often without a salutation, take the horse's muzzle and pull open his mouth to have a look at his teeth. This is a liberty which horses, poor things, never seem to object to. The aficionados, well wrapped and ready to get back into their warm kitchens, would say something like: 'Aye, aye. Well, you're not getting much of a day for it', and let us go on our way.

That time, we turned the horses back to their owner at Perth, and on an impulse fled back to Glasgow, collected our passports, and flew to Dublin for a memorable week. As Kipling used to say so tiresomely, that is another story.

Horses are charming creatures, patient and submissive, and altogether noble. I do not understand why they can tolerate humans at all, far less allow themselves to be taken advantage of in the way they do. Another year we took robust Highland ponies, great beasts on the hill, plodders and amblers for ever and a day, but reluctant to canter or gallop. We wandered for a week or two through the moorish hinterland between Moray Firth and the Mearns, finding amazing old and firm roads among the windings of the upland farm lands, and coming down at night only when it was time to look for a bed and horse park. After a day or two away from their known territory the beasts would not let us out of their sight, presumably since we were the only ones who would eventually take them home, and when we lunched or slept we let them wander far, even with the saddle-bags open and all our gear ready to spill. It went wrong only one day of low cloud when we were in the Abernethy Forest not far from the shores of the Green Loch. For half an hour or so, above us, there had been the intermittent sound of a small aircraft, probably feeling his way to Kinloss or Dyce, and we paid small attention. Suddenly this aerial fellow dived clear through the clouds, and came out a few hundred feet above us. Clearly he was lost, and took this desperate measure to locate himself. He must have spotted the terrain and the directions at once, for he bounced up through the cloud cover and disappeared somewhere in a beeline. But the horses had never seen anything like this, and they took to their heels faster than they had ever gone under our direction. We went panting after them full speed through the high tripping heather, gathering up in the pursuit the costly items of clothing, binoculars, spare sweaters, whisky flasks, and other treasures which jolted out of the bags as they fled.

We got to love these horses too. They were as affectionate as dogs, although I do not suppose they even recognised their own names. Also, like us, they dearly loved chicken sandwiches.

All this was before the family, although we had been married for a number of years already. The two of us made devoted travelling companions, with much talk and laughter and songs and hopes. And I think a fair amount of naïveté. There was one day on that trip when we arrived late at a small country inn which had a few guests, probably couples fishing or birdwatching. They gave us a meal and we turned in. But in the morning we were a little late in coming down for breakfast. You know that silence that falls in a little hotel dining-room when latecomers walk in. Everybody craning to hear what one of you might say. And Dorothy said to me blithely, 'Do you take sugar in your tea?'

Another day we had a simply terrible trek through endless rain, away in the grey uplands of the small towns like Dufftown and Craigellachie, and came down at last to the hotel at Aberlour, where I had phoned for a room and a field. We tied up at the rail at the parking place, and stood dismounted, the rain spouting from every part of us. Mrs Hendry the proprietor, in oilskins, came to her door, saying, 'Come in. Mr Somebody, who farms up the road, is on his way down. I phoned him when I heard the horses, and he will put them into his field and store the tack in his stable. There is a hot bath ready for each of you — one in each bathroom — and when that's over there will be a high tea ready for you in the bedroom, so you don't need to dress up.'

The baths were neck deep, and there was a coal fire in the bedroom. People don't have to do this, but when it happens, you must only rejoice, as at the sunburst of some Golden Age.

About the time of the riding treks I had my long trip to the United States of America on a Smith-Mundt scholarship, set up officially under USA government auspices to familiarise foreigners with the American scene. I was away without Dorothy for three months. In that time she painted portraits of her mother and father — her first attempt in that field; learned Spanish with astonishing fluency, and spent a lone two weeks in the south of Spain. For all the reasons you can think of, I was glad to be back, and we had one of the sailing holidays later that same year, in the familiar west coast. But the clouds were gathering about the

Daily Record. To be sure, we had some editorial triumphs, and it was a good paper, cheaply and ingeniously run. Still, the Kemsley management had not advanced into the 1950s, and some of us foresaw that the future would be an unstoppable decline, with one paper after another being sold off to meet the cash requirements, just like the madness that lies in closing down the branch lines of a great railway system.

This made the years 1954 and 1955 difficult and troublesome, and it cost me some effort to keep clear of a sense of pressure, feeling perhaps too much responsibility towards the carefree mob of my editorial staff. Late in 1955, with hints coming from our top senior administrative staff, it looked as if the sands were running out and that the paper might not last until Christmas. Dorothy and I had not had a holiday for over a year, except for some weekends snatched with our tent in the remoter parts of the near west. Late one week at the end of September I suddenly announced in the office that I was going off for at least a three-week holiday, and put my staff plans in order. This was a Thursday afternoon; by the time I had reached home I was able to tell Dorothy that we would leave on Saturday. I had hired a caravan — neither of us had ever seen the inside of one — and had arranged to have a tow-bar fixed to my old Humber the next day. I made plans for a suitable intake of food and drink; especially a scheme with Skinner's the bakers, where my father had long ago served his apprenticeship.

We didn't know, of course, where we were going, but it seemed clear that the only way to signal the hoisting of the flag of freedom was to get out of Glasgow by the main Highland road and head for the north. Saturday dawned with a cold day of rain that slashed across the street, drenching all. The caravan was to be picked up on the farther east side of Glasgow, but my first stop was Skinner's, for I had ordered a specially decorated cake there. Our wedding anniversary was to fall in the first week of the excursion, and I had designed a suitable inscription to be carried out in icing, with initials and dates. Presumably they had been working on it overnight, for it was already boxed, with the lid open for inspection, when I arrived. The young girl who displayed it to me, before wrapping, was eager to know what it was about, but she courteously refused to ask, saying instead, 'We thought it might be for a club.' So I told her about the caravan, and how our wedding anniversary would be during the trip, and that my wife knew nothing of this cake affair, and that on the evening of the day I would produce the wrapped parcel, open it up, display it, and she would ceremonially cut the first slice while I poured two glasses of special wine, with the gale, no doubt, raging without. As I expanded the narrative — for I guessed she might be a romantic little thing — she stared at me with her eyes widening and filling with tears. Then she gulped a sob, abandoned the parcel, said, 'Oh! Isnae that no' lovely! Inn't it no!' and ran through to the back shop where she gathered the other girl assistants to tell the tale. Eventually she came back, still overcome, and took my money, with the others coming to have a peep at the fellow.

However, Nature would not co-operate in this spirit. The rain, which was to increase and drive for another twenty-four hours, chased me through Glasgow and out at the other side. A small man led me to the caravan, with our car number painted on its stern, showed me how to hitch it on, gave some perfunctory instructions about the gas stove and lighting, as well as a confused set of directions about how to back, and left me to it. The drive through Glasgow was a knotting agony. The Saturday traffic was at its height; pedestrians, hating the rain and wind, simply dashed across the streets; the stopping and starting which set off the caravan's own braking system, shook me and the car like a cocktail. It took me a few miles to get the hang of it. At the door to our building I was exhausted. But Dorothy had already packed everything. We flung the stuff in heaps upon the floor of the van, never stopping to see what the inside was like, and set off before my nerve went. So we crawled that old familiar road, dropping down to Great Western Road in a paroxysm of snatches and jerks, then running more smoothly along, through Anniesland, at least reaching the Balloch Road, Dumbarton, Loch Lomond itself, Luss, Tarbet, going up and over into Crianlarich and then Strathfillan to Tyndrum. There was the climb again on the Glencoe Road, past Bridge of Orchy. Hour after hour passed, but mile after mile too; and at least they were familiar miles, and the rain and sleet streaks on the windscreen were not all that unfamiliar too. At last we were on into Glencoe, and the daylight was going. We passed Kingshouse, and started the descent through the rock passes towards Loch Leven. Almost nobody was on the road. There was suddenly a wide flat of rough parking space on my left, the result of the excavation of a whole hill shoulder in the making of the new road. I slowed and swept in there, drew up, switched off the engine and pulled on the brake. I remember laying my head forward on to the wheel and giving up. As I faded away somewhere, I was thinking that this was what it was like to be old and done.

Dorothy got out and left me. A long time later, or maybe not so long, she was back opening my door. 'Come on in.' She threw a raincoat over my head and we ran for the caravan door. Inside, it was miraculous. Most of the stuff was stowed away, in the fine cupboards and drawers. There was a light, a table erected. Cushioned seats. And on the table — there stood a bottle of whisky, a jug of water, and two drams already poured.

I recovered, fast. Not much was said. It was another of the times when with a stound of assurance and love I knew beyond doubt that the judgement — the choice — the only one that really matters, was right.

That night and the whole next day we took to sleeping and recovering, with sunshine coming at last, so that we were able to wander down by the brown river, or try the near hill shoulders. But on the Monday morning we were up and away, and there was no stopping us. To the far north-west we went, rolling the narrow roads, often finding it hard to get the van off for the night, because landlords, whose instinct often it is in these parts to discourage the traveller, had the trick of ditching the roadsides, or strewing them with boulders, to bend people like us away from a clearing that might have been ideal. From the far coast we turned eastwards to the North Sea shores and enjoyed the Moray Firth ports, southwards from Dornoch and Cromarty. Years later, we were to buy a caravan for ourselves when the sons were young, and make many a sortie. But there was never quite to be the same novel contentment, the same joys, the privacy, the peace. It was amazing to me to find by how far a caravan is superior to a tent. I know that many seem to get pleasure from huddling into great caravan villages, and good luck to them, with perhaps interesting conversation and even games of bridge at night. My job, and Dorothy's, had been incessant meeting with people, and we needed to be away. At the time, this holiday set us up for two hard winters to follow.

There was another excursion of a particular kind that I remember fondly. Twenty-five years after our wedding we ran an outing for the friends and participants of that time to the island of Inchcruin in Loch Lomond where the honeymoon had been spent. Again Alex MacFarlane took us all in his new, bigger, boat, and we cruised the loch, weaving among the islands, dining at Inversnaid, and at length landing, the lot of us, on the island itself. The party strolled romantically about the trees. This time there were children, god-children, nephews, and Granny Halliday, the only grandparent our family has ever had. The house was closed up, and shuttered, but two of us remembered it well. I thought of how, on that first night there, it had looked from the inside. It was built with a long corridor along one side, from which all the rooms opened off. We had been able to take an extra bedroom each by way of dressing-room and storage space. Then I was waiting for her at the door of the main bedroom. She came at length, walking slowly, wearing a dressing-gown splashed hugely with a pattern of gold, and with a lamp in her hand. 'That's my wife', I spoke into the long corridor, which, like my life, was empty but for her.

CHAPTER FIVE
Family Life

On the high walls at the top of the main staircase in our house, there is a minor gallery of paintings. Among the *objets d'art* are eight family portraits in oils. If you paint pictures, the only ones you get to keep are those depicting members of the household. The other sitters all insist on taking them away, whether they happen to have paid a fee or not. When Dorothy was starting up this part of her career she sought among us people who would be content to stand, or sit, if they were lucky, for many hours at a time and into the small hours.

The first portrait that came through with everything of her eventual authority as an artist was her father's, painted while I was in America on that three-month trip round the States. There followed quickly a most searching study of my father, with some of his books and interests about him. It was hung for a season in the annual exhibition of the Glasgow Institute of the Fine Arts, where it was warmly reviewed by Tom Honeyman, the acquaintance of my banking days, who by that time was the director of the Glasgow Art Galleries. My father was inexpressibly affected by this production and its accolades. As a young and poor man he had annually visited the Institute shows, and would never have been able to forecast that one day his own portrait would hang there.

There is a series of three of me, all very different, two of which hung in the Royal Scottish Academy. One was called *The Yellow Jacket*. It shows me black and beetling, but I fear accurately, wearing the upper half of my yachting oilskins, which I had to don because 'painters hardly ever get a chance to paint anything yellow'. To celebrate our coming to Edinburgh and my editorship of *The Scotsman* Dorothy also painted me, large and kilted, standing at a window which framed a dramatic view of Edinburgh Castle. In truth, the window was one of ours, and it frames, not Edinburgh Castle, which is two miles away, but the Mormon Church. I shall not say it is severe, but it is perhaps a shade lugubrious, since the main features of the face and eyes were done while I was still posing, but also watching on the television the Scottish rugby team getting a hammering from the Welsh at Murrayfield.

Our children also feature in this gallery, since they were at the time

61

rather young to be able to object. There is Ninian as a baby with Elizabeth Coghill, our first splendid nanny, and you can see his present features in that five-month-old face. And there is a somewhat older Mungo, wearing a gaucho outfit we had brought back from Peru, and hugging a treasured woolly llama which is now the loved plaything of the baby daughters of an oil sheikh in Saudi Arabia.

Dorothy has always been able to paint exact likenesses. This is not so common as might be hoped. Not that the subject of a portrait is ever likely to be enraptured by how the artist has seen him. Dorothy never used the camera, but she always seemed to achieve the way the person looked. Some, of course, are easier than others. Her memorable portrait of the actor Duncan MacRae — he is now long since dead; a good friend — was made while we were still in Glasgow, and it hangs in the Citizen's Theatre where he towered for years. It was done in his character of Jamie the Saxt. We had to hire the costume, and he wore this intricate pattern of material which was, I recall, more elaborate than what he wore in MacLellan's play. It is a musing study of him, well caught, his hand dropped over the arm of the chair and holding loosely a book, portraying, as it were, the Scholar King. However, Duncan always fell asleep during the sessions, when the book would drop from his hand and fall to the floor of the room, which was some distance below the dais. Since the book was a period one, some rare old volume from my meagre collection, and was disintegrating with each descent, Dorothy took to placing a cushion to catch the battered volume. As a background to this kingly study, you will see the Honours of Scotland, the crown, the sceptre and the sword, and she did a separate study of these treasures, working late at night, locked into the Crown Room in Edinburgh castle.

Roy Thomson, my old newspaper chief, the first Lord Thomson of Fleet, was a keen patron of hers, and she did two portraits of him, one of them going to the University of New Brunswick, who honoured him. There was another Canadian who was a fan of her Lymond books. He commissioned her to paint a picture of any one of her characters from that series of books, and to send it to him naming the price. She selected the purely fictional character of Abernethy, the elephant trainer, and there he stands now in our little gallery, with his broken nose and tough half-bald look, the wee man from Fife who intended that the court of France would believe him to be a Turk; and behind him there looms an authentic sixteenth-century elephant. I say there he stands, for alas, the Canadian patron died as the job was finishing, and his widow wrote urgently to deny the contract, saying the picture would not be needed now. So he joined the family.

People like to have their portraits painted in clothes of their own choosing. Flora Adam, Seumas's wife, was a beautiful subject, untouched by the passing of the years, and she agreed to model for Dorothy who was not finding female subjects. She chose a long silk dress with a most detailed pattern, and Dorothy toiled long into many nights to complete the portrait, working over the tiny design like a needlewoman engaged on a coronation robe.

I took an occasional small role in these activities, sometimes being retained to engage the victim in conversation. But my main role started after the subject had left, and it was commonplace for me to don some robe or skirt and pose so that Dorothy could capture the draping. There must be no mention of the times when I turned a shapely hip, or swept to the dais in a peer's or lawyer's robe, to say nothing of their wigs, and nothing at any time will induce me to reveal what part of these far scattered portraits — what ringed hand, what shoulder, or indeed what other part of the anatomy — I helped to set forth. However, it is good to know that one has been a modest servant of the arts.

Dorothy had at this time also embarked on a three-dimensional contribution. She took a great area of our dining-room wall and started a mural to be called *The Modern Athens*. Here, creating figures in raised relief, she modelled her new Athenians in plaster. These were not fictional characters, but the folk of the present day whom you could see walking the contemporary streets of Edinburgh — heads of state and of departments, judges, bankers, provosts, nobles, artists, musicians, authors and playwrights, university characters, scholars — all of the most eminent who lived and moved amongst us in 1960 or thereby. They were all elegantly draped in ancient Athenian togas and cloaks, and short kilted and fringed garments. Many of the personalities came and sat for her as she modelled them in the upright plaster, which she learned to sculpt in fine lines. This had to be kept damp, and the dining-room, out of commission then for years, was festooned with hanging rags that dripped. We had meant to have a grand unveiling ceremony, to be called the Frieze Warming, but four of the characters never got finished. Ann Redpath, the artist, had her face chiselled off because Dorothy thought it lacked boldness, and Willie Merrilees, the former Chief Constable, still lacks an arm, thus giving point to the title of his autobiography (he is a small man) *The Short Arm of the Law*. However, it will no doubt get done, and the party will be on, but there are sadly more than a few who will now be absent.

For a long time we were a small family, the two of us. For all her other triumphs, Dorothy was repeatedly struck with obstetric disasters, and had many miscarriages, including one in the South of France, when she was carried in the middle of the night out of Roy Thomson's villa and dealt with in the Princess Grace Clinique. We were grateful for the urgent action of the local doctor but I feared she was going to die. Also the affair nearly ruined us; everybody on the case seemed to present separate bills — sisters, nurses, attendants — even the young girl who carried in the Lucozade.

At last, after a full-term and difficult pregnancy, we had a boy born dead. For a few days she was very far away, and I did what was required. I offered the little body to the anatomy department of the university medical department, but they said 'No'. So we buried him in Liberton Cemetery, without a name, for as far as I could find out he had never lived, and I had to conclude that he had not qualified to have a soul. I have not discussed this with any of them, but it seems to be well known that Roman Catholics believe unchristened babies have no entrance to Paradise, and are relegated to somewhere called Limbo. Of course, I do not believe a word of this myself. The Founder has done an adequate job of endorsing the claims of children to whatever present or ultimate citizenship is attainable. But none of us knows. And if, after this, I find it to be true, and there is a heavenly limbo, I shall go there and find him, and take him away. When the tiny coffin was ready, Seumas, my close friend, found me by telephone as I was wandering here and there about Edinburgh, and wanted to come with me to the cemetery. We had done nearly everything together, but this was for me alone, not to be shared. I think he knows that I was more grateful than I was ever able to say.

Then Ninian came, and had a normal and stalwart childhood. There was no name of Ninian in any of his ancestry, but it seemed right for him, and when he was a few months old I took him the long car run to Whithorn and had him christened there in the parish church of St Ninian, our first Celtic missionary, believing that if he grew up thinking in any way like me about these things, he would be glad of it. And if not, it would not have done him any harm. In the way of personal faith, this I think is just about as much as I can do. But I am still engaged in the search for truth.

There were more miscarriages. Dorothy told me one day she had investigated a certain surgical operation which somebody was performing, that she had had him examine her, and she had booked herself to have it done. It was; and then came Mungo.

The logics for his name took a deal of compiling, for a woeful number of people, including of course Dorothy's mother, had never heard of the name Mungo, the beloved patron saint of Glasgow, another old Celt of some sort. One of our overworked family jests is that Granny Halliday thought Mungo was some form of skin disease, but I confess I doubt if I heard her say anything so specific, and it is likely that I burst out with the tale in a moment of the sort of hysteria common on these occasions. I have never confessed this to Mungo, but there is an error in his birth certificate, for when I registered him I gave the day of our wedding as 1956 instead of 1946, and there it is to this day, although I made a late sheepish note in pencil that the true date was 1946. This was after I had gone back to see the registrar to get the thing altered, and was repelled from the counter, after being given the impression that the date, or any other fact in the document, which I had double-checked earlier in his presence, could only be altered by Act of Parliament. I think I doubt that, but at the time I was too weak a character to carry the cause further.

By this time Dorothy was slacking off from her painting and sculpture activity and had turned to writing. The story is that she had exhausted all the available publications of her favourite reading, historical fiction, and that when she complained to me that the supply had run out and it wasn't all that good anyway, I had replied, 'Why don't you write a book yourself?' This is on a par with a celebrated remark of Alistair MacLean, in the course of a television interview with Jackie Stewart: 'I don't really read books. Whenever I want a good story I write one.' So far as Dorothy's capabilities were concerned, I had already seen and read a small masterpiece she had completed to please herself. It was a long short story set in some historical period, with — her characteristic — a profound and yet elusive love story. Never one to fall short of completion, she had also done about four large and splendid illustrations, which any of the current glossy magazines would be eager to publish. So I had no doubt she could do a book.

For probably eighteen months she worked, reading enormously into historical areas she had never reached, first in my own books, then the libraries, then the manuscript collections, and the foreign libraries, and she was quite early discarding the familiar unresearched repetitions of tradition and moving by deduction and instinct to spaces in these old tales whose inmost corners had never been reached. We scoured the Border lands, and the Highlands, following old roads and tracks, seeing the sites and the ruins, the lost harbours, the old streets and buildings of many a town. It absorbed her.

I had no idea what she was writing. I never read a sentence of the many finished pages which seemed to rise in heaps. Fools and bairns and husbands should not see things half done. Even now I never see anything before the completed manuscript; but thereafter, I see it first.

One day after nearly two years of this she handed me the immense pile of pages that formed *The Game of Kings*, the first of the Lymond series saying, 'Do you think you would have time to read this?'

It took me two days, or properly two nights running, each time from about midnight to 6 am. When it was finished I remember laying my head down on the desk, dazed, triumphant. I was first of all aboundingly glad for her, that the time had been so worth it, and even if nothing were to come after there would be a lifetime satisfaction, for someone like her, in the contentment that it could be done. The style was amazing, the scholarship nimbly knitted into a tale, with personalities both historical and fictional, so realised that the whole thing lived and spoke of human dilemmas and contrivance and idealism. Beyond that, I knew for certain that here was a sudden milestone in this kind of writing, and if it got into print it would never stop expanding as people, taking time, would come to find it was unique and unsurpassed.

Five distinguished British publishers turned it down. We never remind any of them about it, although many of the people who run these publishing firms are friends and even professional colleagues. Now and again, one of them will say, 'I wish you had let us know that Dorothy had written a book.' We always let this go. Perhaps they have no means of checking what has been turned down by them in the past.

One publisher, rejecting the manuscript on the grounds that it was too long, encouraged us greatly by sending his reader's report. This person, unnamed, in an enthusiastic recommendation that they should take on the book, said:

> I have read every word of *The Game of Kings* with increasing admiration and pleasure. It is eccentric certainly . . . and monstrous without a doubt. But what eccentricity and what monstrousness! At the end I was quite lost in admiration of the vigour and wit which kept this bespangled, word-crammed, plot-ridden and fantastic tale all in one piece; and I searched in vain to find a thousand words expendable in the whole . . . I have learned to respect Miss Dunnett. She knows practically everything, and her sharp, adroit, level-headed humour kept me afloat, so that not once was I in danger of going down even for the first time in a welter of Scottish genealogy and costume description. Her great thing is *not* to explain. If you don't know what a papingo-shoot is, well then, that is your look-out. Latin, court French, Italian and Spanish conceits flitter impertinently in the dialogue. And so do endless references to things and situations which no doubt held no secrets for Shakespeare, but which present foxers in 1957. She must have the most ostentatious dictionary in the world; else where did she discover 'loricating', 'splanchic', 'tourmalines' etc? The effect is like being in some great murky place, like Holyrood or the Tower of London, but without a guide or any of the little notices telling one where to go, or what this thing was used for. All the dreadful realities and foibles of the past exist hugger-mugger and one reels out, overcome by a mixture of small, cold rooms and huge hot treacheries. Two things extra Miss Dunnett grants — a wonderful way with Scottish women and a grim way with Scottish weather. *How* it rained in 1547! We should be thankful. And for only one of her many bright observations, how about this?
>> 'Mr Crouch, wittingly obese like a middle-aged titmouse, sat enthroned on his stomach, giving tongue. Incidents of his boyhood surged to cataclysmic peaks of pointlessness. Episodes from his career in the Princess Mary's household explored tedium to its petrified core.'

The reader went on to a brief summary of the plot, and to emphasise his enthusiasm for the publishing of the book, mentioning the 'witty renegade named Lymond, who is one of the best picaresque-character inventions I have ever come across'.

There were other gratifying tributes, although none quite so lavish as the unknown reader's, but nobody was prepared to publish the book. An air of discouragement was beginning to hang about us, for it had been a grinding two years of toil and application. There was no doubt that there were uncounted riches of production to come, if we could achieve the first step. So I wrote to Lois Dwight Cole.

Lois Cole was an American publisher whom I had met several times and got to know. When she was working for the firm of Dutton's, I

66

called on her once in New York and she pulled me off to meet the head of the firm, a man called MacRae. He was about the most typical MacRae I had ever seen, looking as if he had come straight from Kintail. But when he spoke about his Scots origins he said that he had been in Scotland on a visit the year before — 'and I am the first of us that has been home since 1723'.

Lois's greatest renown up to that point, however, was that she had discovered Margaret Mitchell, the author of *Gone with the Wind*. This unknown writer had bundles of unsorted manuscript in her home, where she had been writing a Civil War story for years, and Lois persuaded her to part with them, bearing the nondescript parcels back to the publishing office, which was then Macmillan's, for Lois believed in keeping professionally on the move. Reading the stuff, she realised that in these dog-eared heaps of paper, there was a great epic. She persuaded her chiefs to publish it, and to let her edit it. It meant spending endless hours with the author, and a deal of persuasion, suggesting new names for some of the characters. The heroine, for example, was called Pansy O'Hara. Lois invented the name Scarlett, and worked on the author to agree to the re-christening. The rest, as they say, is history.

We turned our backs on the British publishing scene, and I wrote a letter to Lois, saying: 'How would you like to see an astounding manuscript of a story written by the wittiest woman in Scotland?' Bless her, Lois rushed back a brief message saying: 'Send it'. The contract came back in a very few days. Lois used to say to us in her older age: 'I always thought that Margaret Mitchell was my greatest find, but Dorothy Dunnett gave me more real pleasure.'

Lois edited the volume — by this time she was working for Putnam's — and she sold the British rights for Dorothy to Cassell, not one of those who had rejected her in the early attempts.

The course was then set for the next five volumes, which took fifteen years. We visited every place in the books, including the Russian locations; every inch of Scotland and the coast. Much of England, we knew maybe better than the normal native. Norway, all France, Italy, Orkney and Shetland, Yugoslavia, Sicily, the desert places, North Africa, seeking out the essential oases. Dorothy went alone to such places as Turkey and Spain, but it was often in the form of a family holiday that we set out. 'Oh, mummy, not another old church!' the boys would wail from the back of the car as we parked, and we occasionally had to leave them there, eating ice-cream and playing Scrabble while we poked into mediaeval apses and spiral stairs, or paced the distance of the bowshot. It is not likely that these locations will ever be faulted. Several times a year she has letters from readers telling how they have been over the course of the rooftop chase in Blois (*Queen's Play*) or have measured the accuracy of the window placements in some remote royal castle, in the guardroom used by the French kings' Scottish Archers as they stood down from duty. We traced the route of the royal progress from season to season, and know the banks of the Loire. Transcriptions of manuscripts, old maps and prints, the tides and currents in streams and harbours — we have the lot.

I have in my time met some scholars of fair fame and dedication, but I have never known anyone with the intense power of concentration that Dorothy has. She is able to go at it for an immensely long day, and many a time I have come down in the morning to find her still working. Oddly, she is not casually observant. Often I point out to her in passing some incident or feature in the landscape that seems of interest, but which she will not have noticed. Yet when her attention is drawn, she sees suddenly much more in it than I do, and she has to point out the unusual features to me.

In among all this she wrote, between volumes, a series of modern thrillers, where the hero, with bifocals, is a man called Johnson Johnson and inevitably he is something in the Secret Service. He is a portrait painter, with a yacht called *Dolly*; all the stories are told in the first person by the girl in the case, and the titles came through as *Dolly and the Singing Bird*; *Dolly and the Doctor Bird*; *Dolly and the Nanny Bird*; *Dolly and the Cookie Bird*, and so on. When these were first published in America all the titles had to be changed, since the President was called Lyndon Johnson, and his wife bore the unexplained name of Lady Bird. The publishers were wary of offending the White House. Later reprints have restored the original names. But we are no doubt in trouble if a presidential candidate turns up one day called Dolly, or Bird again, or Johnson. Or even Dunnett, a far from improbable eventuality.

By way of a fling between series, she paid some attention to a suggestion from her American publishers that they would like a one-off book from her centred on some well-known historic character, like Mary Stuart, or Bonnie Prince Charlie. She told them that everybody had written a book about these ones, but how would they care for a book about Macbeth, who could hardly be better known, thanks to Shakespeare, although she knew nothing of him herself. They thought that was great, and a contract was signed to deliver the book in a year, or two at the most.

This industry was something of an interruption to anything like normal life. The book got into print some six years later than the contract had stipulated, and was seized on by her devoted fans, including a new generation who had come to know Lymond.

Dorothy has demanding fans, and I must confess I resent, in a way, many of them. Twelve hundred readers write to her regularly, and they get replies, some at inordinate length. She will not put them off nor prepare a friendly stock answer. Many of them are scholarly and academic, others are simply splendid enthusiasts, and the onset of their verbosity impedes her work by months. There are sadly all too many who write to state such information as: 'I have got your book out of the library and would like you to answer the following seventeen questions'. She does. They arrive to visit, often without warning. More than once I have arrived home to discover, most usually, a lady fan, taking a late afternoon tea, having arrived for morning coffee, and sitting on with Dorothy cooking lunch for her about half-time. My discourteous device is to exclaim 'I'm so glad to have arrived in time to run you to your hotel.'

Horses, dogs and children are called after her characters. Lymond fans meet each other in groups on the great horse-ramp staircase at Amboise, or outside Topkapi, with the books in hand, following the steps of the hero's adventures. Groups of fans in such far states as Iowa and California circulate chain letters, of which they send her copies. It is an amazing thing to have married a cult.

We spent much time with our children at all their ages, but we needed help at home to take them through some of the details of growing up. So we had a superb series of young nannies who came to live with us, and became daughters in the house. There was Cathie from Shetland, with whom Ninian learned to speak. And he spoke like a Shetland child, lisping also folk-rhymes and tales. There were two Norland nannies, Elizabeth and Sue; and the memorable Edna; all now away with their own families, and the closest of our friends for ever. These were commemorated by Dorothy in the comic thriller *Dolly and the Nanny Bird* in a moving dedication of the volume to them, which read:

Dear Elizabeth, dear Edna, dear Sue:
This book is for you, and for all those other friends of the young who left, carrying with you the love of two generations. It is also, of course, for your children.

It is easy to give the impression of a grim remote scholarship above the cares and demanding trivia of life. Nannies, anyway, cannot do everything, and they are off frequently. Both of us could do everything connected with babies — the midnight stirrings, and feeds, the changing, the stories, the songs, the caring and holding, the walks with the pram, the long patient slog at entertaining them and of making life seem interesting and adventurous. However tired we were, it always seemed worth while.

So to Macbeth, and it was back to the old story, the long treks to the Alpine passes, to ancient monasteries in mid-Europe, to remote parts of Brittany, and the Mediterranean, to Rome, Norway, Denmark, Orkney, various navigable British rivers with forgotten harbour walls and settlements. In eighteen months Dorothy knew more about the historical actuality and setting of the man Macbeth than did anyone alive. Through his life, in a thin thread of kinship, ran also the contemporary figure of the Earl of Orkney, known to most scholars as a figure called Thorfinn who existed at that time. There was some sort of relationship, for they had the same proven ancestors, and he turned up in references, in historical footnotes, and even in such fiction as had been attempted, as a foster-brother or a cousin of Macbeth. It seemed that he had much to do also with mainland Scotland, and instead of sticking to his Scandinavian kingdoms and the watery passage of the seasonal North Sea, that great basin of commerce and trade, he could be found historically as far south as Fife and Angus and the emerging new Scottish kingdom. I was hearing about this from time to time and, doubtless like the publishers, was awaiting the indications that Dorothy had actually started to write the book.

One night she told me that she had decided, and could prove, that Macbeth and Thorfinn were one and the same man, and given a year or two more of research and topographical and genealogical investigation, the story that would come out in the end would be one that told how this ingenious young prince went far to gathering together the young Scottish kingdom in the shape we know it now, while from his northern strongholds he fended off the envious Scandinavian kings, most of whom were his kinsfolk.

This is the story that turned out to be *King Hereafter*, and my only contribution to it was the suggestion of the title. Again, in all holiday and spare times we went travelling, flying low in aircraft over the sites of great sea battles, climbing to obscure hill forts and towers, scanning the estuaries to place the opposing fleets and forces, trying the terrain where the horses would gallop. It took two and a half years more before she could even begin to write it. By this time she had done genealogical tables for 143 families of the eleventh century, and among other esoteric feats she could name practically every Norman who had taken part in the Conquest, and knew who his grandfather was, and could tell where he had settled in the big giveaway of land by William. There is a master table of the genealogy of all the crowned heads, earls, chiefs, and princelings of Central and Western Europe — it is 25 feet wide, drawn on the back of a strong piece of wallpaper. No doubt these items will form in the future a vital part of some treasured archive.

With four and a half years of research to be held in her mind, where thousands of facts, deductions, problems, developments, people, imaginary characters, and all the apparatus of creative writing jostled each other, Dorothy was ready to start writing the book. Another eighteen months went to the writing of *King Hereafter*. Even this run at the narrative was far from straight, as it had to be interrupted for fresh assaults on some historical source, and there were proving sorties into the backward mists. So the covering wings of the writing task hovered and settled more firmly upon the house, and all of her strength, when she had the time, was directed to sustaining the effort. The household had still to be run, and the boys attended to. Escort duties for them were of course coming largely to an end. For years we had taken them to school and collected them, ferried them to the doctor, the football and cricket practices, the piano, swimming and golf lessons, the parties, the country picnics, the school outings, the buying of shoes and trousers, and all that. They were now at the stage when they wanted to

70

visit friends and come home late; be conned through their prep, and in general look after their own spare time, among the essentialities of which is to borrow a car for some unspecified mission, an arrangement that proves to be considerably more anxiety-making than the mere walking home late from somewhere.

We also held to the idea of family holidays, making them as adventurous as possible, with the one built-in requirement that the holiday had to be spent in some place where one or other of us, or better, both, could use the location and some of the experience in subsequent fiction. 'Will you use that, or shall I?' was a commonplace question we would pose to each other, grinning, as some spectacular sight or incident unrolled itself. During the Macbeth time we spent two Christmasses in Paris, two full-length summer holidays in America, as well as in Madeira, one in the Caribbean islands and two in Crete. It was in Barbados that I discovered that my swimming days were not over after all, since even the Mediterranean had long since become too chilly for me, and as for the west coast of Scotland, to go in at all had always been an ordeal, but in later years I had readily come to the decision, and welcomed it, that the sea was not only too big, but also far too wet and cold. The water rolling in to the south shore of Barbados was like warm and buoyant milk, making my Presbyterian conscience almost, but not quite, ache with the shameless luxury of it. We had no such twinges when sallying out late on Christmas Eve to attend the High Mass in Notre-Dame in Paris. Paris was also a lazy way of avoiding the fearful chore of cooking Christmas dinner. Granny Halliday came to Paris with us. She believes that Christmas dinner is an unvarying ritual, while for me, I'll take a fine Paris meal any time, in or out of season.

Dorothy has got some kind of a contract to produce a series of, say, six to ten novels about a fifteenth-century character called Niccoló, who will be a merchant adventurer and banker based in Venice and Trebizond and such places. So we'll take the high road yet again.

During the first ten years or so of our married life, in Glasgow, we lived in furnished rooms, and then a flat in the street called Glasgow Street, which was within a hundred yards of my old school, though I had never heard of it. We seemed rarely to have visitors there, except for somebody sitting for a portrait. Dorothy and I between us covered a working day of eighteen hours, but we often broke off for the cinema, theatre, or surges into the country, sometimes with a tent. Such entertaining as we did took place in the fine restaurants of Glasgow, now bustling back to their old and couthy splendour.

The first thing we did, when we realised that the editorship of *The Scotsman* meant a permanent move to Edinburgh, was to decide to buy a house.

'It's got to be the right one,' said Dorothy. 'We'll work at it, and get

71

it right, and I'm never going to move again.'

It sounded easy, and I do not recall making any observation other than a kind of agreement. Dorothy saw eighty-four houses, and I saw about nine of them, before we got the one we wanted. She pinned up a huge map of Edinburgh on a wall, and with a series of coloured pins indicated those she had seen, those she had still to see, those she wanted me to see, those which were too decrepit or unsuitable to be worth seeing again, those which might be worth seeing another time, and what not. All this must have been useful toning up for the subsequent ushering of Lymond and others about the world, for we have become a house acutely aware of maps, and the boys too have this tendency.

We got the right house at last, moving in by mid-August 1956. It was while sailing in the cargo boat *Loch Carron* to the Western Isles that I had phoned Hector Ross, my lawyer, to be told that he had clinched the deal for us, taking it on himself to go somewhat beyond the top price I had laid down; we rejoiced in a remote and lovely part of Skye that night, tied up to the pier at Uig. Not long ago on a car jaunt to the islands I was able to point out to our sons the very box from which I had made the telephone call, high on the roadside brae above Uig. The house was to echo fairly emptily with us for years. Dorothy set to, designing every year a fresh room, and having it carried out as funds were gathered and then disbursed. Much of the painting and decorating we did ourselves. Sometimes tradesmen from *The Scotsmen* came to lend a hand, sent out by Jim Coltart, the chief executive, who told me that in his times in the *Express* newspapers, it was the habit and the perk for each senior executive to have a complete room redecorated every year.

With this setting, from being a reluctant mixer and determined not to be a having-a-few-people-in-for-dinner person, Dorothy became probably one of the most notable hostesses in our part of Scotland. The highlight became the time when every year during the Edinburgh Festival, we had parties for over a hundred people. These took place after the shows, when the performers have their main meal of the day, and others have time to attend a theatre first. 'After the shows', we made clear on the invitations, there was an enormous buffet. Then we all crowded into our large drawing-room with fireplaces at each end, to hear an entertainment. It became a great feature of these affairs that, mainly through good friend Dick Telfer, we were able to find good young promising artists to play or perform for us. We had several solo pianists, Moray Welsh the cellist, Daphne Boden (daughter of an old friend, Leonard Boden, the painter) the harpist, and Jimmy Fisher, the folk-song man.

I suppose there may be many about who remember these nights. It is good to think that Yehudi Menuhin and many another figure got some of the Scottish zest in hearing our own music, and by our own talented youngsters. Others met with us, as they had met in many a place about the world of entertainment, not having the time to see the others perform but glad to have a drink and share some nostalgia with them.

72

They were generally and not ungenially true to type. I took Laurence Harvey into one of the crowded rooms on a night when he came late, and said, 'Probably a lot of people here you know.' Being tall, he saw across the heads the immense figure of James Robertson Justice, and with a face shrivelled with dislike, he made for him.

'I was in a film with you once,' he announced to Jimmy, in a voice that begged for trouble.

'Ah, yes, I remember,' Jimmy responded affably. 'You were the page-boy.'

Laurence's face pinched with hate. His voice too. 'I,' he said, 'was the prince.'

What with Dorothy's terrible effort to finish Lymond, to struggle her way through the endless Macbeth agony, and the later pressure to complete a long overdue Nanny book, the huge parties have had a few years of suspension, and in their place we reverted to smaller dinner parties of an old-fashioned sort. But you never know.

There is an odd and intriguing perk and privilege which marriage brings to a man. He is allowed to accompany his wife when she is buying and trying on clothes. This is an unexpected ritual, not to be missed, at least for the first one or two occasions. I imagine the whole performance changes when the woman is on her own, but the drill is tremendous when the man in the case turns up. In no other situation is one so deferred to, while the stripping and hitching goes shamelessly on. All the other assistants, mostly young, find a reason to turn up in the fitting-room, no doubt out of a professional female interest, but making no effort to conceal that their main interest is to have a look at the man who, presumably, is paying the bill. For a good many years this latter has not been my role, and I have thus not been to the fore in exploiting the occasion, but don't miss it, at least once, I say, if you qualify.

There are equal hazards in buying clothes for a wife and, let us say, a little surprise. When I did my three-month visit to the United States, it was at a time when there were no clothes worth looking at in the British scene. I got Dorothy to give me her measurements, and determined that she would have some truly stunning outfit as a result. At the end of the trip, which had been necessarily modest in terms of outlays, I gathered up the rest of my dollars and went into a famous New York store, heading for the spectacular beachwear department. At this time, beachwear was, on home shores, a dreary affair, that consisted of mainly black one-piece bathing suits, enlivened occasionally when some lady bather would adopt a costume of white cotton, which when wet became transparent in the most agreeable fashion. I settled on one outfit all in yellow. It consisted of long pants, short pants, a bikini top, a skirt, a little jacket, and a hat, six pieces, all beautifully made. I handed out the measurements, and they made up the set.

You know the rest, I am sure. None of them fitted, except maybe the hat. I should have known better. It's not that women are not numerate in matters of importance. It is that they live in a gentle world of self-deception. After that, I always measured her.

Buying a hat was always easier, since we have the same size of heads. Not much attention is paid, even in fashionable milliners, when you try on a woman's stetson, but the transaction becomes dubious if you are looking for a small feathered number. This is a good test of one's ability to carry off a situation without appearing to notice the shudder of enquiry and perhaps even vulgar disapproval. Not for nothing do they make those wretched little fellows in Eton and Harrow wear those daft hats. It is to inure them to the sniggers of peasantry. I should say I don't go in nowadays for this kind of purchasing, because Dorothy would much rather buy her own.

Writing is the most fearful drudgery in the world. With someone capable of such sustained effort as Dorothy is, people who are in any way interested in having a view fall into two groups. One lot thinks merely that writing is easy for such as she. If it was as easy for them, they would be doing it. The other group tends to have a little more understanding, and to say 'I just don't know how you get the time to do all that you do'. But this second lot also includes the dangerous ones whose motto is: 'If you want a job well done you go to a busy person'; and they lumber her with such things as addressing small-scale meetings, and then they go back to their television sets while she slogs it out through a night to prepare speech notes. I frankly do what I can to protect her from this, but she has a sense of obligation as well as duty, and that is a perilous combination.

Still, she has done much outside of writing and painting, and making the happiest home that I could have believed possible. She has been for many years a Trustee of the Scottish National War Memorial in Edinburgh Castle, the shrine of Scots men and women who have fallen for world causes of one kind or another. She is also, in her own right, a director of Scottish Television, and seems to be making a fair contribution.

I am a privileged man, and I know it. Once, at a leisurely reception, we sat together and had a drink at a small table. Later a woman friend we both knew and liked said aside to me, 'You two are amazing. I would never guess you are married. There you were sitting and talking and laughing as if you were strangers who wanted to get to know each other.'

I said, 'She is the most interesting woman I know.'

CHAPTER SIX
The First Victim

More than any other influence in my boyhood, it was the Boy Scout movement that set me free. And yet I joined the Boy Scouts with some reluctance; spent the most energetic years of my teens and my early twenties in it; and eventually repudiated it in public for the bureaucratic authoritarianism and loss of the early flexibility with which it became afflicted in the post World War I years.

I had wanted to join the Boys' Brigade. My father had been in the Boys' Brigade and the three sons of the Mowat family, who were my cousins, Jim, George and Jack, were all enthusiastic members of our local Brigade Company, the IIIth Glasgow — or, as it was affectionately known in the city, never at a loss for picturesque descriptions, 'the three caun'le-sticks'. Sir William Smith, the founder of the Brigade, was a Caithness man born and bred and he had come to Glasgow where this interesting organisation with its Church associations was set up. As a very small boy I attended his funeral, in the middle of the wartime, about 1916. A huge parade of boys in their uniforms, with bands, gun-carriages, flowers and tremendous solemnity, paraded through Kelvingrove Park and my mother took me to see this spectacle. The band drummers' instruments were muffled with black cloth with only a three or four inch diameter section of parchment exposed, on which the sticks tapped. Even in that time of death great crowds turned out, and we felt we participated in an enormous mystery which, however, was continuing in the form of lively companies all over Glasgow, the headquarters of the BB, and to us at that time the centre of the world.

I used to be taken to the annual concerts and parades of the IIIth Company which remained a good quality amateur show as the years went by. However, I was more enchanted by the military parades where in some large drill hall the boys would march and countermarch, do rifle drill and form fours with great precision. They also performed gymnastics and pyramids and swung Indian clubs as well as signalling with noisily fluttering semaphore flags. This was great stuff. They drilled with authentic-looking rifles which, although they did not fire anything, could be cocked and trigger-pressed with an appealing rattle of musketry. Compared with this, anything I had seen in public of the Boy Scouts seemed to show them forth as a straggling mob with no bangs or precision and their drill lacked fire. Moreover, I ached to join the IIIth because my three cousins were there. Jack was my contemporary in age. He became an ordained minister of the Church of Scotland, later served with the University of Aberdeen and wound up a conscientious ministry in the Church of Scotland in Rome before retiring to the Mowat's old family place in Freswick. George, who was about the age of my own brother, George, trained as an architect and surveyor and served for many years in the Department of Agriculture in Scotland, especially in Argyll. Jim became a director of Beardmore's and probably one of the leading experts on steel-making in the west of Europe. At the end of World War II he was unexpectedly given a spectacularly senior military rank and sent as head of a British Commission to see what could be done about restoring the steel industry of defeated Germany. He had, in the meantime, leaving our old church of Finnieston, founded at the other end of Glasgow what was said to be the biggest Sunday school in Scotland, while George had devoted many years of his life and his unending energy to raising funds to build and furnish the church of St Bride's in Oban.

But my father felt that the Boy Scouts were more in my line, and one night I presented myself at a basement in the old YMCA hall in Partick near where we then lived in Hayburn Crescent. Here was a spirited group of about twenty-eight youngsters in all ages of boyhood and I quickly got on terms with them. We met every Friday night in the uniform with the mushroom hat and swotted to win badges — learning to tie knots and bandage the broken-limbed, studying the principles of the combustion engine, and finding out how to tend our bicycles if we had any, cook primitive camp food, read compasses and maps, calculate the height of adjacent peaks (there were none in Partick) and salute with three fingers of the hand upright, the pinkie in the meantime being held down by the thumb crossing the palm. This last was a feat I never mastered. Four rollicking young men supervised us as officers and there were some helpful senior boys, one of whom, Ian Paterson, the younger brother of our chief scoutmaster, was to become my brother-in-law.

The first glimpses of personal liberty of an undreamt quality came to me in this setting. I was on good terms with my classmates in school, but that atmosphere was hideously poisoned by the home requirement to be the best at everything. By this time the doubled-up home lesson period inaugurated by my father had apparently passed by, since the school was piling on homework to an extent that gratified even him; but the pressure did not ease up. There was the terror three times a year of bringing home my school report and presenting it to him, because we had to take these reports back, duly signed by our parent. There was one I remember where the results read something like '1st in English, 2nd equal in French, 2nd in German, 3rd in Science, 4th in Mathematics . . .' I waited while he perused this document grimly and hoped for a word of cheer. 'You're pretty weak in maths,' he said eventually.

Nothing of this overshadowed the Boy Scout nights and activities, and I was able with a fairly free heart to engage in their artless fun. There was also much talk of camping, and when the spring came and the early summer, off we went indeed to one or two modest weekend sorties in country pretty nearly within walking distance of our headquarters. This was an amazing release and I seized it with passion. All of it. The pitching of the tents, the songs round the campfire. We found ourselves taking on young political groups in debates, particularly about the condition of Scotland, and in other ways made ourselves fairly notable and perhaps even intrusive in our refusal to accept conformity. At that time most public gatherings and certainly cinema and theatre entertainments finished with the playing of the National Anthem, with even at times a few wavering voices joining in. We took to singing this lustily, concentrating on the anti-Jacobite verse which was a central feature of the song in its early days and in otherwise hushed choral endeavours our voices rang out with:

God grant that Marshal Wade
   May by Thy mighty aid
Victory bring
   May he sedition crush
And like a torrent rush
   Rebellious Scots to crush
God save the King.

Few meetings organisers and few inoffensive members of the public knew how to deal with these outbursts.

At this time we were in the forefront of an endeavour to obtain at Auchengillan, on the borders of Stirlingshire near Glasgow, a large moorland Scout camp for the City of Glasgow. Our lot helped to build it and we spent nearly every weekend under canvas there from Easter to late autumn.

One learned how inadequate was the supervision which brought to the fore in various Scout troops a generation of bores and bogus psychologists to run these organisations. There was one bullying schoolmaster, who was also a scoutmaster in an adjacent county, who turned up from time to time and on an occasion gave a morally religious address at the Sunday parade we called 'Scouts' Own'. He devoted himself to the future of these young fellows in the field of sex. He talked obscurely of the delights they would experience, using not crude terms for which he might have been forgiven, but allusions of the grossest indelicacy. But not, he warned, 'until a plain gold ring has been put upon the third finger of her left hand'. Boys squirm at such public references and, as an assistant scoutmaster, I would not let this man come back to us again. Other scoutmasters with handicapped members in their troop, knowing little about how to deal with afflicted youngsters whom they had promised 'to treat just like any other boy', must have shattered some of these unfortunates for life. We once played a scratch game of football, choosing two teams from a mixed crowd of teenagers. Two captains were needed to pick the teams and we nominated one of our side as one of them. A group from another troop thrust forward their champion as the other captain. He turned out to be a boy with one leg who moved about with a crutch. The game was a nightmare of farce with this boy playing as centre-forward being given the run of the field, his own mates seeming to tackle him and bouncing off so that they fell on the ground with their legs in the air bemoaning their inadequacy and praising this genius of the pitch in mock expiry. Young boys are prodigals of decency if the cause is made to seem authentic.

I remember also a ghastly campfire which I ran, attended by two or three hundred boys. After a few opening choruses and general bon homie, I called for volunteers to perform. Immediately there were cries from one sector 'Jimmy Thing, Jimmy Thing', pointing to one of their number. I said, 'Okay, Jimmy, you give us your piece', and he launched boldly into what appeared to be a song delivered with the most appalling hare-lip and throat deficiency I have ever heard. It was quite impossible to make out a single word. The company sat stunned through this gibberish, and when it finished his loyal little gang burst into tremendous applause shouting 'Encore, encore'. Whereupon he immediately launched into another piece, to receive the same ovation. There was no doubt in these instances, and many more, of some fragments of an intention of goodwill which had gone astray, but all round it could have been nothing but harmful, especially to the chief artists. One wondered what happened to them when they had to face the actuality of life with no kindly gang present to deceive them.

At an early age I made a break away from mass camping. By the late spring of 1926 I had already been working for nearly a year in the bank. Summer holidays were on a rota basis with not more than two away at any one time, and as I was the youngest I got a fortnight at the beginning of May. I decided to take to the road. Black's of Greenock had a tent shop less than a hundred yards from the office where I worked in West George Street. There I bought a small one-man tent for seventeen-and-sixpence. It was later marketed as the Guinea Tent, so that I was early in with my bargain. I bought from the Army surplus stores an old army webbing pack and also a solid pair of stiff boots which I prudently refrained from wearing until I could take to the road. I had one blanket sewn into a wide bag. In fact everything was wrong about the expedition except maybe the spirit of it, and there were times when that dwindled, for it was a cold and stormy spring. It was, moreover, timed, but not by me, to coincide exactly with the General Strike. My father travelled with me in a bus to Balmaha on Loch Lomondside, and there I parted from him with our new affection. I had of course no stove, but would have to light fires for the modest cooking which I had planned. My first night was on the shores of a bay south of Rowardennan and I slept little because I was shivering so violently. Later I took to wearing most of my clothes, only daring to take them off if there was sunshine in the middle of the day. The second day I climbed over the shoulder of Ben Lomond to Brig o' Turk at the Trossachs. It was on this ascent that I became knit forever to my native land. I was laden with useless gear, including a number of books. The new boots were chafing my feet to the drawing of blood, which they were to do for the duration of the journey. I could hardly bend my knees on the climb, since I had bought a pair of army breeches obviously made for some slim cavalry type with no knees worth speaking of, and I had later to unpick one of the seams in each leg to let me step out. But there below me, 2,000 feet or more, rolled the length of Loch Lomond with its islands and woods, its streams, its bays, with shadowing hills and fields, the plains to the south and the bulwarks of bens to the north, and all these I was seeing like this for the first time, teeming as they were with the songs and stories that I knew already, but had never located.

As I climbed I stopped often and looked back, to dote in a daze upon this amazing new relevation of beauty and endearment. I often spoke aloud to the scene — I still do this in the right places — pledging some sort of commitment. I remember I had tears to shed, just as some women do at weddings and probably for much the same reason. I went as far as Rannoch on this inland voyage, which lasted for ten days. There were few signs of the General Strike. No trains and buses seemed to be running, but shops were not short of supplies and I got and sent mail regularly. Although I was far from appearing like a militant figure, I was once accosted by a countryman who asked me, 'Are you one of these agitators sent out to stir up the country?' I travelled by Callander, Strathyre, Balquhidder, Lochearnhead, Killin, Kinloch Rannoch. I slept on Rannochside in the barn of Ardlarach farm and the next night in a surfaceman's hut beside the railway line at Rannoch Station. There was a night when in my tent beside Loch Tay I lay awake all night jerking with cold, and in the morning there was much frost on the ground. At Fortingall there is erected a statue to Stewart of Garth, the historian of the Highland Regiments. I copied down the Gaelic sentence from the inscription: Cuimhnichibh air na daoine o'n dh'thainic sibh. (Remember the men you came from.)

I made a poem or two on the way, and on the whole route I carried my preposterous load with a selection of books, including the Bible and a Gaelic testament and dictionary, a mouth organ, some writing paper, and a practice pipe chanter with a book of tunes to learn.

On the second last day I walked the whole of the railway line from Rannoch Station to Bridge of Orchy, since there is no road, and at night in Bridge of Orchy I camped in the school playground which was the only level little bit of grass available. People were good to talk to and they showed much kindness. I did not feel young, but I must have looked it. I got an occasional meal; a kindly bed once at Glengoulandie farm on the road to Rannoch; and I made friends, some of whom I kept in touch with until they died. Once a man came from a nearby modest cottage where he was living with his father. He turned out to be an old pupil of Hillhead High, my own school, but much older than me. However, he said that the night was cold and could I do with an extra blanket or two, an offer which I eagerly accepted. The blanket turned out to be flea-infested and I carried these little travellers back with me to Glasgow, which I reached as the General Strike stopped. I picked up a train at Stirling, got to Glasgow Central Station and went home.

The next year I travelled in the company of Stanley Smith, an indomitable and witty school-mate who became a chartered accountant and proprietor of an estate and house agency firm. We took to the Border country and explored all the famous Border towns and vales, striking afoot as far south as Thornhill and Moniaive and then north by St Mary's Loch and Cappercleuch, through Yarrow and over the hill to Loch Talla and so by Ayrshire and home.

The boon companion of these years was Jim MacDougall, a year younger than me and the younger brother of Jack MacDougall with whom I was running the Scout troop. Jim turned out to be the most resourceful of companions, up to all kinds of novel notions; and like me, passionately devoted to any kind of unorthodox travelling, especially in the north and west. I think he was the one who invented hitchhiking by sea. When I was not able to go with him he used to go with his kit to Balloch, hire a rowing boat for an unspecified week or two, row down the River Leven to the Clyde and from there across the widening Firth to Greenock. He would then lie off the Tail of the Bank, awaiting the arrival of an outward-bound puffer, one of the small steam-driven barges with a three-man crew who serviced cargoes and goods throughout the Western Isles and the Highland shores. It never seemed to be difficult for him to hail one of these and get a lift wherever they happened to be going. They would take him aboard, hitch up his rowing boat astern and there he would make himself useful for a few days helping with the cargo, making the tea and cleaning up, adding his spirited store of narrative and adventure to theirs. If they were coming home too soon he would unhitch and pick up some other puffer and go farther, for in those days he could always get one coming back empty from round about the Firth of Lorne or the Sound of Mull.

My own nautical adventures of a solo sort, apart from holidays, could, I found to my delight, be prosecuted within the bank's working day. If you got up at 4.30 to 5 am you could walk or get an early tramcar into the centre of Glasgow, and in Kingston Dock or the Queen's Dock you could pick up one of the fleet of Clyde tugs. There was almost invariably one about to leave to take an outward bound tramp steamer down river on the tide and there was no difficulty in getting the skipper to take you aboard; so you could be away on the tide by 6 am and in less than two hours the tug could put you ashore in

Greenock harbour, having cast off the steamer somewhere downstream from Donald Quay Light past Bowling. You then got the bus or the train into Glasgow and paraded smugly at the bank, perhaps even a little earlier than usual.

But for the holidays Jim MacDougall and I went far afield. If it wasn't camping and climbing it was on the cargo tramp steamers round as far as the Outer Hebrides. These were of course bigger than the puffers, and they carried a superior contingent of about a dozen cabin passengers, while we always travelled steerage. They called at every single little port and I often go to these derelict piers in a mood of fond nostalgia, for many a happy time we had in harbours there.

Our great friend was Alasdair MacRae, a Marconi-trained radio operator who was the wireless man aboard the SS *Hebrides*; a Highlander, a shy but marvellous writer, a very good piper and a great companion who used to come ashore with us and climb the hills, or take his pipe and pace along the foreshore of the likes of Loch Harport or the quayfront at Lochboisdale. He was an ornithologist of note and wrote some beautiful pieces for us for the *Claymore*, about snow buntings and the rest. He died a year or two ago but I kept up a lifelong friendship with him. The time came when he left the dying cargo boat trade and became a long-range radio operator on the big airliners flying to such places as Australia. The last time I met him was when I saw a familiar kilted figure in the middle of the road between Muir of Ord and Inverness, standing with binoculars looking up to the sky at some birds. Dorothy and I at the time were driving home from our very first caravan trip, and we parked at the side of the road, put down the legs of the caravan to steady us all up and had a dram or two and many an old jest.

One of the many surprising things about life is that one seems to be able to remain in intimacy with someone, although you may have met only six times in a lifetime. That was how it was with Alasdair MacRae — a few voyages and that last meeting on the Muir of Ord road, itself now long ago — but I remember long nights talking with him in his cabin and operating-room on the *Hebrides*. It was high amidships, a little fortress of its own where he had his bunk and ablution arrangements, and the desks and panels where he tapped out his messages. Sometimes when the night was rough and the seas got up he would rise with a patient grimace of dismissal, pulling down his concealed washbasin because he was about to be seasick, an affliction he carried with him like a tenderfoot for over thirty years at sea. The deeps of me are stirred by the undimmed memory in my ears of the notes of his pipe at sundown in Hebridean harbours.

From then on it was Jim MacDougall and me, by land or sea, in the search for the reality of the Scotland that more and more belonged to us. He shared my passion for a future for Scotland more than for a past, but we built on that past the better to understand what we were losing. He sang the songs I had made, and was too generous about things I had written and said. We did many a mile on the water or the roads and the hills. By this time we knew how to do it in comfort. Our small pressure primus stove would cook anything simple and would heat a tent on the bitterest of nights. We rarely had to light a fire except occasionally on seashores for spectacular satisfaction or to sit at twilight dreaming. We did not feel the cold any more under these conditions. By the time I was three or four years past my first long trek at the age of seventeen I was pretty skilled at looking after myself. Now I often think of how I used to lie shivering; and I wonder, since nearly sixty years have gone by, how it is — and what agonising fates am I tempting by saying this? — that scarcely a twinge of arthritis or rheumatism or some other contortion affects me even now.

Once when camping near the River Beauly we called upon Monty Mackenzie — later Sir Compton — at Eilean Aigeas in his loved house on an island in the middle of that foaming river. He gave us his blessing for our immature pilgrimage, and this was a useful preliminary to the many hours I spent in his company in Barra and later in Edinburgh. We went to Wick once and stayed, both of us crocks with knee injuries, with my old Aunt Min in Sinclair Terrace. It was at Wick we had our first of many overnight trips away with herring fishers in a steam drifter, the WK 12, called the *Silver Drift*.

I met in the harbour there the skipper of a ship called the *Mayberry*, the drifter which on a wartime assignment with the Royal Navy had taken Kitchener out to join the *Hampshire* the night he drowned. The skipper recounted how terrible a night it was of wind and rain, and on boarding his craft at the harbourside the warlord shouldered his way into the wheelhouse leaving the door open.

'Shut that door behind ye,' the skipper ordered. 'It's all very well for ye with all them greatcoats, but I've only got a thin ganzie.'

They exchanged no more words until they were alongside the *Hampshire* from which a rope ladder with wooden rungs was dropped over the side to get Kitchener aboard. 'I'm not going up there,' he said. 'Can they not put down steps?'

'There's nae other way,' said our skipper. 'If ye are going that's the way ye go. Ye'd better climb.' He climbed grumbling, and that was the last of him.

Unless they can afford their own boats, which no doubt many of them can, the twenty-year-olds nowadays are hard put to find unorthodox methods of travelling. The great feature of the old cargo steamers was the freedom with which one could inhabit the whole of them. Of course we travelled steerage, paying shillings only, to get to the likes of St Kilda and the remote Hebrides. The cabin passengers paid as much as £10 or £12 for the round trip of ten days and they had sumptuous but set-piece meals where they had to attend in spite of the attractions of shore-going. For our part we had the universal privilege of all steerage passengers of being permitted to use the ship's galley to cook our own food, and this we did, fitting in the operation with well-timed darts ashore and on to the hills as soon as the steamer tied up for a cargo landing of three or four hours. One cannot share a galley for a week or two with the rightful inhabitant without getting on pretty good terms with him, and the cooks we tended to meet were generous to the extreme, sharing our disapproval of high-paying passengers in any case, and they would clinch this covenant by slipping us enormous slices of prime beef and plum duff intended for the privileged. These extras handsomely eked out the supplies of sausages, eggs and corned beef which we were able to buy in the stores ashore. In this way we were able to see the most desirable parts of our own land at almost no cost.

On land we were able to make contact with people just as congenial. There were the memorable John and Kate Sinclair, a bachelor brother and spinster sister, who farmed at Gartnafuaran in Balquhidder. We camped in their fields at odd times for years and knew the Braes as well perhaps as they have ever been known. John Sinclair had been an ironmonger in Fort William, and then for the sake of his health he had to take to the open air and so became a sheep farmer in Perthshire, his sister, a nurse, coming with him to housekeep. He was a gentle, jovial, romantic, full of stories and ploys. She was a character of great vigour who mothered us severely with endless kindness. She loved an argument. They had family connections in Argyll but it was in and around Fort William where most of their earlier life had been spent. She told us once how she got into some argument with a surgeon in a hospital, refused to concede the point he was making, and finally heard him burst out, 'You're a dour, proud Argyll woman.'

'How dare you say that!' she answered. 'I'm a dour, proud Lochaber woman.'

When I go on the hills today I carry with me a shepherd's crook which John Sinclair carved for me when I was twenty. We would yarn with him, telling of our modest adventures, or going with him to see some of his neighbours, all of whom seemed to be dramatic and special. There was Mrs Colquhoun, an elderly woman who lived alone, and she and her people had been for centuries in Balquhidder. Although my own grandfather, George Dunnett, was born in 1815, it was Mrs Colquhoun who gave me my most astonishing historic bridge into the past in terms of someone I have actually known. Her own grandfather, she used to describe, was out in the '45. There was no reason to doubt it. He had married late in life and his son, her father, had married late in life, and there she was, and every time I saw and spoke to her, the most part of two centuries vanished and I was stirred by great deeds and lost causes.

Another eccentric was John MacDougall who kept the King's House Hotel at the end of the glen — not the King's House in Glencoe but the one beyond Strathyre where the Lochearnhead road starts. John was no mean sampler of his own wares, and some of his repartee in his own bar was renowned. He was one of the early twentieth century Scottish Nationalists, so it was no surprise to anyone when at a local displenishing sale he bid for and obtained a dubious engraving purporting to be that of William Wallace the Patriot. This he carried home in triumph, and pending his discovery of an important place in the then dingy hotel in which to hang it, he stood it on the table in the entrance hall where the anglers laid out their fish for weighing and admiration. A party of anglers from England bent on a joke took the picture and hung it in the men's lavatory, where it bided for some days while John, knowing very well where it was, didn't say a word.

At last he was asked, 'Well, Mr MacDougall, did you see where we hung your picture of Wallace?'

'Yes, indeed I did, and I couldn't myself think of a better place for it.'

'Why — how is that, Mr MacDougall?'

'Well, if there was one chap that could knock the shit oot the English, it was William Wallace.'

Travelling with Jim MacDougall was a strenuous undertaking. I think it must often be the case that people who are to die young, pack their short lives with as much joy and achievement as those who are to run the whole course. One of our favourite ways of spending a hot summer's day was to walk up a hill burn through the lower woods, past the waterfalls, sometimes wading in the very bed, up on to the moors and to find at last the head waters and perhaps a little loch or two where we could swim. On the way up we often used to shed our clothes. The shoes and stockings would come off first and be put under a rock, then the kilt and sporran and the shirt, and I've seen us reach the top trickle of the burn with nothing on either of us but our wrist-watches.

In this way I peched after him, up every possible hill and along every river and lochside. When we had had our midday bite I liked to rest and contemplate; he would forage about to see what he could get up to. On a moor he would build a lean-to of branches, and thatch it with heather. Often we slept in these at night. At a lochside he would start to build a raft and launch it away, shouting with delight. It was a precarious form of navigation, because there never were anything but gnarled and shapeless branches for the craft, and he never had brought any rope to tie it together, so that he devised bindings from rushes and bracken stems which parted shortly after he launched and he would disappear to immersion, laughing amid a congeries of twigs.

About this time also we discovered Ireland and took to it with almost as much pleasure as we took to our own country. I made my first trip there in the early 1930s and went back many times, studying the ways by which the people of Southern Ireland were trying to revive local industries or plant new ones in remote areas to help to abate the curse of emigration which they shared with us. I came to know some of the good young civil servants in Dublin who were working on these problems and made many friends there and in the country. Jim and I never went to Ireland together, but we used to follow up each other's friends.

84

His last trip to Ireland was at the start of the summer of 1939 when he set off, carrying his kit, indeed in a haversack which I had lent to him, and soon I got a postcard from the Gaeltachd, where he was smiling his way among the Gaelic speaking inhabitants. I waited to hear the familiar phone call arranging a meeting with me at the end of his fortnight to tell of his new adventures and the songs he had brought back. After a day or two of silence his older brother, Jack, phoned me to ask if I had heard anything from Jim, because he hadn't come back. We waited nearly a week and then went to the police in Glasgow, where the very helpful chief superintendent of detectives discussed the situation with us and passed us on to some of his young crew. The thing that mainly interested them was that Jim had been employed in the head Glasgow office of the Bank of Scotland and they immediately went there to discover if Jim's books were all right. There was no cash defalcation. Assured on that they lost interest, on the grounds that, as was no doubt officially proper, he was a grown man, it was a free country, and a responsible citizen had the right to go anywhere he pleased. When we told them we would go to look for him they helpfully put us in touch with their opposite numbers in the Dublin Garda.

We went there and toured Ireland in vain for three weeks, following every clue and hint, and looking, sometimes successfully, for his name written in some bed-and-breakfast boarding house book. There was a helpful Inspector Nangle in Dublin and he issued for us a description of Jim as a Missing Person which was sent to every police station in Eire, as well as broadcast several times on Radio Éireann. The farthest place and the latest dates we could get for him were in the Dingle Peninsula, near a small village called Ballyferriter, and we haunted and raked this place for days. A local Garda man helped us to find some fishermen who had seen him on the cliffs of Clogher Head from their curragh. They said they had shouted to him to ask if he was all right and he had smiled and waved Yes. When they rowed past that way an hour later there was no sign of him, and orange peel was floating on the water.

I made an arrangement with the policeman, persuaded Jack to go inland to follow up another clue, and went out with the fishermen in their curragh to drag the spot below the cliffs where Jim had been seen. Distraught as I was by our blank days of failure, I took time to note the techniques by which these men manipulated their boats. light shells only of tarred canvas, stretched over thin ribs, the only solid parts being the midships thwarts where we all sat. There were three men rowing, each with a pair of oars, without blades, so that they could pull these poles quickly through the water, and I rode with them for hours across the huge Atlantic swells, noting that their stroke never varied from thirty-six to the minute. They had a mysterious code in what I took to be ancient Irish Gaelic and I hope that some of the folklore people in Ireland have noted it all down, because I doubt if there is much sailing of this kind in the West Coast of Ireland, even now. The stern man or stroke kept an eye on the 120° of wild sea that he commanded from where he sat; the midships man watched the 120° between the bow and the strokeman's sector on the port side and the bow man watched the starboard or weather side from the bow to the strokeman in that sector. In this way they commanded the whole sea and they talked to each other incessantly, apparently describing the kind of wave and how it was coming and whether it was breaking, lurching their bodies to lean in to the wave and never breaking the stroke for a moment. Below the rocks they attached a rope to the grapple they had brought with them and we dragged for a long time for Jim's body, eventually giving up and rowing home to their sheltered harbour among the cliffs, stepping into the edge of the tide and lifting the boat upside-down on to their shoulders to walk up the loose beach like a giant beetle. For days more I walked the turf cliff top looking for what I cannot think, but once I seized upon an empty discarded cigarette packet which had been assembled in Glasgow, remembering reasonably that Jim did not smoke.

We traced him from house to house, finding occasionally one where he was remembered, and ached to get the trail going inland from these cliffs. I could not believe that Jim had fallen off the cliffs. I went down myself to the spot where he had been seen by the fishermen — a ledge about 40 feet above the water — and there was nothing in the descent that would have worried Jim in the slightest. I was aware that I was developing a habit of looking into every face I passed, sometimes into gardens of houses and pursuing young men along the streets whose back view might be something like his. It occurred to me that I might well go through life like that, looking like Rachel for the young one who would not return, and who in my mind would not grow old.

The last night before we returned to Dublin, after three weeks, we spent in the boarding house of the O'Dea's in Galway where Jim had spent many pieces of holiday and where he had slept a few nights before he had been seen on the cliffs of Clogher. There was a daughter of that house called Maeve whom he had thought was the very spirit of Ireland — a schoolgirl and a singer and a merry lass. She and her family gave us great comfort and even set up a little party for us late at night with discreet music and a great sense of warmth and solace. I asked Maeve to sing a song and she stood up artlessly and sang 'The Lark in the Clear Air' which I had never before heard and which now chimes in my ear like an endless blessing. Before she went to bed Maeve asked me to write something in her autograph book and I sat apart and wrote:

I needed songs and then you sang, and back my banished laughter
    Came soaring in on wishing wings above the salty bay;
The burden of the grievous years that lie before and after
    Was lightened in the gallant tune I got from Maeve O'Dea.
I gathered up my bits of rhymes, and put this beannachd down
    To the lark's song in the clear air, and yours in Galway town.

We came back to Dublin, had a drink with kindly Inspector Nangle and went mooning about the docks for a day or two, watching the ships leaving for the Clyde and the people who boarded them. There was one crowded ship where I was convinced I had suddenly seen Jim on the foredeck. I broke through the ticket men at the gangway and rushed up there and through all the decks, finding none. We came back then ourselves to Glasgow, telling those who cared that we had failed. There was one girl who cared greatly. A month later Jim's body was washed up 40 miles north of Clogher Head. The villagers and the police gathered these remains and buried them with a religious service, not knowing that in the Garda office the notice of Jim, with his description, was hanging on the wall. We brought him home and buried him in Killermont looking to Dumgoyne in the Campsie Hills, on whose summit he and I had once slept all through a summer's dawn until nearly noonday, after a night of climbing, to awake, each man with one side of his face burned red with the sunshine and the other white, like parti-coloured clowns.

We shall not know this side of life how he died. A good man on rocks and anywhere. Like the Gowrie Conspiracy, we shall have to await the truth. One thought came to us from Robbie MacLean's father shortly after the funeral which was only a few days before the war broke out. By this time he was an old man, brosey in the face, and with a mane of fluffy white hair, looking, as Robbie said, like a Celtic saint. He said, 'Jim MacDougall was the first victim of the war that's coming.'

Robbie himself, not long ago, sent me a newspaper cutting reviewing a book which told of how, all during the summer of 1939, German U-boats were cruising and surfacing off the West Coast of Ireland, apparently testing water depths and seaward bolt-holes. Old MacLean may have had some insight and it could be that Jim saw something that he was not supposed to see. How can we know? There were busy days ahead, and by the time the conflict was finished, many another flower was to be taken from the forest.

CHAPTER SEVEN
Seumas

There cannot be many people who have inaugurated a lifelong friendship and partnership through meeting on stage while playing in pantomime. This was the case with James Seymour Adam and me. He was playing the part of Prince Charming and I had been cast in the name part of the Sleeping Beauty. It is hardly necessary to go into the squalid details of this affair, except to say that it wasn't our fault. We had fallen into the hands of a grown-up enthusiast for Scouting, a young English actor who was playing a season for the Macdona Players in Glasgow. I have mentioned how at that time — perhaps still — the Boy Scout movement frequently attracted odd folk who got the bug late in puberty and they would turn up at our Auchengillan camp, eager to embark on some fanatical enterprise, not knowing that we had come there to lie on the heather, or in the tents, and talk and laugh with our cronies until it was time, on the Sunday evenings, to walk home. They were generally English, these fellows, wearing knee-length khaki shorts and faded neckerchiefs; they had spindly legs, and they spoke a version of the King's English which lent itself richly to our coarse mimicry, as we affected to be politely bending our pure vowel sounds to match their distortions.

This performer came to the camp for a number of weekends while his company worked their way through the Shaw repertory. He seized upon the idea of producing a pantomime, his own, far from laughable, version of the classic story. This was given official blessing. He recruited and cast some of us extroverts to set forth this horrid production, rehearsing it with us for a few successive Saturdays, and arranging almost professional billing. I remember little of the result as staged, save for the climax, when, daubed with superfluously uglifying make-up, I rose from my couch, panting to receive the prince's kiss. Instead of bestowing it upon me, he seized a tent mallet and brought it down on my pillow. It is well over fifty years ago, and I remember the clout of the mallet as it grazed my ear, and his ever-twinkling eyes, that were to look at me for years in bare rooms, in tents, in lashing seas, in poverty-stricken lodgings; and eventually across boardroom tables, and in the back seats of limousines, and in Pullman trains and padded aircraft.

James Adam — I have always called him by his Gaelic name of Seumas — was by this time a regular habitué of Auchengillan, where his mission was something on the same lines as mine, but with young boys who were even more underprivileged than my troop. They lived in the depths of Partick, from which it was difficult to escape. Their fathers were out of work or their mothers were widowed, and it took a bold stretch of Celtic imagery to see beyond their tattered-arsed actuality to the men they might become. Maybe Seumas and I overdid some of it; although it can be asked whether you can ever overdo the input of idealism to the young. At that time we had both found, in our separate ways, that the whole aspiration of the Boy Scout movement, as conceived by Baden-Powell, was infested with the glories of the Red Indian cult, which made it necessary for the youngsters of Partick and Kirkcaldy, and perhaps also of Liverpool and Penarth, to make heroes of individuals called Little Bear and Sparkling Fountain Water. In our endeavours to eliminate these far-flung traditions we were happily met more than half way by the built-in cynicism of small boys who had been sharpened rather than cowed by their deprivations; and who, falling back upon such native traditions as anyone had bothered to instil in them, or that they had picked up even in the prejudiced emotionalism of their surroundings, out of a sheer desperate need to survive, had come to the conclusion that they and their kin were as good as anybody, and better than most. Some of this sentiment found its way into the slogans and the songs that they had grown up with.

In a sense, then, the fields were white for harvest. And in setting out to develop this essential pride, we were already fostering what was to be a lifelong and (if people care to look on it with a spirit of proper reason) an ineradicable belief that what Scotland had done through the will and determination of her people had added to the long inheritance and had given her modern citizens much to be proud of. At that time in the 1920s there were already some signs of a crude nationalism, and there was a spirit of correction abroad intended to persuade us that these sentiments were parochial.

Undeterred, we set out to instruct these boys in the richness of their inheritance, and we found ready listeners. Many of the kids came to tell us of things their parents and grannies had remembered from the family's own past, and we encouraged them to find more, and to write it down. In fact they were young clansmen in their own right, bearing names like MacGregor and MacFarlane and Robertson, so we led them towards some understanding of these great family groups. Through modest cash-raising efforts we got kilt funds going so that these fragments of noble families, stranded by misfortune in the receding backwash of industrial failure, were able at last to buy kilts of their own clan tartan, and wear them with pride.

The next thing was to take them back to their clan lands, if only for the sadly few days of summer holidays. They went with us to camp sites, sleeping in what had been the free air of the people they had come from, and by day walking the hills like young princes. There were sparks here that smouldered. Soon this was spreading far in the West of Scotland Scout movement. The kilt of your own tartan became an essential, especially in the senior Scout section, or the Rovers, a company of which I had formed out of the older lads in our Scout troop who wanted to remain and be stimulated by the spirit we had.

By the late 1920s the Rover Scout movement had become the most powerful youth body of its kind in Scotland, and unique in that it recalled specifically the national values that many had thought were long since gone, and others had worked energetically to eliminate. The world we lived in had a great share of old-style conformists, holding to some ideal of the British raj which was all right for the home counties but had long since stopped being relevant to what we knew. On the last great Sunday church parade, a day in 1932, of the Glasgow Rover Scouts, many thousand of youths turned out, with their pipe bands and tartans. Hardly a pair of trousers was to be seen, and we had taken, all of us, to wearing our balmoral bonnet headgear instead of the orthodox wide-brimmed South African hat which Baden-Powell held to be proper.

We were never to meet again in such spirit and numbers, for the Chief Scout almost immediately issued an edict that the balmoral hat was to be banned. We were given a year from then to equip ourselves with the mushroom hat, or quit the movement.

In a stroke, to use a phrase since much used in politics, the beloved and ill-advised founder of the movement killed his creation in our part of the world. I am told it has crept back to some strength, and that there is no question of anyone having to wear the ridiculous hat. But the thousands at that last parade never reassembled. Before the year was up they had found better things to do.

It was necessary, however, to meet the challenge head on. This was the first situation in which Seumas and I collaborated with a purposeful resolve. A few others gathered with us, and we arranged meetings of those who would not conform and who resented that the mass of others should be made to conform. A revolt grew. The newspapers supported our cause, often without greatly understanding what the origins of the arguments might be. They readily used our logical arguments. A valiant ally was Harold Dickson, chief reporter of the *Glasgow Evening News*, a stylish character full of flair and initiative, a man who was barely literate, but one of the truly greats among newsgetters. 'After all,' he wrote following one of our briefings, 'do not the Indian Scouts wear their turbines?' This was significant support for the cause. Senior officials of the movement played no helpful part in this, and attempted to stop the protests, on the grounds that orders were orders, a reasoning much resorted to in other authoritative situations.

Probably the peak of the propaganda came when Seumas commissioned me to write a song. It was one of the brightest of his lifetime run of inspired editorial ideas. A contemporary song was going the rounds,

'In Eleven More Months and Ten More Days', telling of a man sentenced to a year in jail, looking forward to his release just as he had started his sentence. I wrote a parody of this lyric and Seumas sang it to tumultuous acclaim on the first available Saturday at Auchengillan.

The first verse ran:

We got the news from London and our hearts are filled with fear,
Our old balmorals must be banned before another year.
But instead of bonnet bonfires you'll see beacons far and wide
And fiery crosses all the way from John o' Groats to Clyde.

the chorus ran:

In eleven more months and ten more days I'll not be a Rover Scout,
In eleven more months and ten more days they're going to chuck me out.

There were several more verses and a final additional chorus which went:

In eleven more months and ten more days I'll be dressed like the English chaps.
In eleven more months and ten more days I'll be wearing a hat — perhaps!

All this was fine fun, and a useful trial run in the creation of public opinion. Exactly at this time, though, there were taking place in the lives of Seumas and me important changes which were to throw us more closely than ever together.

Seumas, like me, had left school at an early age, and after serving for a spell with the firm of Colville's, the steel people, gathering up an accountancy qualification in the passing, he had joined the *Daily Express* in Glasgow to sell advertising. Suddenly the paper's management decided to move him to Edinburgh, where he was expected to set up a sales office for the East of Scotland. Precisely at this time my bank superiors announced that I was to be transferred to the accountant's department of our head office in Edinburgh, goal of the ambitious bank junior. I got less notice than he did, learning of the move on a Friday afternoon and instructed to start in Edinburgh on the following Monday. So that I was already installed in a room with a landlady in Forrest Road by the time Seumas entered the capital two or three weeks later. Being paid on a sumptuous scale, as it seemed to me, he was able to afford much more superior accommodation. No doubt his employers thought he was worth it all. Within a month or two of his arrival he had sold the first-ever full page of colour advertising to appear in a British daily newspaper, a promotion for a tweed fabric called Glamis Red, intended to celebrate the childhood home of the then Duchess of York. He had many another triumph, and we worked our way through the first winter. We joined a Gaelic Society called Comunn Tir nam Beann, which met and danced, and listened to the old songs, on a Thursday night. Also we became founder members of the new Edinburgh Camanachd Association, which ran a shinty team. I had been brought up playing shinty. We two used to meet at the end of Forrest Road at seven in the morning, and run through to the Meadows, whacking the leather ball along the wide greens, and easily outpacing such rangers as attempted to stop us, especially one who had, surprisingly, a Cockney accent. We climbed Arthur's Seat often, and swam off the Granton breakwater. But we hankered for the satisfaction that we had found in trying to sustain, in ourselves and others, a dispersed Scottish consciousness. At times we had Jim MacDougall and Robbie MacLean and Johnnie Burt through from Glasgow to stay with us for the weekend, when we would take to the Pentlands.

Apart from our own Glasgow intimates, Edinburgh was to allow us to enter a circle of intimates somewhat more dazzling than Glasgow had been able to provide. I had already a family contact with Bertie Black, who was producing a weekly magazine called *The Freeman*, devoted to essays on Scotland's literary heritage and present output, and also to the realities of present-day nationalism. R.M. Black was a Highlander from Oban, a member of the family of William Black the novelist, who flourished towards the end of the nineteenth century, and who in his lifetime was almost immediately outshone by Neil Munro. The Blacks had owned one of the Oban newspapers. A year or two earlier, when he was assistant editor of a significant monthly periodical called the *SMT Magazine*, Black had accepted for publication an article I had written about the north-east coast herring fleet; an article which was swiftly repudiated by the editor, Inglis Ker, as soon as Bertie had left the magazine to found his own. I wrote occasionally for *The Freeman*, which had the added eccentricity that its main function was to promote the beliefs of C.H. Douglas, a Scot who had devised the Douglas credit system, involving a formula by which the money supply always kept up with the demand. Nothing in my elementary banking wisdom enabled me to grasp the principle of this theory, which prevailed for a time in the province of Alberta in Canada, but which I assume was overtaken by the sharper-edged tenets of prosperity.

Around him, in his small office above the Grassmarket, Bertie Black had gathered a devoted band, skilled in writing, unskilled in finance, except that they had come to some arrangement by which Bertie appeared to be sustaining them all in a meagre way of life. Chief among these was Christopher Grieve, better known as Hugh MacDiarmid the poet, who had been existing in some way in London; but learning that his old friend was publishing his own journal, Chris loaded his wife and baby son — the infant Michael — aboard some old motor car and headed north. When they reached the border they got out, Valda and Chris, and danced a reel on Scottish soil, convinced, like many another home-coming exile, that with their presence all of Scotland's problems were solved. They then drove to Musselburgh and moved in on the

Blacks, where they stayed for many months. Another contributor was George Dott, a thick-set kilt-wearing man, brought up in the coal trade, who wrote a Hugh Miller style of economics, and made diplomatic references often enough to the Douglas credit system. Another hanger-on was Tom Douglas MacDonald, better known as the novelist Fionn MacColla. I think at that time he had written only one novel, *The Albannach*, which had been swooped upon by the Scottish cognoscenti for its rudely pro-Celtic chauvinism. There was an Indian scholar, often crudely addressed in anger by Black as 'You bloody nigger'; and a self-effacing little man, lately left Edinburgh University as a brilliant student, called Matthew Moulton. A Caithnessman, he was later to be a colleague of mine on *The Scotsman*, where he became my chief leader writer. He was to become the one in my view who could best express, in the short essay, an essentially honest and logical Scottish purposiveness.

Seumas and I did not need Bertie Black's strained bounty, so we happily wrote for his paper without fee. It struggled on for some years, and he was no doubt sustaining it from his diminishing private funds. One of the great educative elements of my life was to join Black, MacDonald, Dott, Grieve and Seumas, for a scanty lunch occasionally in a small café near *The Freeman* office, in Bank Street. Most of us took bread and butter and tea, which was all we could afford, but Black at times, mindful like an Eskimo head of house of the need to conserve his strength, sometimes ordered a single tomato on a separate plate. He would cut this into eight pieces, let them fall open, sprinkle them daintily with salt and pepper, and eat them piece by piece with a fork.

But the conversation was memorable. All the others were outstanding debaters, accustomed in long days of intellectual idleness to use their skills in conversation, to concede, to come to conclusions or to lead others to that end, so that a stumbling exhorter like me would sit in a daze, hearing the apt solution, and thinking the New Enlightenment had come as Pentecostal flames seemed to fall on each head. Seumas, emerging like me from a solitary sojourn among a generation less eloquent, was no laggard in these bouts. It was easy to come to the conclusion that man's problems were soluble by the fit phrase, and that the dawn of our day was at hand.

If so, it would not be by these sterile exchanges, and Seumas and I decided we should have to hasten the sunrise ourselves. We were not unmindful of the earnestness of that little group. But they did not seem to be driving hard in any special direction. We thought there might be a way of getting to the goal sooner, and of making ourselves independent in the by-going.

There was no particular dramatic flash in the invention of the *Claymore* idea. It grew out of our many dialogues, none of which we shared with *The Freeman* group. In a night or two of planning and conversation the two of us had resolved on a plan which would be commercially successful and would go far to recall Scotland to all that for years she had been cheated out of. We would found a weekly adventure magazine for Scottish boys.

No range of Scottish periodicals existed [I wrote in my book *Quest by Canoe.*] 'There was consequently little market for the Scots writer who cared to depart from the stock view of his country and its people. The only possible sustaining force of any people is the virtue of patriotism, with as many separate graduations of appeal as there are citizens. In Scotland in the nineteen-thirties this was a gravely spent force. For adults there existed a narrow choice of opportunities for national favour — crude enough, but something to be going on with until the country could be shocked out of its second childhood and drawn to a mature focus. There was *Para Handy*; the Glasgow Comedians; international football occasions at Hampden and Murrayfield. Extracts from this list could bring to mind the zest, if not the dignity, of the place to which they belonged; where most of them would live, work, and see out the end of their days.

But for the children there was not even this short list of enthusiasms, while their literature painted a greatly different scene. The boys' weeklies in existence had a wide range of stimulus. They led their readers adventuring into all parts of the globe — except one. The repetitive pattern of their tales dealt with young explorers up the Amazon or down the Congo; South Sea planters' sons; English boy football stars; pet gorillas which played cricket; jabbering and excited foreigners ready to be cowed by clean-cut types; Zulu chiefs who would change herds of cattle for alarm clocks. Only one part of the world did not pulse with these thrills. The weekly wave of adventure never reached the Scottish shore: not even on the home front, which was held to be adequately covered by stories of English public school life. In this grand pattern of events no British schoolboy could hope to be a hero unless he had been a fag and a fourth former in his day, with plenty of high-class japes. The "bad yins" of these tales, apart from an occasional genteel cad, were coarse errand lads, usually discovered twisting the arms of small boys, although these villainies were mere by-products of the major crime of working for a living.'

It was in this general context that we set out on our mission of correcting the distortion. We also felt like doing it with as much good humour as could be assembled, since although there were many political and polemical pamphlets and publications abroad in Scotland, dealing sadly with the terrible decline that had happened in our attitudes and way of life as well as our economic condition, this was all being done with a fairly grim and humourless style of writing; and in spite of the earlier example of Tom Johnston's *Forward* (which I describe later), nobody had thought much about using even the satirical joke as a style of corrective.

We decided that the *Claymore* would give to our readers a picture of Scotland as the Land of Adventure. This was an enormous novelty and great numbers of young people in the event responded to it. If we needed young explorers, we had better ones than anybody else; just as we had better footballers and rather more rumbustious and even hilarious schools. We took many months to plan the style and attack

94

that our paper would develop and we went to the wholesale newsagents to ensure that they would distribute it when it was published. Our main team reduced itself to five people, Jim MacDougall, Robbie MacLean, John Burt, Seumas and me. Robbie would do most of the illustrations and the rest of us most of the writing.

Even looking back at the filed copies of the magazine in the bound volumes in which we preserved them, the stuff looks not too bad and one or two of the items were published in book form later, including my serial story 'Treasure at Sonnach', which became a young person's best-selling book in 1934, published by Nelson's. (I was later to become a director of Nelson's and took over the copyright of the book so that I might be suitably poised for further offers.)

One of the oddities of the illustrations, which were splendidly done by Robbie, was that we had not realised fully that Robbie was left-handed. Accordingly, in the great battle between the stranded Vikings and the Celtic defenders of Sonnach Island, every man jack is wielding a sword in his left hand. Or was in the original drawing, but Seumas cunningly reversed the negative of the block so that they turned out more or less normal like the rest of us.

Seumas left his *Express* job and rented a small office in York Place in Edinburgh. Nearer the publication date towards the end of 1933, I left my job in the Bank, and Peter Irving the chief accountant was very good in letting me go quickly. I told him on the Thursday and left on the Friday night.

The paper was different in a number of ways. Each week we had a different action picture covering the whole of the front page. We had a page full of very lively jokes which we rewrote with witty skill to such an extent that we had the gratification of seeing grown-up newspapers and magazines lift our jokes and their frequent punning headings to fill the ends of their drearier columns. Bertie Black of *The Freeman* wrote a heavy-going series called 'The Unconquerable Folk', telling the tale of the Picts and their centuries-long battles with the invading Romans. He used to come up to the office with his weekly contribution written precariously near press time in pencil on different scraps of paper. On one occasion he never turned up at all, and, working through the night, I wrote the next instalment. And since his fictional narrative was becoming turgid I brisked up the whole action, staged an enormous and fairly conclusive battle in which one or two of the Roman villains were killed. In this also I composed a song which the Picts chanted as they marched south to victory and again north in triumph. Bertie was grievously wounded by this liberty, and sat down somewhat sulkily to write his next instalment in which one or two of the slaughtered characters came back to life and in an obscure series of political manoeuvres the battle appeared to be less conclusive than I intended it to be, since it outdid anything I had lately read in the Old Testament about what the Israelites did to the Philistines.

I have told some of this story in the Canoe Book, since it was an essential preliminary to that adventure. The greatest of the adventures, however, was to keep the *Claymore* going, because we had no earning income now and it was a long time before the wholesalers' cheques started to come in. Seumas had earlier moved in to my own room in Forrest Road, but this proved ridiculously costly, and we gave that up and set up our camp beds in the office in York Place, unknown to our landlord. There was a gas ring on which we cooked some meagre meals, but we had great difficulty in finding cash to pursue our essential business transactions.

One day we had no food in the place at all and no money except twopence which I had to use for a strategic phone call to the main wholesalers in an attempt to extract from them some interim payment for the papers which they had already sold. I went to a nearby telephone box, and before inserting my twopence I hopefully pressed button B, to be greeted by a small shower of coppers. Eightpence descended into the receptacle and I grabbed it. I put through my wheedling call to the wholesalers and then sped up the road to a nearby small grocer's shop where I bought two pies and a small loaf with the eightpence, bearing them back to the office so that we could both scoff the loot. A few years later I assuaged my conscience in a ridiculous fashion by buying eightpence worth of postage stamps and tearing them up into a wastepaper basket.

Other ingenuities were called for among these neo-literary labours. I went one week to Walker's the printers in Galashiels, to put the paper away to press, and discovered that a rousing article by Seumas on the Border Rievers was about three inches short of the full page which it deserved. He had talked of the great cross-border raids which went on for centuries, with English incursions into Scotland and reverse ones by our folk, with the driving off of the herds of cattle which formed the main wealth of the people of that disputed territory. To fill the gap I stood aside in the print room and wrote out this small verse:

Lament of the Border Cows
I've hiked in years o' riving,
   Ilk weary border track,
Ae nicht the Scots are driving,
   Then South men herd us back.
When rievers' scabbards rattle,
   And roof trees light the howes,
Think on the spoils of battle —
   The footsore border cows.

We didn't know then, but we know now, that boys don't read much in the summer time since there are many other things to do, so our sales slumped badly as we came to midsummer. In a desperate endeavour to gain revenue and keep things going, Seumas made a few brilliant sorties into the adult world of space-buying, and booked a number of advertisements from such as oatmeal merchants, cycle and tent makers, wooden bowl and horn spoon manufacturers, and others of a vigorous character. This produced a small toiling revenue. We both took time — although I don't know how we made it — to canvass round the doors of the Edinburgh tenements and managed to book some subscriptions with signed coupons which we handed to nearby newsagents so that they could deliver the paper to the gallant mothers whom we had persuaded to invest in healthy reading matter for their young. Jim MacDougall, writing and working endlessly for us in Glasgow, wrote a short story at his kitchen table while his mother was dying in another room. Norman Adam, Seumas' young brother, rushed round Glasgow on a motor bike, fly-posting our bills on forbidden hoardings and walls. John Burt wrote a serial about two Scots shepherd lads who went abroad and took their dogs with them to give demonstrations of sheep herding and sheepdog working. One of the difficulties about John's enthusiasm was, in his rush to get on with the narrative, he often omitted the dogs from his story altogether, and we had to sub-edit his matter carefully, inserting a few sentences here and there to indicate that the dogs were not only alive but barking. Two staff artists employed by D.C. Thomson of Dundee, the firm which manufactured most of the boys' adventure papers, did brilliant drawings for us anonymously, glad to be working outside of the trashy standards they had normally to employ. Seumas' mother lent us £50 and my mother gave me £50 also.

All this was not enough, and in addition we were exhausted. Walker closed us down eventually, and in retrospect he can hardly be blamed, although it was bitter at the time. One of the last adventures we described was a canoe trip made in single-seater canvas sectional canoes through Hebridean waters by some of our team and it was in this direction that Seumas and I turned on the failure of the *Claymore*. We got two of these canoes and made a trip lasting three months throughout the West Highlands. Seumas finished it the following year by making a brilliant solo paddle across the Minch and into the Long Island, where I joined him with another canoe, coming by steamer; but the trip of the first year was a great highlight, since it gave us a platform of precarious adventure from which to write newspaper articles mainly concerned with social conditions, economic setbacks and the requirements of a totally neglected people and way of life.

Throughout the West Coast and the Islands we became known as the Canoe Boys, and there are probably some around who still remember us more or less being washed ashore on remote beaches. We camped at night and grew to tremendous fitness in our encounters with south-westerly gales which bore us north on great swells of sea, off the like of Ardnamurchan Point. I have described the last days of the *Claymore* and the whole of the canoe trip in the book which the publisher insisted in calling *Quest by Canoe — Glasgow to Skye*; a pedantic label which I later persuaded subsequent publishers to change to *It's Too Late in the Year* — this being a phrase which had pursued us on our whole voyage, it being

97

the ready pronouncement of the despairing senior inhabitants of that part who had much to be pessimistic about. Night after night we had long planning sessions crouched in a small tent and scourged by the endless winds of that coast.

At the end of it we secured an agency for the canoes from the maker, John Marshall of North Queensferry, who agreed we could have a substantial commission for every canoe we could sell, and we set off for London to try the big stores there. This turned out to be an abortive venture, because we got to London at the end of November and it soon became apparent that for the next four or five months no store was going to think of buying canvas canoes. So we were in for another hungry spell until about the end of February when Willie Ballantine offered me a job on the *Glasgow Weekly Herald* of which he had lately become editor. The pay was £3 15s a week, but I was able to stay at home and from this base I gave my mother a pound a week and sent a pound a week to Seumas in London to help keep him. In a month or two he turned up in Glasgow having secured a job in an advertising agency. They were about to publish a series of guide books and his assignment was to visit every hotel in Scotland and the North of England and collect advertisements. A car was supplied and to secure the job Seumas had refrained from telling the agency that he could not drive. Dauntless as ever, he got someone to give him lessons for the whole of one Friday and the following Saturday morning. On the Monday morning he collected the car and set off on the space-selling mission which he sustained successfully for a year or two until we found ourselves in the daily newspaper scene. But that was a long way off.

The *Glasgow Weekly Herald* was immediately a stimulating education for me, and suddenly I was able to do the things I most wanted to do and probably did best; and could also pay my way at the same time. Willie Ballantine happened to be the brother-in-law of Seumas, having married Margaret Adam his sister. He was a quite unique character, tall and a little vain with a great mind for the stories that might lie behind the ordinary news. During the bleakly hungry days of the *Claymore* he had commissioned from me — and somehow I had found time to write it — a ten-part serial story for the *Glasgow Weekly Herald* and the £15 from that kept us going for a few weeks longer than we might otherwise have managed. The paper had a small staff: Alastair Borthwick, since renowned as author and broadcaster and climber; Leslie Ker Robertson, who became the deputy editor of the *Daily Sketch*, and fled from it, I imagine, with a suitable handshake just before that paper folded, bought the Dunvegan Hotel in Skye and as something of a local laird in that island remains a good friend; Sidney Harrison, another good friend, who later edited the *Scottish Field* and became a newspaper proprietor in the West of Scotland in his own right; and there was the rumbustious Bill Thomson who acted as staff photographer and indeed as chauffeur to the rest of us as we went on our feature story excursions.

For the most part I was able to pursue the theme which had been behind the canoe trip and which indeed had been to some extent the subject of my serial story already published. It had been called 'Tomorrow's Tale' and dealt, inevitably, with the Highland problem, and the endless dilemma of the Scot who seems to be able to make a go of it in every country of the world except his own.

In those bleak 1930s there were few hopeful stories to tell, but our researches turned up one or two. I unearthed a firm on the outskirts of Glasgow which had been in business for many years manufacturing silk handkerchiefs. Most of the other firms in that old Scottish industry were going out of business because gentlemen no longer wanted coloured bandanas in their pockets. Some genius within the firm decided that if they made the same sort of article, but twice the size, they might be turned into head scarves and neckware. The sample batch they produced was turned down by every retailer in the West of Scotland. But the manufacturer took his lot to Paris, where they were seized upon and displayed in the top shop windows with splendid follow-up orders. The American buyers came in that year to Paris, saw this product and launched large orders for themselves for the profitable shops in Fifth Avenue and elsewhere. They boomed in New York too, and the following year the London buyers in New York also grabbed these and they turned up in the West End of London as the latest fashions from Paris and New York. In due course the Glasgow shops came into line and followed suit with this latest fashion from the arbiters of taste, unaware that they were manufactured within a few miles of their own doors and that they had already turned them down.

I persuaded Willie Ballantine to let me go to the Moray Firth with Bill Thomson, and we produced a series of articles about the terrible decline of the herring industry, and the boats and men that had made it great. At that time there was a fleet of many hundreds of steam drifters, each manned by eight or nine men who were shareholders and part owners, who had known boom times and were hanging on for the boom to come back. In the meantime they were on their beam ends. We found one drifter whose owners and crew for some years hadn't been able to raise the £5 required to have her pulled up on the slipway out of the water so that her hull could be examined. After a few years they raised the £5 in desperation and got her out. Below the boilers of these coal-driven vessels it was the practice to lay a great bed of cement to keep the fierce boiler heat off the hull plates; this ship's bottom plates had rusted away completely and, for God knows how long, they had been sailing on the bed of cement.

I went to Aberdeen then to produce and print there a northern edition of the Glasgow daily newspaper, the *Bulletin*. I had four pages and hardly as many staff and the feature of it, which I played with in full gusto, was a centre spread of pictures, as well as the two other pages of news. It was intended to be local news, but we picked up late stories and ran them with great effect if they had international significance.

Like the night when we broke the story of King Edward VIII and Mrs Wallis Simpson.

I had offered to file stories for some of the national newspapers with whom we were in contact in London. There was a night when we discovered that a trawler had gone ashore somewhere in the remote parts of the Shetland Isles. We gathered what information we could from the coastguard and the local police; but an irritated news editor came on from a Fleet Street paper demanding more. I was explaining the logistics of the situation when he interrupted me with, 'I like what you've sent, but we need some colour. Can't you take a taxi down to the beach yourself and file us an eye-witness account.'

Of the tiny team involved, two people were special to me. One was a teenager called Raibeart Scoular with whom I shared rooms in Gilcomston Park, and who stayed on in the regular Army after the war as a Major. The other was the gentle and scholarly Cuthbert Graham, a poet who wrote journalistic prose like an angel, but who was almost immobilised by polio which had long past crippled him hopelessly. In due course he became the literary editor of the *Aberdeen Press and Journal* and wrote memorably in poetry and prose about the hills he loved, though he had never been able to see them except from some roadside. Years later I was to surprise him by having him brought to Aberdeen airport, where I met him and got him aboard a helicopter which took us over the tops of all the hills he loved and on none of which he had ever set foot. We landed him on the summit of Lochnagar by special royal permission from Balmoral. All I wanted from him in return, I said, was that he would write a poem about it, which he did, in the form of a long epic interspersed with narratives. The *Press and Journal* ran it in three long instalments on successive Saturdays, and they should probably publish it in book form as well.

Unknown to me, Clem Livingstone, who at a very young age had just been made editor of the *Daily Record*, was looking at my daily picture spreads in the *Bulletin*. He asked me to come to see him and offered me the job of art editor in the *Daily Record* — that is the man who looks after the photographic staff and the main picture pages. Nothing to do with art and very little to do with editing. So I came back to Glasgow and joined him, in 1937.

But this was meant to be Seamus' chapter. I shall be looking at how we came together in newspaper executive scenes in the *Daily Record* and *The Scotsman* group; but this was a time of sundering. He was gone until the outbreak of war with his advertising sorties into the remote parts of England and Scotland; was called up to the Army and slogged it out as a signaller, turning up eventually as a staff officer in Northern Ireland Command. He wasn't long there before he married the beautiful Flora McDonnell. She was the private secretary to Sean Lemass, who was a cabinet minister in Dublin at the time, and he went on to become the Prime Minister and then the President. Her home was in Limerick. They were McDonnells of Glengarry, which they had left two or three generations before, but retained such strong Scottish Highland links that every member of their large family had a Scottish Highland and not an Irish Gaelic name, while their house in Limerick was called Invergarry.

After our long *Scotsman* chapter together Seumas went off to found a new newspaper, now called the *Chester Chronicle*, and after some years there he became the managing director of the Middlesbrough Newspaper Group from which he retired, coming back to Scotland at once. What he has done since is to be, until lately, the mainspring and inspiration of the world-wide organisation for the International Gathering of Scots. Ask anyone about him in any gathering of Scots in the whole world and they know his name well. He goes occasionally and speaks to them, reminding them of our inheritance. He has taken to writing poetry, biblical ballads from the New Testament along the lines of the work that W.D. Cocker did for the Old Testament stories. And these ring, albeit jokily as required, with his own immensely high standards and moral attitudes, from which he has never in the slightest wavered in all the time I have known him.

CHAPTER EIGHT
Daily Record

Immediately I felt at home in the *Daily Record*. It was the place for me, and I was at once in tune with it. My paltry previous experience of adult newspapers had nothing like this clean-cut purpose and editorial drive. The *Glasgow Weekly Herald* had been a superb experience, and it had almost been a continuity of the *Claymore* in the sense that it tested one's ability to explain things and to find the significance and the stories that lay behind the hard news, which was not the road along which most of the newspapers travelled. Investigative journalism and feature reporting only occasionally turned up and then almost by accident, but in the *Weekly Herald* I had realised that I had an editorial mind, and longed for an opportunity to put this into practice in a substantial daily newspaper. The *Bulletin* also saw me develop something of a management style and this was to be my main role for most of the time I was in daily newspapers. It had been a quite unique undertaking that I had enjoyed, although I had had no leisure at all. However, in both these chapters it had been necessary to create an entirely novel form of journalism, and in one case at least I had no local tradition whatever.

Here at the *Daily Record*, there was a going concern. Clem Livingstone had taken an outmoded, somewhat eccentric, newspaper and brought it sharply into focus with a lively young team responding to his very skilful editorial impulses. The ponderous John Simpson was somewhat older and was firmly established as chief reporter, but his deputy, Jimmy McDowell, was a great newspaper man who was to be a leading war correspondent, and was later given a dying newspaper to edit, but too late. Jimmy Cameron was the sports editor. He was to command his own ship at the D-Day landings and came back briefly to be my sports editor after the war. There were half a dozen of us about the same age, and Clem at 27 years of age was the youngest editor by far in the Scottish daily newspaper scene. He felt it necessary to edit the paper by being its chief sub-editor. He sat at the centre of the sub-editing table, designed all the pages but mine, selected the stories for each page and was able to shout across the open floor to the news desk to get reporter follow-ups. He did this with an attractive enthusiasm which brought forth tremendous response from his sub-editing team, and the paper took a whole lively air upon itself. In addition, Clem was a great talker. He would discourse at great length on everything and in public, a habit of which the more taciturn of our team disapproved, but at least the editorial direction of the paper was seen and recognised by its staff. Although he had great firmness in his expectations of what he wanted in the paper, Clem was a modest man, and he should have been seen more in public and at large, making the necessary contacts with public figures; but he had his own way of doing things.

I found myself inserted into this vigorous scene to bring to the photographic illustrations of the paper the same vigour and style, and perhaps to add something of my own. Up to that point the pictures had been mere insertions. Apart from the illustrations to news stories, the centre spread of pictures, which at that time was a feature of the 'popular' type of newspaper, tended to have the deadest of fashion pictures: 'Latest London fashion — a tasteful toque with semi-veil seen at millinery show in . . .' or 'A merry group at last night's Draper's Ball in the Ca'doro . . .' or, worse still, 'The wind played tricks with the bride's veil at the pretty wedding in St Mary's Church yesterday of . . .' No theme ran through these snapshots. They served, no doubt, some purpose as a kind of national family album. I had always felt that pictures positively added to the news and indeed that the right pictures could eliminate the need for a news story. It wasn't long before I was telling my team of photographers that our job was to make the reporters obsolete. The right picture and the right caption — and I would do the writing of the caption — should be able to do away with some of the news stories for which the photographer had accompanied a reporter, merely to illustrate what the reporter thought was a visual impression, adding some percentage to his story.

Fortunately I had a lively platoon of photographers, very good craftsmen who were glad to be rid of the chore of writing captions, and who saw the point of taking their own visual concept of a news story, rather than being directed by the reporters. I took to having long briefing sessions with them, designed to persuade them that almost anything dramatic and visual could be made a whole story, provided you went at it boldly; and I often went out with them and directed productions, so to speak. So the centre picture spread of the *Daily Record* started to look different, and to match, I felt, what the paper was doing in general editorial terms.

One of the first coups was when I sent Charlie Barr, himself a considerable golfer, to take pictures of the American Walker Cup team practising on some Scottish golf course before the contest which was due to begin the next day. We took the whole centre spread for this, and perhaps it's safe to say that nothing like this had ever appeared in a daily paper before. The main feature was one or two immense — larger than life-sized — pictures of the American stars demonstrating their hand grips, and when the first edition of the paper came up from the print room, the floor of the editorial room filled up with journalists practising with umbrellas, walking sticks and even broom handles, while those who had a bag of clubs in a corner issued the necessary implements. They swung to such an extent that Clem couldn't get on with the second edition and good humouredly phoned me in my room on the top of the building to come down and see the havoc I had created. The photographers enjoyed this greatly because they had ceased to be mere illustrators of news stories which had not necessarily any great visual quality or content; and they were turned into creative journalists themselves with the power of pictures added, and one was perhaps able to show them what that power could amount to. In early days I took advantage of some anniversary, it might have been the fiftieth year of press photography, to take the whole picture spread to proclaim my own photographers. There were four of them, and I wrote them all up with an identifying picture, as well as asking them to select for publication on that page the most dramatic picture which they had ever taken. This was a prestige issue which was noticed here and there, but the morale boost to my small team was considerable. The press photographer had in those days a harder task than the reporters. However difficult the reporter's job, once he had his story, he simply got to a telephone and got rid of it, and went to bed somewhere; but the photographer had to get the picture back, and I was at pains to see that they were recognised for it.

We set up a lot of events like that. I once went with Jimmy Morrison, the youngest of the photographers, to the Tam o' Shanter pub in Ayr to take a series of pictures to celebrate 25 January, the annual Burns Birthday Festival in Scotland. I got permission from the local magistrates to have the pub open and some controlled drinking going on there after hours, and I compiled from among the regular clientele a cast list of characters who could be put together in still pictures to illustrate the opening scenes of 'Tam o' Shanter', the great narrative poem by Burns which he set in that very pub. Most of the players responded zestfully, stimulated perhaps by the fact that they were drinking out of hours and at someone else's expense, so that we could show such a scene as:

As we sit boozing at the nappy
And getting fu' and unco happy

or,

The landlord's laugh was ready chorus

or, pointing to the original ancient clock in the corner,

Nae man can tether time nor tide
The 'oor approaches Tam maun ride

The final result for a half day's shooting wasn't bad at all and it made quite a stir in the appropriate circles. To be sure a certain stiffness came into the amateur efforts. The landlord, whose name I have forgotten, played the part of the original landlord, and he had a slightly disapproving face which did not lend itself very readily to the idea that the landlord's laugh was ready chorus. Nevertheless he mouthed open a semblance of a laugh and his efforts allowed us to get some jolly pictures of the other boozers.

We had something of a novelty in the captions, since it occurred to me to go to the Mitchell Library with Jimmy Morrison and photograph the relevant extracts from the facsimile original manuscript written in Burns' own hand. Accordingly the spread of pictures showed these authentic scenes in the very place of their creation, with the explanatory lines underneath each one in Burns' own handwriting.

Another time we went round the various Ayrshire and Dumfriesshire farms where Burns had toiled as a tenant or hired man, illustrated them as they were in the present day and described the differences in the current farming procedures and crops raised, comparing Burns' day with the middle 1930s. There must be a lot of research history buried in these old *Daily Record* files. But it was not necessary to seek great national events. Any good story that has reasonable implications can be enlarged into a whole documentary of human events or procedures. We did a whole spread once of a dance on the island of Lismore, the central feature of which was that the band which played there, a five-man piece, I think, were all granite quarry men from the Bonawe quarry on Loch Awe, and the photographer showed them sitting as a band; and then we photographed them sitting at their sett-making tasks in the quarry in precisely the same positions, but instead of musical instruments they had hammers and other gear with formidable protective boots and clothing. The practice grew in the paper that, provided we had the right picture, I could by agreement take over from the news desk the reporter's story and render it into a written caption below the picture and so relieve the news columns of a need to find space for that story.

Nowadays a prominent inside page of every daily newspaper is set aside as the so-called features page, with articles commissioned from outside, giving a platform for controversial subjects which do not necessarily appear in the hard news stories in the paper, but must be developed by the writer, who is named. This took a long time to develop, especially in the popular style of newspaper, and at the time I joined the *Daily Record* there was no such thing in its pages. I described this lack to Clem Livingstone and at his request put the idea down on paper. He accordingly appointed me features editor and told me we would start from Monday week, which meant the additional task of finding six good and varied articles every week. I took this on and although there was no extra money going — indeed for the three or more years I spent in pre-war time with the *Daily Record* I didn't get a rise at all — I was called art and features editor thereafter, and I made sure that both the art and the features pages were distinctive and memorable. I suppose this is what is called learning on the job.

There were other old-fashioned bits of the paper simply dragging along and they hung on until the outbreak of the war. One was a page of small paragraphs entitled 'This Morning's Gossip' compiled by a scholarly and attractive little comrade called Eric de Banzie. It was a mere clipsheet of gossip, mainly compiled by underpaid freelances, or sometimes staff men, from such a source book as *The Book of Days*, with small paragraphs which embarked on their communications role with such words as 'A correspondent has been reminding me that it is a hundred years ago today since the town of Seville in Spain . . .' or 'An amusing story is told of a visit paid by the Turkish Ambassador to . . .' or 'Many of my readers will remember the striking statement made by the late . . .' Nothing illustrates the sharp-edged change which has come over newspapers more than these turgid pages with their paragraphs which turned up in some form or another year after year. Every paper had one. The page in the *Bulletin* was called, wittily, 'Pertinent and Otherwise'. The most successful of them all was a column in the *Evening Times* called 'Gossip and Grumbles', written with splendid Glasgow spirit and introducing every other day or so an *oeuvre* from the pen of Paddy Coffey the dockside poet. This bard used to celebrate among other heroes such a figure as Humphie Dan, 'the champion crane man o' Finnieston'.

These features were all swept away and never came back after the war. Every now and again some superior newspaper starts something of a much more sophisticated character with paragraphs strung together, and I've often been asked by editors how they should liven a back page, if they have no set-piece items there already. I always tell them to get someone who can write short witty paragraphs because there is something in that formula, the provision of talking points and mild gossip, which give great variety to the morning reading. However often these features are started, they almost invariably degenerate into one long heavy essay, almost a political pamphlet, and you find them on the backs of newspapers, some of them running to 2,000 words long, with the chap who should be writing the 'shorts', pontificating on a subject that has already been thrashed to death in every other item of the media. Lord Kemsley, who was a good newspaper man, although by the time I knew him he was embedded in a pretentious way of high life, once said to me, 'If you want a fund of good ideas for your newspaper, look back in your files of twenty-five years ago.'

I often hear members of the public, and even journalists, who should know better, lament the passing of good evening newspapers which have seemed to them to reflect the salty nature of daily life in the cities where they circulated. Many of them have shut down, and the ones that remain are mostly fading away. There is a simple explanation. I once asked little Tim Watson, a Glasgow journalist who took to the writing of plays and who made a good living at it for many years, with robust scenes from Scottish historical or industrial life, what was the secret that had given him this marvellous ear for the true east-end dialect of labouring cities.

'Alastair,' he told me, 'it's easy. Live up a close in Glasgow.'

This is the secret that the modern journalist has missed. He does not stay up a close in Glasgow. He does not stay in Glasgow at all. He is enormously well paid, and if his paper is in Glasgow he has his home in Helensburgh or Girvan, with a large garden and a paddock and all the rest, and I rejoice in his good fortune. But he is not the man who should be editing a paper in working-class Glasgow, nor anywhere else.

But the world was catching up with us all and some of our endeavours, good or bad, were about to be bundled away for ever. One night in 1938 Clem phoned from his desk to where I was sitting in the art department and said, 'Oh, Alastair, an amazing story has just broken. Neville Chamberlain is going to fly to Berchtesgaden to see Hitler.'

'Clem,' I said to him, 'that's the most humiliating thing I've heard this whole year.'

Clem, superb newsman, had very little political conscience or even interest. 'But Alastair,' he said, 'it's the most marvellous story for years. I thought we'd build up Berchtesgaden and the whole run up to this in pictures.'

I went down to see him and we decided to throw out the whole centre spread and build it all up again with Berchtesgaden and the hopes of peace and all that sort of stuff. It was good contemporary daily journalism at the time, and in any case it was too late. War was a sure thing from then on, and when it came to us on the *Daily Record* it took a long time to bite.

The first impact, of course, came with the evacuation of the children. The most memorable story I read then, or have ever read since about this great exodus, was done by James McDowall, and it stays on the file there as perhaps the most moving thing of its kind ever written. It was done in the context of a man filing stories to catch an early edition of a daily newspaper — a quite beautiful essay about parted families, and sorrow and fear and the terror of the unknown that politically we had been pretending for years would go away or could be bought off somehow. The evacuation of the children also revealed, in a clash of thunder, the social conditions and deprivation of a great part of our population and the level on which they lived and which now, torn up by the roots, mere dauntless courage in familiar squalor could not cope with. The photographers were out at the stations and the bus depots and some of them went to the not very far places where the children were arriving and were being picked up by families and taken away. Jimmy Morrison, who was by no means a soft fellow, came back from such a place as Callander and sat weeping on a chair in my room, but was able to tell me the incident in a short time. Families had turned up and taken, in ones and twos and threes, the various little groups of children who had been dumped on the station platform, until there were only two left, two extremely grubby and unprepossessing little boys, a slightly older brother and a young brother whom he was holding by the hand. The young brother was crying and the older fellow, perhaps just eight or nine years, was trying hard not to cry. Nobody wanted them. They were too appallingly dirty and undesirable, and as the platform cleared except for them, Jimmy saw the older boy lead the wee fellow up to a dubious adult and say, 'We can wash the close and go for the messages and we can run alang the railway line looking for coal.'

As the months passed and virtually no war was going on anywhere except in Finland, these stories took a remote hilarious turn, like the true one which Tom Johnston used to tell. He was at that time Regional Commissioner for Civil Defence and Lord Rosebery was his deputy. The Countess of Elgin had taken in a group of very scruffy little evacuees and she wanted to have Tom Johnston know of an incident that happened the night they arrived at her home of Broomhall. However, the story was not of a ladylike character, so she resorted to the device of telling it to the Countess of Rosebery who told it to her husband, who then told it to Tom Johnston. It seemed that the children had been so dirty and ragged and smelly that the housekeeper and Lady Elgin stripped them of clothes and filled a bath with hot water to immerse them. One little boy screamed at the sight of the bath, spread his legs and arms and would not let himself be inserted, and all the while he was yelling some unintelligible phrase which meant nothing to Lady Elgin at all. At last she said to her housekeeper, 'What is he saying?' And the housekeeper replied, 'He's saying, madam, that it's ower fuckin' deep and it's ower fuckin' hot.'

The war, however, was real. John Simpson came into my room a few days after the war broke out and said, 'Gerry's got *Athenia*.' The Clyde ship, an Anchor liner, had sailed from the Clyde and had been torpedoed, and many lives were lost, including those of evacuated children on their way to the safety of Canada. In a day or two the survivors, young and old, were being landed in the Clyde again and this was a terrible story. One of those covering it was a fairly senior reporter, Elma Waters, whom I used to visit in the 1950s when she was working in the United Nations building in New York. She too sat and cried in my room.

Four or five of us took to staying late, sleeping overnight in a dormitory that had been made up in the building so that we could be on hand to produce a late edition with some specially dramatic news; but that was scarce and I was away by the time Hitler made his thrust towards the continental coast. We used to play exhilarating games of football on the editorial floor after the final edition had gone away, and James Cameron used to fry steaks for us. This was followed later, generally, by a session when we smoked from my clay church-warden pipes and pontificated at large. A church-warden gives you the chance to have a long cool smoke through that elegant stem, which can also be pointed meaningfully here and there as you solve the problems. Sometimes the late reporters would pick up a stray or two from the streets or the station. One of these stragglers was often Benny Lynch, then far gone in liquor, a down-and-out, who would be ejected from pub after pub, where he would go seeking a drink from some of the hangers-on who had battened on him when he was the flyweight boxing champion of the world. We used to let him sleep and have a shower in the morning and a canteen breakfast. One of the reporters heard an exchange of views in which Benny participated in some drinking den, where a well-meaning citizen was berating the little chap, now fat and bloated, saying, 'Benny Lynch, you ought to be bloody well ashamed of yourself. Just look at the sight of you. You ought to be setting an example to young people instead of getting yourself into that state.'

And Benny, swaying, pulled himself up and looked blearily at the man, 'I was the world champion. Whit were you?'

One nocturnal visitor was a young lad from the Outer Isles who had been trying to get the late train to London and had missed it because the connection had been late on the long journey from Stornoway. It turned out that we knew something of this young fellow, still in his teens, who had been a junior seaman before the mast on a ship which had been torpedoed in the Atlantic 600 miles from the Outer Isles. Most of the crew had got away in boats and as morning broke this lad found himself in a ship's lifeboat where he was apparently the only person who knew how to sail small boats, or how to navigate at all. He got this collection of engineers and cargomen to rig a mast and sail and he steered the little boat the 600 miles to his very village where they came ashore. This was all reported by the local coastguards and eventually reached the ears of the Admiralty in London, who summoned the boy to meet them, omitting to say that they wanted to commend him in some way. Accordingly the lad, as he told his story to us, was very troubled because he thought he was to be reprimanded. 'There was an onshore sea running when we brought the boat in, and we damaged one of our planks.' When asked how he had managed to make the landfall exactly at his own village, he said, 'But you see, it's my home.'

But in the paper we were already cutting down. Some of the staff had been called up because of Territorial Army commitments. The Kemsley Organisation had decided to fire a number of people because newsprint was getting scarce and a smaller staff would be sufficient to produce the daily number; and we had to cut back on our lavish picture and feature displays. One of the items I was very sorry to see disappear was what we had been perfectly justified in calling 'the world's first real life comic strip'. This was a pictorial feature directed by me and photographed by John Stewart, called 'Kuddy the Kid'. It featured the real life comic adventures of a family of father, mother and small boy of three. It was worked out by Duncan Ross and me. Duncan was a remarkable impresario who at that time was living in Glasgow with his wife and two little boys and was the manager of the largest cinema in Glasgow, the New Savoy. I had first met him in the *Claymore* days when, in his early twenties, he was manager of a cinema called the Regent in Abbeymount, Edinburgh, a building now derelict but which he endowed with remarkable life and excitement. He was an artist and sculptor of some note as well as a producer of stage entertainment, and every year he seemed to get the top award given by his chain of cinemas for the manager who was best at promoting the films on show. He used to fill his vestibule at the Regent with great 14-feet long models of crocodiles and he once built a 9-feet high talking robot in metal with flashing eyes and twitching, riveted, limbs. Now at the New Savoy he was packing in the crowds, and doing all sorts of things to decorate the theatre, like creating in bronze relief a beautiful wall sculpture in the ladies' lavatory into which I was sneaked at an off moment to see the masterpiece. In our strip, Kuddy was played by his three-year-old younger son, Brian, while Duncan played the father and his beautiful wife, Sheila, the mother. They were all extroverts and it was a joy to work with them. Had we had more resources we could have got a lot of serialisation of the feature. I was to be a colleague of Duncan's for a period in the wartime when after some strenuous months as a film operator with the Ministry of Information he joined the Paul Rotha Organisation. After the war he became a scriptwriter of some renown with the BBC in London.

For our family the outbreak of the war was signalled by the breakdown in health of my brother George who had been working night and day with the new Ministry of Food. He went back to work shortly after, but he and my mother decided to go and stay in our little cottage at Minard, and I drove them there early on the morning of Sunday, 3 September 1939. I had to turn and come back immediately and at 11 am — the moment when our British ultimatum to Germany expired — I stopped in the deserted Glen Croe in Argyll where no traffic was running, and the only sound was the endless voices of the hill burns, and imagined the whole Maginot Line and the other frontiers flaming as the guns opened out. None of this happened, as it turned out, and we had many months to wait on our side of the action before a gun was heard.

On the Monday morning Seumas and I and Leslie Robertson went to join up at the OTC office in Glasgow University. To our surprise they wouldn't take us. I wanted to join the Argyll and Sutherland Highlanders and Seumas was eager for that squad too. The officer in charge advised us to go away and wait until we were called up — 'It's going to be different this time.' But he seemed to be offering us a commission in the Green Howards, which at that time did not sound to us to be a very valorous setting for our military enthusiasms. In due course it was announced that I was already over-age in a reserved occupation and in any case an old rugby knee injury had written my ticket. Seumas eventually turned up as a statistical staff officer in the Northern Ireland Recruiting Depot at Lisburn; while Leslie Robertson found himself in the Glasgow Highlanders and leading squads of soldiers through France and into Germany. I found myself engaged in a largely bloodless war in a variety of government departments and after Hiroshima, Clem Livingstone, who was by this time managing director of the *Daily Record* Group, asked me to come back and edit the paper.

When I arrived back at the *Daily Record* in 1946 the paper had been running for a number of years with eight tabloid pages to contain the whole story of what was going on in the local, Scottish and world scene — the three-sided role which a Scottish daily of any stature has to perform. Most of the conscripts were already back and in place and others drifted in, so that it was a team I was perfectly familiar with and they knew something about me and what I could do. One of the first pieces of information I had to digest, and I did it with eagerness, was that newsprint supplies had immediately been liberated and in a very few weeks time we would be leaping up from eight tabloid pages to twelve. There was an opportunity here to promote the announcement in editorial terms. For about ten days I ran a short story on page one, each written by a different feature contributor, telling how the extra pages would at once enrich the store of information we could give to news and foreign readers, letter writers, sports fans, music and book enthusiasts, readers starved of pictures, others aching for controversy or comic observations on human affairs, the general hunger of a community no longer to be fobbed off with censored short staccato miseries. We built up expectantly to the day, which happened to be timed to arrive in the middle of my honeymoon, since Dorothy and I were marrying a few days before the first twelve-page paper would burst upon our readership. So we had to cut short our honeymoon on that island on Loch Lomond and come home, so that I could demonstrate 50 per cent more of editorial flair. This may partly account for the fact that all our holidays have been of the character of a honeymoon ever since.

It must simply be terrible to be a good and competent editorial executive on a worthwhile newspaper, and never to be editor at all. This is what happens to most journalists. Some of them do not care, if their work is reporting or certain types of feature writing. They consider their job to be much more important than that of the insiders who sit at desks and mutilate their copy and pictures. I suppose it must happen in almost any business or profession that a great number of people in the middle ranks, not lacking in ability and devotion, wonder why opportunity has passed them by. For all the time I was in newspapers I never had a job of any kind which I asked or applied for. Every chance and advancement that came my way I was offered. There may well be some style that marks out some people from others. All I did was to do whatever the job was as well as I could, and as far as I was able to carry the performance beyond the line of duty. If this is done at all, it has to be done, I am sure, in a way that does not distinguish one as an ambitious and thrusting bastard.

However, editor or not, or boss or not, there is always something that clouds over the full enjoyment of the job. In my case it was a good old friend called Jacky Robertson, a great enthusiast for life who had been a young RAF pilot in World War I, and in World War II, in his spare time at weekends, taught RAF recruits to fly. He had been a good evening paper reporter and also wrote showbiz paragraphs in the years before the war; but some time during the conflict he had leaped to senior rank and when I reached the *Record* as editor, he had been installed in the group — not only the *Daily Record* but the *Sunday Mail* and the *Evening News* — as editor-in-chief. I may say I do not believe in the title of editor-in-chief, or the duties it is supposed to perform. If you have an editor you have an editor, and I've only known the job of editor-in-chief carried out with any kind of executive flair and efficiency in one case, and it wasn't ours. Jacky tended to brood over me and my staff with amiable clumsiness. He would push into my office, thrusting the door wide in his passage and unregarding as to whether I had anyone in or not. He would ask my staff to account for some editorial practice of which he disapproved loudly. The time came when I simply wasn't getting on with Jacky at all and I had to ask him to keep back and deal through me; but as we say, in every job there's aye something. The time came when he was given the editorship of an ailing Sunday paper in Manchester and he saw it to its deathbed, returning at last to Glasgow after I had gone, and where, with no status at all, he most calmly carried on with his small showbiz paragraphs.

Clem Livingstone was a great strength, a great reconciling element in these difficult early times, although his devotion to goodwill and the covering up of trouble led him to stand off from some of the personal conflicts. Job definitions were out of the question. Big Jacky liked to be in on everything that was successful and to be seen to be in the forefront. In staff matters he thought it was proper to share these fifty-fifty with me, especially in matters of staff dispositions. He hired and I fired, until the time when I made it clear that that wasn't the way I was going to work it.

However, we were making an impact, and of course we had the people to do it. A great number of the old guard had been hired by the eccentric David R. Anderson, who had been the editor and general manager of the paper for many years before the war and he had picked up people, or they had insinuated themselves on to the payroll, without anyone knowing what systematic training or aptitude they had ever had. The place was full of 'elderly stout fellows who sometimes sub-edited sport, especially greyhound racing, and also appeared to have the running of the staff canteen or to be responsible for preparing the rota for the backdoor commissionaires and the messengers who ran to the station for the parcels of copy from correspondents. As for some of the others, I never really discovered if they were journalists at all. There was an elderly journalist on the *Evening News*, and so far as I could discover his only distinction was that he was fiercely anti-semitic. His favourite theory in the 1930s, when I first encountered him, had been that the small actress, Shirley Temple, was not in fact a child but a thirty-seven-year-old dwarf Jewess.

There was also a redoubtable man on the fringes of music called Herbert Bennet, an Englishman from somewhere, whose arrival on the paper no one seemed to be able to trace. He persuaded D.R. Anderson that the *Daily Record* should become the official organ of the brass band movement in Scotland, and this it did, running the annual brass band competitions which I had to attend with Dorothy once I became an editor. We used to sit for most of a whole Saturday once a year in a box in the old Lyric Theatre listening to these dire blasts of brassy chords; first the solos, then the quartets, then the full bands. After the presentation of the cups and prizes the winning bands would crowd on to the stage and we would be conducted in some monstrous classic, the baton being wielded by Herbert Bennet himself, or even by so renowned a visiting personality as Mr Harry Mortimer. After I became editor, Herbert Bennet used to visit me in my room repeatedly to assure me of countrywide devotion to brass bands and the eagerness with which at least half the readership of the *Daily Record* bought the paper for the brass band notes alone, which he wrote under the name of 'Bass Clef'. He was a great, hulking chap and he used to loom over me speaking closely and spitting faintly. His lips were corded with muscle as a result of a lifetime devoted to developing the necessary embouchure to play his beloved instruments. His lips indeed were a frightening spectacle, and since I was a small and insignificant physical specimen compared with him, I used to have a fanciful notion as he bent over me that some day he would snatch me up and play me.

In this gallery also was John S. Clarke, a Yorkshireman who had somehow become attached to the *Daily Record* and who put himself forward with such success as a world authority on Robert Burns that he became much sought after for the proposing of the Immortal Memory on 25 January. John was also an animal lover who brought small monkeys into the office and even larger creatures. His role was vaguely to do with the writing of general interest articles and this was another editorial hazard. The paper as I found it in the first year or so after the war was still lumbered with a number of rights apparently belonging to members of the staff who, having been refused a rise by David R. Anderson, had been promised by him — or so they claimed — that they would get at least one publication a week of some useless article written by them and placed in the paper for a small fee. I had to clear out a great deal of this material in the hope that we would have some general and recognisable editorial theme running through the paper. Not that the articles and observations were required to be entirely homogeneous; but nothing gives a paper's editorial policy away more than the fact that it is a dumping ground for old-fashioned 'articles' on nothing in

113

particular, when the whole post-war scene is throbbing with impending problems that have to be dealt with. Quite early we devoted the whole of page two to letters from readers and built up a splendid controversial platform.

One lesser handicap of having the very helpful Clem Livingstone now as the chief executive of the group was that he was almost too well known about the building, in which he had started as a boy of sixteen. He knew everything about the staff and the methods of the production and advertising processes and almost everybody in the building referred to him as 'Clem' although he was punctilious with the older ones and addressed them gravely as 'Mr — '. He almost invariably had a string of people in his room every day, talking about the paper and their part in it, and where there were difficulties of persuasion in a new direction it was common in the beginning to have some of them say to me, 'Well, I'll need to speak to Clem about this.'

There were of course many in the staff who rallied round magnificently, especially some good young reporters whom we made into a team which could beat anything in the West of Scotland both in newsgetting and in the distinctive lively writing style we developed in the paper. One of these was Max McAuslane whom I had known since he was a small kilted boy in the church in which I had been brought up and where his father was the organist and choirmaster. Max was the best news editor I have ever come across and I was to take him, in that capacity, to *The Scotsman*, which had never before had a news editor. Later I made him editor of the evening paper in Edinburgh after we had bought the *Evening News* and amalgamated it with our own *Evening Dispatch*, and he ran it in brisk news terms until he retired.

Eddie Campbell was another whom I put in charge of films and theatre criticism and news, and he excelled at that, building up a ponderous filing system which he no doubt transferred to the *Evening News* in London where, in due course, he became literary editor. Eddie's hobby was the unexpected one of taming lions. From his boyhood he had been associated with Wilson's small zoo in Argyll Street in Glasgow and when Wilson, prompted by Eddie, bought a litter of lion cubs from some travelling circus, Eddie brought them up and trained them until they were fully grown. He was well known to all big circuses, Mills Brothers, Chipperfields, Billy Smart and so on, and he used to take me to see the acts and to roam behind the scenes where all the people and the animals knew Eddie and considered him a professional. The Mills Brothers offered him a permanent, well-paid job with them as a breaker of new acts, but he decided to stay in journalism.

In many ways the star turn of this splendid young team was an exuberant, lively teenage sprite, called Cliff Hanley, whom I discovered sub-editing news stories as one of the chief sub's team, and rewriting dreary ones so brilliantly that I called him into my room one day and said, 'Cliff, you're not a sub, you're a writer. Out you go.' And I more or less flung him on to the street with a column to fill every day. He did.

At an early age he left journalism to take a chance as a freelance writer, producing novels, plays and everything, including popular songs, one of which, 'Scotland the Brave' to an old pipe tune, appears still to yield him a comfortable figure of royalties annually. He is now a visiting professor of English here and there about the world, and a renowned broadcaster and teller of tales, as well as a great friend. Like all confident small men, he married a splendid, tall, handsome girl, called Anna. In the early days of their happy marriage they both came to the *Daily Record* staff dance one night about Christmas time. There was one of those embarrassing dances where the music stops from time to time and some busybody or master of ceremonies announces a particular forfeit to be performed by the couples on the floor. In one pause we were told that the gentlemen must lift their lady partners and waltz for the next dance round the floor carrying the fair burden. The Hanleys did not hesitate. Anna snatched Cliff up and danced round with him, both faces beaming with hilarity. It was at one of these dances when I was playing a strenuous part that the announcement was made that there would be a prize for the first lady who rushed up to the platform with a pair of gentleman's braces, or suspenders as the Americans call them. As we stood embarrassed and sheepishly waiting for someone to make the first indelicate move, a purposeful lady, dancing nearby, having discovered manually that her partner was wearing a belt and not braces, dashed over to me, rummaged about my waistline to discover that I was wearing the required article and with practised fingers that had no doubt taken down the trousers of many a small boy, she stripped me of the braces and rushed to the platform to claim the prize, leaving me standing holding up my trousers.

There was a brilliant man there called Harold Stewart who under the name of 'the Gangrel' wrote a daily comic column of scholarly wit and spirit. His invented fictional characters ranged in their adventures over the whole scene of satire and political ineffectuality, interspersed with heroic and comic tales from Celts and Vikings and sardonic or sometimes pure love poems. He was an inspired jester and scholar, turning after a lifetime of fairly ordinary reporting to his outpouring of magnificent and profound commentary. There is nothing like it in existence, and in my view it outpaced 'Beachcomber' of the *Daily Express* at that man's best. Another memorable figure was John James Miller who had been a carter and farm labourer of ambition. Endowed with muscle power and a determination to be prominent, he had taken to the Highland Games and become a heavyweight athlete of renown, even hiring himself out for a season as a labourer on a farm in Cumberland so that he could learn the local wrestling styles. He used to clean up the prize money at the North of England Games as well as in Scotland. He started writing articles for the *Daily Record* and David R. Anderson gave him a job. At his best he refused to call himself a reporter, putting himself forward as a 'descriptive specialist'. In quite old age he became fat and flat-footed but shuffled bravely about the country sending in the results of agricultural shows, until a wasting disease seized him so that he was loose inside his immense suits; but he met his fate with courage, and better still, with style.

The *Daily Record* had great fame in the field of sport and it used to be thought that people would buy newspapers to read accounts ostensibly written by famous sportsmen themselves, so that at one time I had five former Scottish football internationalists on my staff. Not one of them turned out to be a Hugh McIlvanney — he was there too — but they wrote all their own stuff and tried very hard. Another great little trier who wrote up our boxing stories was Elky Clark who had been the Scottish, British and European flyweight champion, and had gone to New York while suffering from the flu to meet Fidel la Barba for the world title over twenty rounds. La Barba beat him on points and blinded him permanently in one eye. Elky used to tell how he was so ill before the fight that he had to be carried on a stretcher aboard the steamer to take him from the Clyde to New York, and when he was just up and about, but far from being in training, a photographic team had arrived at their hotel with a 'kilty' outfit, the like of which Elky of course had never worn, and had made him dress in it and had taken him to some park where he posed in the snow. He never could recall the fight from round six to sixteen during which he got his eye injury, and was obviously fighting instinctively. When he came out for round seven he noticed from the big boards at the back of the hall that it was round seventeen and he assumed they had simply made a mistake. He had been going for ten rounds unconscious. Elky was very far from literate but an immensely likeable chap, and Harold Stewart used to write useful cliché-style phrases which he could incorporate into his copy, like: 'the strong two-fisted little Wishaw boy soon warmed to his work' or 'after four rounds of this the lanky Liverpool lad was about to cry quits'.

Elky's proper Christian name, I think, was Willie, and he never could understand how he had come to be called Elky among his boxing associates. He once told me how he had been able by this means to preserve a remarkable anonymity even in his own home where they knew nothing of his boxing career. He was already European flyweight champion before he mentioned to his father that he was a professional boxer, and on one of his successful defences of the title he took his father along to see that worthy's first ever boxing match. The old man was staggered at the violence of it and said afterwards, 'Willie, that's bloody murder. Ye've got to stop that sort of thing.' To which Elky replied, 'Faither, I'm afraid it's got a wee bit too far for that.' He had a crumpled ear, an ill-fitting glass eye and a bad stammer, but he remained a courteous hero.

An editor has always got to be analysing what is the function and purpose of his newspaper. Through the *Record*'s preoccupation with the results of greyhound meetings, horse racing and the overwhelming supply of news and gossip about football, I found it useful to be able to describe our paper to Fleet Street pundits as 'a working-class *News Chronicle*'. It reflected in my view truly the aspirational intellectualism of even our under-privileged, and until I left the paper we ran a full page of book reviews and also reviewed in serious terms, and at length, the major art shows in Scotland and in London. We were not short of people who were able to write on these lines. One of my staff was William Power, whom I had known for many years and admired. He was certainly one of the best literary essayists Scotland has produced. When as a schoolboy I read his book of essays *The World Unvisited*, I used to try to detect from the clues in that book the very house in Great Western Road in which he lived in Glasgow so that I could go and hope to catch a glimpse of him entering or leaving. Another of my heroes was George Blake, staff writer, novelist, playwright and broadcaster. I had hardly reached the age of ten before I had read his book *The Vagabond Papers*, a collection of itinerant essays which had been first published in the *Evening News* under the editorship of Neil Munro. George was a pugnacious and patriotic Scot, and although I realise that by the time he was on my payroll he was elderly and out of breath, I suggested to him that his written contribution to post-war Scotland would be *The New Vagabond Papers*, another itinerant collection which we would publish weekly and would update our looks towards the future. Talking about the idea to George I felt that he was somehow almost stricken with the impossibility he felt within himself to recapture that first, fine, careless rapture. He was old and heavy and he turned the idea down, although I would have relieved him of all problems of mobility and logistics. I think we were both very sad about this.

Another companion of those days was John Robertson, who was unexpectedly in charge of all the advertising for the whole group of newspapers. He was a distinguished and scholarly man who read books, studied opera, went to all the new plays, knew about pictures, and his conversation was urbanely scattered with Latin phrases. When he died in his early fifties and I wrote about him in the *Daily Record* I gave him a Latin phrase to see him off. He was as far away as can be imagined from the present atmosphere of space-selling with its targets and phone-in, and indeed phoney, jargon. A man to be loved and cherished. The whole scene has moved vigorously into another era and no doubt one would be rated as far behind the game to have employed such a figure as John Robertson, but in his time we were making profits. He was bringing in the revenue and the newspaper managements who would repudiate him now seem to have very little to show for their advances in revenue-getting techniques and effectiveness.

But in the meantime, of course, we were getting on with the job of running the paper. Quite early on in my editorship I determined that the feature side would have to be run by Seumas. On coming back from the Army he had got himself into a minor job in the subbing team of the *Evening News*, but this was really ridiculous. Without mentioning it to him I found myself being pressed by Jacky Robertson as to any staff changes I thought were desirable and I told him that I wanted James Adam as features editor. Jacky made no observation on this to me, but he sent for Seumas and offered him the job as features editor of the *Daily Record*. I was angry with Jacky about this, but I didn't make an issue for Seumas' sake and he joined me in a day or two. Immediately the features side of the *Daily Record* started to be what it should have been. Sharp-edged articles, controversial, lively, humorous, everything that was required to supplement the hard news elements we were developing in the rest of the paper.

Apart from outside contributors Seumas picked out the right members of the reporting staff, like Gordon Frogatt and gave them feature spaces every week or so along campaigning lines. Some of his series on public argument were memorable, particularly the famous 'Flyting of the Makars', a long-drawn-out debate lasting for many days in verse, bringing in the leading poetic figure in the Scottish scene. It started because we had on the staff then quite an elderly character, the pawky figure of W.D. Cocker whose speciality was writing memorable comic verse describing biblical incidents as if told by an old Scottish bard — about the flood, and David and Goliath, and other heroic or cataclysmic incidents in which much of the less scholarly Old Testament Calvinism of Scotland was rooted. Seumas got him embarked on a new series of these, and a young poet called Maurice Lindsay objected to these primitive manifestations from which he believed he and his fellow versifiers were steering the Scottish ethos. Seamus got the idea of making the whole thing a series of poems illuminating the Scottish attitude to nearly everything, so he got Willie Cocker to respond to Maurice Lindsay, printed nothing, but in the meantime set them up in verse and sent proofs to other poets. They readily came in on the series, attacking each other with tremendous swinging strokes of the broadsword, and eventually he had a series of about fifteen separate poems which he then printed on successive days. It was of course a quite unique idea and a great talking point, always helpful in drawing attention to a paper which apparently had very little to spend on its publicity in other directions.

We also found David Stephen, who was to become probably the leading practising naturalist in Scotland. At that time he was working obscurely in a local authority job as a welfare officer, but from his boyhood he had been studying wildlife and was already an expert on the badger, the roe deer, the fox and all the rest. He was to become a great friend, to such an extent that a walk with him through woods or on moors was a revelation since he could see things one simply could not see or recognise. It has to be confessed that he was very far from being the only one I enticed out of a safe job to come into journalism. Reading something he had written I sent for him one day to have a look at him and asked him if he would write for us, and before the end of our first interview he had agreed to write a number of weekly articles. This turned into a series which went on for years. During that first visit I told him that we had a young chap on the staff who was an animal man and I sent for Eddie Campbell. Now David Stephen is a man of excessive gentleness towards animals, but his style is firmly masculine and he tends to snort when speaking to strangers. Eddie came in, small and pale-faced as ever, and I introduced them, whereupon David said to him aggressively, 'What's your racket in animals?' Eddie replied quietly, 'Lions.' And I really don't think David Stephen ever recovered from this mild reply. Years later David followed me to *The Scotsman* and he is writing there regularly still, having produced a great list of magnificent books about animals, many translated into a handful of the European languages.

If you have David Stephen for a great friend you take him as he is. He happens to be one of the people with whom once, for a blinding few seconds, I was perhaps more enraged than I have ever been with anyone. His daughter Kathleen's twenty-first birthday happened when we were all together on the *Record*, and David and his wife, Jessie — who, by the way, is one of the great experts on wolves — invited us to their home. I told David that in addition to any little thing we brought for Kathleen I would like to get her a twenty-first birthday cake, because things were still a little scarce and I knew a good baker who would stretch the regulations to produce something special. So on the great day we turned up and I handed over the cake to Kathleen to be produced at the feast. When we sat in to the table it was there in a place of pride in front of Kathleen. However her father, fortunate in being the head of a household which probably never queried his actions, reached over towards the cake and drew it to himself with a view to cutting it up. The main decorative feature of the cake was an enormous, beautifully sculpted rose in red sugar embedded at the centre of the icing at the top. Before plunging in the knife, which I had assumed would be the privilege of the girl whose birthday it was, David with a large hand prised the rose loose and unceremoniously stuffed it into the gaping jaws of his large slobbering black labrador which always sat at his side. I said nothing simply because I was quite unable to.

I believe the editorial ingenuity of the *Daily Record* reached its peak with the establishment of the Pat Roller column. Our main circulation area was of course the City of Glasgow and its immediate neighbourhood, and for a long time I had been concerned about the disturbance to the paper, and the costs of replating whole pages and holding up the printing for the last edition, to accommodate all the small and medium-sized paragraphs which dealt with late-night accidents, adjacent murders, rapes and near rapes, social and romantic gatherings which often turned into mayhem. These were not in themselves by any means major page leads; but coming out of the vigour of Glasgow such incidents mostly deserved more cover than could be carried in purely objective little news items scattered throughout the paper. I decided the way to do this was in the form of a new style of near-gossip column, to be located permanently on column one of page three. The late night staff would achieve a homogeneous style of writing and would put in their paragraphs, the whole thing to be carried by an obviously contrived but personal-looking name. The first problem was to find the name and I asked for suggestions. I put forward the name of Bill Winkie, derived from the attractive bairn rhyme:

Wee Willie Winkie
Rins through the toon,
Upstairs and doonstairs
In his nichtgoon.

On deep reflection I came to the conclusion that this was perhaps slightly frivolous for some of the serious references that would have to be made in the column; and Cliff Hanley came up with the masterly suggestion of Pat Roller. I hesitated for a little because I thought the name was so obviously a rendering of 'patroller' that no one could possibly take it seriously. But I was wrong about this.

Finally we launched the column, and its heading on its first night and for the years it lasted went as follows:

In Glasgow
Last Night　　　LOOKING FOR TROUBLE
By Pat Roller.

The column built into an enormously potent and entertaining, indeed hilarious, morning revelation about the late-night activities and thuggeries of Glasgow. In a short time the Chief Constable of Glasgow, old friend Malcolm MacCulloch, had given instructions to his staff that the Pat Roller column was to be the top item on his desk when he came into his office every morning. He used to read it and then phone a few chief superintendents who often were waiting in apprehension for his call. The rougher element in the Glasgow population knew the column as Pat's column. When they saw the editorial car about the town they used to hail it, 'Hello there, Pat. How's it going, Pat?' and so on; and the less literate of them, whose reading was restricted to the greyhound racing columns, knew the feature as 'The Rollo'. It was a column that could get involved with the community. It rejoiced with their miraculous escapes from death when they fell over windows and bannisters or were plucked uninjured from below Corporation buses after pub closings. Some of these near-victims would appear in the splendid style of the writing as heroic figures and local heroes in their tenement closes. Small incidents, because of the essential human drama involved, became astounding in our canon and the three or four reporters who did the regular pieces strained smoothly towards a picturesque idiom. An immortal paragraph written by George Martin about some obscure mishap opened with these words: 'If old Harry Inglis of . . . [address] is ever nearer to death's door, he'll be able to look through the keyhole.'

There were unexpected by-products of the renown which Pat Roller accumulated to himself. Frequent invitations came for him to open East End sales of work and jumble sales and other events. He was regarded as some sort of patron figure of charity, and Christmas toys and gifts for disabled children came pouring in. Groups of small girls in the summer evenings gave concerts in the back courts of the tenements and used to deliver gravely their sums of money to the office, these being duly recorded in the last paragraphs of the column. Thousands of pounds came in and were distributed and, especially at Christmas time, the editorial floor became encumbered with parcels of toys for the children who could not come home from their hospital beds; around that time the editorial cars and the parcel vans had to be requisitioned to load up this bounty and distribute it round the wards.

It was in this context there occurred the nearest thing to a miracle to which I have ever been a party. It happened one Christmas Eve when things had quietened down in the office and since we were not publishing the next day there was only a standby editorial staff on the floor. A call came from the local telephone exchange saying they had some toys for the hospital distribution. Everything had gone out by this time and the telephone ladies were apologetic that they had been so late. The story was that one of their number, who had been stricken by some disease, was bedridden at her home, but being a fine needle-woman she had spent some painful months dressing, quite beautifully, five dolls. They were so handsome that the telephone people had gathered up a subscription and bought in the five dolls that very night, and there they were to be handed over to children. Our reporters collected the toys and went straight with them to the most notable children's hospital for long-term cases. In the entrance hall they asked to see the matron and after some delay she came from her room, a tall, austere woman, not young, but perhaps slightly distressed. 'What have you got?' she said crisply to the reporters. 'Five dolls,' they said. And this firm capable woman, who had looked with detachment on so much sorrow and anguish, was suddenly standing there before them crying. 'Come into my room,' she managed to say.

In her room, more composed, she told them. She described how, in one of her wards, there were twelve small girls, more or less permanent invalids, and how in the weeks before Christmas there had grown up among them a belief that they would all get a doll from Santa Claus for Christmas. She and her nurses had gone to great efforts to get a doll for each of them. '. . . but by the time they were all down for the night we had only been able to get seven dolls, so we've all been making up other parcels of ludo and snakes and ladders and card games and other things for the five girls who couldn't get dolls. And when the nurse came to say you were here, I was on my knees in this room, praying for five dolls.'

We could have been doing with such divine intervention in other parts of our affairs, although most of us working on the paper saw little

121

sign of the impending doom. Even I had never been shown a balance sheet nor had I ever been given a budget for editorial purposes; I spent little and if the sum seemed excessive I used to get sanction from Clem Livingstone to spend it. Tony Bowman, the company secretary, told me later that for many months the Kemsley interests had been trying to sell the *Daily Record* group of papers as one of the healthiest going concerns which the organisation possessed, but which required capital expenditure and a good deal of commercial input and know-how.

But it would not be right to leave my own recollections of those challenging and on the whole most happy days without remembering one or two more of the people who distinguished the group's performance. A young woman reporter turned up whose name was Jean Macauley and she had not been long on the *Evening News* before I asked her very orthodox editor, Willie Goldie, who she was and why he did not give her a by-line, as her material was so distinctive and her personality so attractive that she would have been a great frontline personality for his paper. A year or two went by before he even gave her a by-line, and she immediately became notable. At a time when I was responsible for editorial innovations on all three papers, she came in once to ask me if she should accept an invitation she had been given to go and open the annual town fair in a small burgh somewhere on Clydeside. I agreed most heartily and spent a little time bolstering her enthusiasm, because she would have to make a speech as well. When she came back she reported to me and it was one of the most engaging and rollicking accounts of introduction to public life which I have ever heard. It seemed that when she alighted at the station of the small town where she was to be the most distinguished personality of the day, there was no one to meet her, and she had a little difficulty in discovering anyone who knew about the forthcoming great events. She eventually found her way to the house of the provost of the burgh who had signed the letter of invitation to her. There she found the house in some chaos, 'for the provost could not be disturbed as he was writing his speech. His wife and daughter had somewhat fallen behind with their household duties. The kitchen was in a muddle and the ladies were panic-stricken about their forthcoming appearance in the festivities. Capable Jean set about at once washing all the dishes and tidying up the kitchen. She then ironed the dress of the provost's daughter and helped the provost to type out his speech, adding no doubt a felicitous phrase or two. They all struggled through the ceremonies one way or another with Jean apparently keeping the morale going and she finished off her account of the whole affair to me with: 'So there you are. You sent me to be Queen of the May, and all I got was dishpan hands.'

It was about this time that I had to take John Simpson out of the chief reporter's chair and give it to Max McAuslane. John, ponderously putting on weight, had become more enigmatic and mysterious with the years. His attitude to me had been one of amused tolerance and foot dragging and I never got much of a response from him, especially for

Above. 1900: My father, David Sinclair Dunnett, with his parents and four of his sisters. My grandfather, George Dunnett, was born in 1815.

Below left. 1900: On left, my father, David Sinclair Dunnett. On right is his friend Danny Mowat, who saved his life at the Ibrox Disaster.

Right. 1904: The engagement picture of my parents, Isabella Crawford MacTavish (Bel) and David Sinclair Dunnett.

Above left. 1920: George, Doris and Alastair.
Right. 1934: Alastair and James S. Adam (Seumas) on Auchengillan moor. The photograph was taken by Jim MacDougall, 'the first victim of the war'.
Below. 1944: To emphasise the Secretary of State's devotion to Scottish primary foods, especially in wartime, I organised a press 'porridge party' in St. Andrew's House. Tom Johnston in the centre. On the left is Sir Horace Hamilton, Permanent Under-Secretary of State.

Above. 1944: On the set (at Chelsea Barracks) of the film *We'll Meet Again*, starring Vera Lynn. Left to right: Patricia Roc, Sir Alex B. King, Vera Lynn, Alastair, leading man, and Captain (later Sir) Iain Moncreiffe of that Ilk.

Below. 1951: This is the best picture I have of Willie Ballantine . We are with Vera Ellen on the set in Hollywood where she was shooting a film with Fred Astaire.

Above. 1960: In Berlin, James Holborn, Editor of the *Glasgow Herald*, Willi Brandt, Alastair.
Below left. 1962: Portrait by Dorothy, which hung in that year's Royal Scottish Academy. 'I shall not say it is severe, but it is perhaps a shade lugubrious, since the main feature of the face and eyes were done while I was still posing, but also watching on the television screen the Scottish Rugby team getting a hammering from the Welsh.'
Right. 1965: James Robertson Justice is laying down the law to me. A good friend, I represented him on the Edinburgh University Court when he was Rector.

Above. 1960: In the western borders of Ross-shire. Michael Powell, Bill Paton and Alastair. The picture was taken by Seton Gordon.
Below. 1967: As Editor of *The Scotsman*.

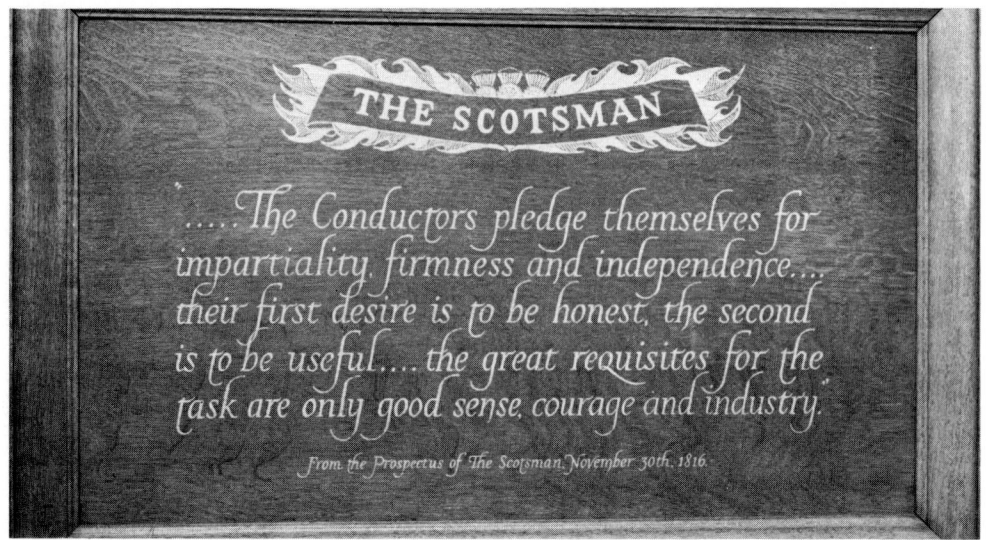

Above. 1967: Extract from the 1816 prospectus of *The Scotsman*, painted in gold for me on the panelling of the Editor's room by the calligrapher Avril Gibb (Lady Watson Stewart).

Below. 1972: When I left *The Scotsman* to enter the North Sea Oil business, they gave me a first edition of Speed's map of Scotland. Left to right are Dr Ronnie Selby Wright, *The Scotsman*'s chaplain, then Moderator of the General Assembly, Roy Thomson, Eric B. Mackay, my successor as Editor, and David Snedden, my successor as Managing Director.

Above. 1971: In the North Sea, being heaved from HMS *Abdiel* to HMS *Belton*.

Below left. 1970: Stuart Boyd, Pictures Editor of *The Scotsman*, tells me that this is me 'telling one of my stories'.

Right. 1972: The Dunnetts awheel. Mungo, Ninian, Dorothy and Alastair.

Above. 1975: Somewhere in Fleet Street. This was one of the times I was chairman at a press gathering for Prime Minister Harold Wilson, a relaxed and co-operative statesman.
Below. 1981: Mungo took this picture of me at the old Oykell Bridge.

the newer innovations. He had resisted the Pat Roller column and other novelties, but he had once been a very good news man and still fancied himself prowling the outback and coming in with tremendous exclusives. At least once a year he would come to me with some mysterious project, using such a phrase as, 'There's something bloody funny going on in Stornoway.' I would say, 'What is it? What have you heard?' He would answer, 'Well — they can't tell me on the phone. It's bloody funny though.' And I would say, knowing the drill, 'John, why don't you go there and look at it yourself?' This, of course, was what he was after and off he would go for five or six days, during which time not a word of copy would be filed. Then he would turn up in the office again and when I asked him, 'What about Stornoway?' he would say, 'The buggers must have heard I was coming.'

I gratified these unproductive sorties for a time but they were far removed from our need to produce better hard news stories in reality than any of our competitors, and they did nothing for the leadership required of our good young team. Max transformed the scene. Although he was hardly older than most of them he had the greatest of instincts for news and the way to tell it.

The year of 1955 ran towards its close. One day Clem Livingstone called me into the room and told me that the Kemsley interests had sold the *Daily Record* group to the *Daily Mirror* organisation, and would I keep that evening free for a dinner where we would meet our new proprietors. He told me how the transaction had been going on for months, that everything would be fine — no staff changes and that I particularly would be wanted to play a prominent part in the new organisation. He was going to remain as chief executive, to be called managing director instead of general manager as heretofore. There would be money to spend and new facilities such as we had not enjoyed in our time. I have heard this story since so often that I should be most wary indeed if I ever heard it again, but at the time it seemed some relief from the Kemsley ownership. I told Clem how glad I was for his sake but my own concern was, 'What about the *Record*? Do they want to turn it into another *Daily Mirror*?'

He was reassuring. 'Not in the least, Alastair. They like the *Record*. You're to continue as the editor with absolute freedom. This is a great day for all of us.'

The celebration dinner for the takeover took place that night in a private room in the Central Hotel in Glasgow and it signalled the start of the worst six weeks of my life. Cecil King presided over this, a grim and, as it seemed at the time, a menacing figure, who had driven the *Daily Mirror* to tarty success over the past number of years. His fellow directors who attended were obviously whooped up by their success in getting hold of us. Some of them spoke freely and unguardedly about the changes that would be taking place. At the end of this feast of joy Cecil King spoke briefly. Clem didn't speak at all but a number of us did. One of the participants was the astounding character of Hugh

Gillespie, a Catholic bachelor who had become the head of our advertising team, a job he carried out with great success. He was a very rough and ready East End of Glasgow chap who had become a full colonel in the wartime and had turned up immediately on demobilisation, still in his uniform with red tabs, apologising to Clem, since they were the only clothes he had at the time. He wanted to forget about the Army and come back to civilian life. He was also an unswerving fan of Celtic Football Club of whose chairman he was a guest at every home match in the directors' box. He had a brother who was a priest and had been a parachute regiment officer, and I think there was a sister who was a nun. He had a terribly scarred face arising not only out of war wounds but a severe motoring accident in which he had been involved at some time. Hugh rose to his feet to make a pronouncement. He did it with the aggressive truculence which those of us who knew him loved and cherished, but which was a little disconcerting to people in business who imagined themselves to be more urbane.

'We don't need you. You need us,' he told them. 'We are doing well here. Maybe after this we can do better, but I'll tell you one thing — with your beauty and my brains we're gonna be all right. With my beauty and your brains — we're out of business.' That was all.

A *Mirror* director sitting beside me was aghast and said, 'He's had it! He's out!' In about three months the *Mirror* director who had made this observation had been fired, and Hugh Gillespie was on the Board.

I wasn't. I had been offered a seat on the Board and of course a continuation of the editorial task. It became clear at once that in spite of Clem's well-meaning assurances the old order had gone for good and the *Daily Record* was fated to become another *Daily Mirror*. The whole idea revolted me; otherwise it would not have been difficult technically and professionally to go along with the plan, for the tricks were simple if one had the stomach or the conscience for them. There was the raking around to get some nineteen-year-old blonde into the story at any cost. The searching for the piquant photograph; the false indignation and editorial demonstrations of almost anything that would feed some semi-illiterate mass prejudice; the hounding of public figures; the manipulation of facts into headline patterns — all the tricks that have proved bitterly possible. I had been in competition all my journalistic life with the papers which did this and I had always believed that sooner rather than later some element of continued education would ensure that public taste would be gradually upgraded so that people would reject the strident vulgarities. I felt that with the *Daily Record* we had achieved a compact with our readership which did not affront their dignity and which allowed them to accept our modest innovations with pleasure. I have mentioned some of these, and there was time now to look back on others which were shortly to disappear as I was myself.

There was 'Marcia' for example. I had been looking for a way of eliminating the dreary group photograph of staff parties and social events which was assumed to be a feature of our kind of newspaper but which did little to entertain the general public, and did not gratify more than the inevitably po-faced people who appeared in the pictures. I tumbled on the idea that some of our fashion design illustrators could be better employed in developing a new sense and going out to these functions, selecting the best-dressed woman and drawing her and her gown with all the usual elegant exaggerations of this art. It was, however, essential that the likeness of the model in the drawing had to be an illustration of the woman and not the conventional angular bone structure favoured by the illustrators in the fashion magazines. I sought out the teachers of Glasgow School of Art and eagerly described to them this creative breakthrough, telling them what a splendid opportunity it would be for some of their more talented students to make a reputation and earn some money, and would they send some of them to me so that we could try them out. To my consternation this notion was greeted with horror by the Glasgow students whom it greatly offended, on the grounds that artists of nature or the human form have nothing in common with fashion illustration and the idea of combining the two was contemptible. None of them would touch it. I often wonder what happened to these purists as their careers developed.

Eventually I discovered a woman who was a commercial artist and who, under the name of 'Marcia', did the job superbly, so that she received invitations from all the main functions, and crowds would gather round her as she selected the model and made the drawing. The paper would carry this with reference to the event in news terms and also a technical description of the gown. It didn't take the paper's new masters long after my departure to drop this feature and I haven't seen it appearing anywhere else.

I look back with pleasure, too, on some of the other innovations and article series that we did. The *Daily Record* was the first paper in Britain so far as I know, to discover the 'teddy boy' and to describe his habit and vocabulary as well as to photograph his clothes. This was done by Max Hodes, who I see is still running his column in the *Daily Record*.

Also in the very early days, I am certain we were the first to make a systematic investigation into the predicament of old, lonely people. Some of our stories indicated to me that there was a substratum of these elderly unfortunates in and around Glasgow, and I sent Liam Regan to produce what turned out to be a memorable series which was as revealing as the forgotten, great stories by Jimmy McDowall about the evacuated children and their unguessed way of life. There were old women, far past active age, still living on their own, helped in and out of bed by kindly neighbours and long since abandoned by their family and relatives. There was an old woman of over ninety who was enduring this kind of living death, and she said to Liam, 'Every night I pray to the Lord to let me die, but he'll no tak me.'

I often wonder what the editors of the extreme 'popular' papers think of as their average reader. In the *Daily Record* we personalised him. While I had been art editor before the war I had invented a little character called Mac, who appeared in the centre picture spread as a small couthie figure commenting on the main picture feature of the day. He generally had something to say on political or social items, or delivered himself of comments that reflected mild prejudices, most of them mine. We now got him drawn in colour 4 feet high and he was pasted to the wall of the big editorial room so that one could readily say to the editorial individuals, 'Would Mac understand this story?' As his legend grew, Mac turned out to have a family with a wife who was a devoted household manager, interested in fashion and gossip and children, and although their thirteen-year-old daughter (someone invented her in due course) had few interests outside film stars and modern dance music, he had a son with his Highers. Naturally all this targeting material went by the board in the paper's subsequent drive for the unthinking.

I decided to quit. There was no future for me here in any kind of context that I could find palatable. Although I had enjoyed the executive jobs I had had in newspapers, and especially in my editorship, I had always regarded myself as a writer, and now it seemed I was going to have the chance to prove it. I told Dorothy that it would be hard going for a long time, if not for keeps, because I had made the *Daily Record* my life and although I had often written there, I had nursed no other contacts of any significance. I think she was glad that I had made the decision, for she saw how troubled I was. This was long before her fiction writing days, but she would be happy to keep going her industrial research job with the Board of Trade and, being alone, we could cut back and manage somehow. I made Clem Livingstone aware of this in confidence and also Seumas and another close friend or two. I thought it best to stay on for five or six weeks to see how the staff would settle down. Most of them had given me rousing and loyal support over the years. Later I was to try to rescue one or two of them from the shame into which I felt we had all fallen, and was surprised that few regarded this situation so distastefully as I did. I suppose that professionalism is a great saviour.

In the meantime, another phenomenon threw me. The majority of the senior executive staff had suddenly discovered that they had two or three weeks holidays due to them and they poured away from the battlefield, leaving the paper very thin in feature and investigative talent, so that what with this and my jangled nerves the papers which appeared under my weeks of *Daily Mirror* proprietorship are pitiful. I remember the great struggle not to feel bitter about this because I felt I had been suddenly abandoned by my nearest and dearest.

It was of course many months before the screws started to be tightened up by the new chiefs, and, even at the worst, I don't think it ever got to look like a Murdoch type of operation. Still, I had four or five *Mirror* directors looking over my shoulder almost every hour of the day, and not diffident with their criticism. I really was on quite affable terms with them all. Hugh Cudlipp discovered a great passion for

126

haggis served with mashed turnips and potatoes, and he, Alec Little, Roy Suffern and I used to sally out most nights and dine, almost ritually, on this dish in a favourite cubicle of mine in the Café Royal in West Nile Street. Another week or two went past and I still was damned if I was going to tell them that I was leaving. Every now and again there was reassurance about the editorial freedom I was to continue to enjoy, along with the status of director of which the Kemsley organisation had never considered me worthy.

Two or three more weeks of this passed. One day we were sitting round the conference table in my room with Hugh Cudlipp, Roy Suffern, Alex Little and perhaps another, although not Cecil King this time, when the phone rang on my desk. It was Jim Coltart asking me to come to Edinburgh as soon as possible to have a discussion with Roy Thomson and him. Without mentioning names I agreed to have lunch with Jim next day in Edinburgh; we agreed on a time and I hung up and came back to the table. We all went on coolly with the discussion, although I was seething inwardly with the possibility that this might be the offer of editorship of *The Scotsman*.

Jim Coltart was to become one of my closest friends. He had been general manager of the *Daily Express* in Glasgow and a few months earlier had joined Roy Thomson as his managing director and chief executive on *The Scotsman*, which Roy had recently bought — his first purchase of any kind of business on our side of the Atlantic. Jim was to become Roy's dynamic right-hand man, their partnership forming a tremendously innovating and exciting chapter in much of British industry and far beyond newspapers. Earlier, the editor of *The Scotsman*, Murray Watson, had wanted to retire and one or two people had already told me they had suggested my name to Roy Thomson, whom I had met vaguely once or twice. Murray himself once ·asked me in Edinburgh if I would like to succeed him, but at that time I was happy with the *Daily Record*. A little later Roy sent an envoy, a fellow Canadian, to seek me out in Glasgow and ask if I cared to be considered as a possible for the editorship of *The Scotsman*. The whole proposition was so vague that I even remember feeling somewhat offended at the lack of precision, although, in my own terms, editing *The Scotsman* would be the very top of the profession, since I had made up my mind long ago never to live and work outside of Scotland.

Over that lunch Jim did indeed tell me that he had persuaded Roy that they wanted me to be the next editor of *The Scotsman*, and he proposed to take me to see Roy immediately after lunch. It was an immensely friendly and uplifting gathering with Roy very enthusiastic, and Jim putting in the wise and wary word from time to time; and, looking back, I suppose what I found most encouraging of all was that my burden rolled away as I sat in that room where I was to preside later for many years. Roy asked me my age and I told him. 'That's about right,' he said.

Then he asked me how much the *Daily Record* were paying me. It

127

wasn't much for I hadn't had a rise for three years. £2,500 a year,' I said.

'Alastair,' said Roy, 'would you come and edit *The Scotsman* for twenty-five hundred a year?'

I don't know if I may be considered a particularly quick-witted person, and although I didn't hesitate, I gave to Roy the best answer I have ever given to anybody in my own interest. 'Roy,' I asked, 'is this an offer?'

Roy was startled. He hadn't expected this quibble and he was suddenly hesitant. 'Eh, well . . . Well, yes it is, Alastair. It's an offer,' he told me. 'I'll be honest with you, there's another fellow I've been talking to but if you accept the editorship of *The Scotsman* now, I'll phone this other guy right away and tell him I've filled the job with someone else.'

That was it. He asked me if I wanted a contract and I said No. I didn't believe in contracts for the editorial type of job. 'What do you feel about front page news?' he asked me. I told him we'd have to do it and quickly. There was some more talk and some joking, never a difficulty with Roy, and we parted, all of us, I think, very happy.

As Jim showed me out I asked how soon I could get a letter confirming the appointment, and he told me he would go right back to his room and dictate it at once. Dorothy and I didn't even celebrate when I got home. It was important to get the letter with its firm undertaking that I had the job. It came by the first post to my home next morning.

It didn't take me long to shake clear of the *Daily Record*.

CHAPTER NINE
The Scotsman

Jim and Roy and I had agreed that there would be no announcement of my appointment until a day or two before I actually started editing the paper, which was to be 16 January 1956, so that although I told them I was leaving, nobody knew where I was going, if anywhere. There was no farewell party or formal drinks, no hearty votes of thanks, but I have never known anything like the relief I knew as I walked the streets of Glasgow, which I thought I had served not badly. Only the closest of friends and relatives were told and they were prepared to be secret. Dorothy's mother simply couldn't believe it. She had recently been widowed. We were all she had and, living as she did in Edinburgh, she felt we were very far away.

On the morning of the day I got the letter of appointment from Jim Coltart I went to the office and told Clem Livingstone that I was going, although I didn't tell him where and he didn't press me to know. I said I wanted to leave there and then. He knew why, because we understood each other very well and I owed him much. I denounced nothing and he defended nothing, but he begged me to stay for the moment, fearing as he said, an exodus of the staff and a demoralisation. He thought I really should be seen around the office for another week or two at least, although three weeks had passed since the takeover. So I stayed.

Characteristically few of my staff, even those nearest to me, came to speak to me direct about the circumstances of my going, although those few who did were canvassed feverishly after they met me in the search for information. One or two of them told me bluntly that if I was leaving, they were leaving. I told them not to be daft, not to rush at it, but to decide personally, if and when they wanted to leave, and in the meantime stay within their own speciality and get on with the job, waiting at least until the smoke cleared away. The fact that I was going to *The Scotsman* never leaked out at all, although Alex Little guessed at it and he used to rib me diffidently in such an aside as 'I don't suppose for a moment this is how they do it in *The Scotsman*' and other unremarkable banter out of the side of his mouth. He was edging towards the editorial chair and although one of my last suggestions was that John Lees should be made the editor, it was Alex Little who took the job over. He was a quiet, well-informed man who had learned how to apply considerable mental agility to the painstakingly cheap formulas of the *Daily Mirror* style; and he was never quite to recover from a severe charge of contempt of court in the pages under his direction. Lord Clyde in the High Court in Edinburgh inflicted a monstrous fine and was on the brink of sending Alex to jail for the offence although the Scottish daily newspaper editors combined to muster defence for him. After a few days I cleared up and left.

Dorothy and I hired a removal van to take our modest household plenishings to Edinburgh. This turned out to be an exercise fraught with more detailed agonies than we had bargained for. We had lived for ten years in furnished flats and were under the delusion that we had no impedimenta of our own. This proved false, and eventually we knew the normal nightmare which afflicts people who move house. For one thing we had sixteen shelves of books. They were to go along with the bookcases which belonged to us and which we had commissioned from a nearby joiner craftsman. We had acquired from somewhere odd chairs, suites of furniture, bedding and even beds, kitchen equipment and all the rest. We suddenly became aware of this crushing responsibility thirty-six hours before the van was due to arrive on a Friday morning and we worked all that time without sleep, trying in vain to junk some of the stuff and not finding anything too unnecessary to throw away. The stuff almost filled the van and about a dozen tea chests filled with old newspapers — thank God there's a use for them — into which the tough men packed our crystal, decanters, fragile cups and saucers and souvenirs, all with deft fingers, breaking nothing. They demonstrated a smart instinct for comfort in the furniture removing business when they held out to the very last a large sofa and my most comfortable armchair which they loaded into the back of the van facing the road. They installed at each side of this grandstand two brass upright ashtrays on legs. On this lot three of the men reclined at once with practised ease and started smoking my cigarettes and drinking the beer I had handed out. I was to travel in the cab with the gaffer. Dorothy stayed behind for an hour or two to hand out keys and sign off somewhere. We took the high road.

Near Harthill, halfway between Glasgow and Edinburgh, we pulled in to a transport café. As we all filed in along the counter I passed, at its edge, a tall, standing mirror into which I gave a glance and laughed in surprise. 'Aye,' said the gaffer to me, 'you fairly get a few laughs in a place like this.' I gave no hint of the timely cause for my outburst. What I saw in the mirror was a rascally figure in a filthy old beret, his face streaked with grime and two days' growth of beard, with grubby hands holding together a duffel coat over a boiler-suit. In *The Scotsman* of that very morning, the day agreed for the announcement of my appointment, there had appeared a picture of me as a dapper figure looking as svelte as I could manage and with no sign of two days' shadow, accompanied by a text which made the most of my achievements to date.

In Edinburgh we moved in to the home of Dorothy's mother until we could find one of our own, and stowed the furniture in her garage. I paid off the men, apologising for depriving them of their comfortable seating for the run home.

I was to arrive in *The Scotsman* on the Monday. On Sunday afternoon I phoned John Buchanan who had been acting editor for a number of months and whom I agreed should be my deputy. He was a short, quiet, scholarly man, unassertive, in no way a leader, and he was afflicted with a devastating stammer which made him diffident about communicating. He turned out to be the least talented of the old style of *Scotsman* leader writers, his essays consisting merely of summaries of the news story or situation and hardly a sentence of opinion. Still, he had his following within the building, and I was bound to expect some disapproval. His chief ally was James Smellie the literary editor, who cultivated an Olympian style and disapproved of change, on the grounds, as I was to discover, that he assumed his own performance was at the peak of excellence. On one occasion in our early days I had a long talk with him about the book reviews — how the writers were chosen and in short what was the kind of service that *The Scotsman* should be giving to its readers in matters of books and their merits. It was a negative exercise. I inserted in it as much good-humoured reason as I felt capable of without lessening my expectations, but at one point I had to mention to him that there were other newspapers reviewing books as well as *The Scotsman*. Some of them had achieved a fair standard of acceptance in the literary pages and perhaps he was being slightly defensive. He drew himself up coldly and said, 'Sir!' (When they call you Sir like that you know you're on a loser.) 'I think I have something to defend.' I remember saying to myself, although I didn't say it aloud, 'By God, that's clever. I wish I could think of replies like that.'

James Smellie was the man who requested that he might make a speech on the day that we gave John Buchanan a retiral party a good many years after all this, and after I had spoken about the great service John Buchanan had rendered and how much respect he had gained within and without, and had handed over the gifts, I called on James Smellie. He did not quite blackguard me, but he asserted in some prepared phrases that John Buchanan had been unfairly dealt with and he should undoubtedly have been the editor of *The Scotsman*, giving a number of unconvincing proofs of the matter. Many years later I went to John Buchanan's funeral which was attended by a small gathering among whom I did not see anyone who was currently, or had been previously connected, with the *The Scotsman*. James Smellie was already dead by this time, having spent the years of his retirement most worthily running a hostel for elderly men in the City of Perth, but it was strange to see no others of the old guard at Buchanan's funeral.

In fact I got on very well with John Buchanan, and we had an amiable, if cool, relationship. He had no managerial skills at all and was out of touch with any kind of technical developments or even editorial techniques, but on that first Sunday in Edinburgh I phoned him and asked if we might meet and have lunch the next day, my starting day, so that we could then go into the office together and he could introduce me to the key figures. He readily agreed and we had a most affable session in a restaurant in the Grassmarket. It could have been much more awkward than it turned out to be although I still didn't know what to expect when we walked back to the office. There was no doubt he was a very disappointed man. What had happened was that on the retiral of Murray Watson, the previous editor, who had been a good friend of mine, it had occurred to Roy Thomson and Jim Coltart to give John Buchanan, the then deputy, a chance to see how he would fare. He was made acting editor for the term of a year; but long before this time was up it had become obvious that he wasn't the man for it, so they had asked me. I tried not to look too wary in his company on that first day but I had to be ready for any eventuality.

When we got to *The Scotsman* building we came down the Fleshmarket Steps and walked along the back corridors towards the editorial department. On the way we passed about six or seven handsome marble busts of previous editors of *The Scotsman* at which I tried not to glance, I suppose out of some delicacy of feeling for the situation. However he mustered his halting tongue and said to me, pointing to the busts, 'You'll never be one of these.' Well, I thought to myself. This is it! We might as well have it now. And I was assembling a script in my mind when he rallied once more and delivered himself of a gallant pay-off line: 'They're doing portraits now.' Decent man. And I was glad I had held my tongue.

The leader writers were an able lot and the chief executives seemed up to the job they had been doing so far. I knew many of them already and spent the time talking to those whom I knew while asking them to introduce me to their colleagues and ones I didn't know. So the first afternoon passed and I set to finding out how this paper got out. There was no news editor. David Terris was the elderly chief reporter, a willing man, fairly well-informed on local affairs. I wasn't able to find a foreign news specialist. There was a good chief sub in Gordon Anderson and I spent some time with all of these finding out what was happening that day and what shape the paper was likely to take for the Tuesday morning. In the midst of this towards the evening there was a tap at the door and a rubicund face, with thick pebble glasses came round the door.

'Can I come in?' he said.

'Roy,' I told him, 'I can't imagine anyone who has a better right to come in here than you have.'

And in he came although he wouldn't sit down. He was there simply to greet me but not a word said about the paper or its contents and he offered me, as he was to do on so many occasions, all the help that I needed to make it the paper we felt it should be, and could be. He told me to be sure to get any new staff I needed. And I replied, and meant it, 'I don't want to get anyone new in here until at least a year has passed. I think I can do *The Scotsman* with the people I find here.' He was pleased about this and said so. I had also inherited a ramshackle old rolltop desk. 'To begin with, Alastair, I think you should throw out that desk and get a decent one.' And I replied, because it was my room and my job, 'Roy, there's a lot of people in this office obviously needing new desks. I'll get mine last.' That pleased him too.

I found that there was no tradition whatsoever in *The Scotsman* of editorial conferences on any subject. I thought I had better start with the leader writers and I summoned them in to discuss this. It seemed that leader writers in *The Scotsman* had become an élite, though they were a very vigorous and attractive lot. What had happened in Murray Watson's day was that some time between 5 and 6 pm the chief sub-editor would bring to him a handwritten list of the main stories of the day with no summary of how they were developing. It was simply a list of titles. The leader writers would gather round his door and eventually he would open it with the list in his hand and point to one writer, saying, 'Coal'; to another, 'Egypt'; and to a third 'Highland Transport'. He would retire behind his door again and the three chosen would scatter to the library and elsewhere to get old cuttings and to the news desks to find out what the developments had been in their subject, while the others went back to their cubby holes to browse over something, probably book reviews.

By my third day, the Wednesday, we were holding our first leader writing conference ever in *The Scotsman*, and it has gone on every working day since. We met in the splendid panelled room next to my own and where, unless they have turned them to the wall or even hidden them in the cellar, there hang the portraits of Murray Watson which I had had painted after his death, and also my own which I unveiled and might well have wisely left covered. They were a likeable and lively lot and many a good session we had together over the years. I knew some of them already. They were Robert Warren, James Vassie, Matthew Moulton, Fraser Cowley, Arthur J. Arthur and, of course, John Buchanan. Later I was to add Andrew Hood to cover the foreign and world news as a speciality. By the end of a year I had come to the conclusion, and it still is firmly in my mind as a matter of judgement, that in the whole newspaper scene in the United Kingdom we had from that lot the best economics leader writer and one of the three best foreign commentators. They were terribly tongue-tied to begin with, but that passed in a week or two and soon they were giving me as good as I gave them. I expected them to come to the conference already well aware of what was happening in the world of their speciality and we could, with such a team, afford some specialisation. For the first two or three conferences I gathered up myself early galley proofs of stories already through as well as the first Press Association and Reuter schedules of international and home news, while I got David Terris to

133

type out for me on a sheet, so far as he knew them, the stories which were developing from his own Edinburgh staff and our branch men and correspondents throughout Scotland; so that we had on the table before us some indication of what sort of paper it was to be the next morning.

There was never enough time to write leaders myself, but I did so occasionally. What I did, however, was to see some of the leader writers individually after our little conference, discuss more fully their chosen subjects, and then see the completed job, making possibly a few amendments before it went down to the case room for setting. I found in the early stages that I often had to write the first sentence and the last sentence to point up what the opinion was to be about. In this way I remember taking the excellent and analytical leader written about a certain budget by Jim Vassie and heading and tailing it in this way. It was the budget by Harold Macmillan as Chancellor which we had all looked forward to and indeed, for some days before at least, the responsible press and commentators had been looking forward to busily, in the confidence that it was to have so attractive a content in terms of tax release and facilities for industry that the whole prosperity of Britain would surge forward into a new chapter. In the event the main item of this budget turned out to be the establishment of premium bonds, a kind of national lottery or raffle. And I remember writing on to the end of James Vassie's leader, with his approval of course, the tailpiece 'This was to be our day of destiny. What we got was a day at the races.' These sentences were extracted and quoted, presumably round the world, as *The Scotsman*'s summing up.

We hit upon a pattern of procedure and held to it for my time. We would discuss as a team the whole range of events of the day, looking also to forthcoming events or to some themes that had floated about for perhaps weeks and which we felt it was time to bring down to earth. So in verbal exchanges that got very lively as the months passed, we kicked these themes around with everyone taking part; as the discussion went on I started to detect what the three or four, or sometimes two, leader subjects would be; and after a few minutes, who would write them. I then allocated the themes, we added a few more pointers as to what might be said, and away they went. I never asked anyone to write about a theme, nor to give *The Scotsman* an opinion, in which he did not himself believe. They were expected to understand what *The Scotsman* should say about matters, and not give personal views. *The Scotsman* would be there for a long time, while we would come and go. Most of them turned out to be full of gratifyingly creative ideas. Such a person as A.J. Arthur, for example, developed a remarkable flair for scientific subjects and wrote frequently, and with great insight, into the subject of flying saucers. Eventually he came to me and said that the night before, walking home from the office, he had seen one, so I steered this subject away from the column altogether in due course as one we had suitably exhausted. At a much later time, when he had written wisely, and most acceptably, about the difficulties that were likely to arise out of the deployment of nuclear bombs and defence mechanisms, he admitted to me privately that he had, after pondering the matter for a year or two, come to the conclusion that he did not feel in conscience that he could write anything more about nuclear arms or disarmament. So I released him from this chore.

The next stage, and it started in a few days, was to inaugurate a news conference when all the heads of departments and main editorial executives could come together to discuss the content of the news pages of the paper for the following morning. This was a large-scale conference, because it included the people who selected and arranged the letters from readers, the man doing the obituaries, the sports editor, the chief sub-editor with home and foreign news schedules, the chief reporter with his list of developing stories from his own staff and the branches, and all those who had responsibility for some section of the paper. The leader writers also sat in with us and when the main body of the conference had dispersed they would stay behind and we would proceed with our leader writing assessment and decisions as well as talk about the weight of the paper's contents and how we could progress or improve some of the items we had heard about. I gave all the leader writers the status of assistant editor so that they were available for direction and at least suggestion in the areas over which they had an insight. There started to be created, I think, a feeling of a network of responsibility and an outlet for talent and decision. Editing cannot possibly be a matter of making all the decisions, although some have to be referred. It is more a matter of leadership and involvement and an expectation of firm purpose, and above all a constant interpretation and reinterpretation of what the paper is and does, and how it sounds and reads. It must seem a grim affair, but these conferences turned out to be often uproarious sessions from which laughter reverberated throughout that wing of the building to such an extent that the staunch Agnes Watt, who was my secretary for all *The Scotsman* years, used to say to me when I emerged, 'That sounded like a good one today.' As we went through the schedules, often light-heartedly but with growing confidence and professionalism, some of the readiest comical responses came from John Forgie who succeeded to the job of pictures editor, having been a skilled photographer himself. We never could make out if I was the comic and he the straight man, or the other way about, but we seemed to feed each other to the satisfaction of the gathering. His puns were invariably fresh and quite splendid. I do not happen to think that the pun is the most degraded form of wit. There is a lot to be said for any kind of word play and John was good at it.

One way or another the whole thing quickly got into place as a team. These men who had, during their time in the paper, been dispersed into moribund and undemanding categories were coming now together, being led to believe in the vital needs of a new and thrusting newspaper, and they were at the heart of it. There was brisker journalism everywhere coming to the fore and I felt very satisfied that I had told

135

Roy Thomson I wasn't going to make any staff changes in the near future. I got great support from this large team of executives and departmental heads and I like to think they got some benefit from it all as well. Not many of them left in my time. After I went into the oil business, John Forgie was offered an interesting assignment out of journalism, to become the National Trust for Scotland's representative in the island of Arran in the Firth of Clyde. He pursued such activities as looking after the beautiful Brodick Castle with its chamber music concerts in the great rooms and was also made custodian of the mountain of Goat Fell, so he became in a way, virtually the laird of Arran, and a many-sided laird at that.

On the paper it was a long, slow process of improvement and updating, with something moving pretty nearly every day. During my first week I was stopped in the corridor by a senior editorial writer whom I knew very well, who told me 'It's always been a great pride of *Scotsman* writers, Alastair, that we never have any alterations to our copy. Everything we write is sent straight to the case room to be set in type and goes into the paper directly.'

This self-indulgent practice stopped almost forthwith. We had a good chief sub-editor in Gordon Anderson, who married Jessie Anderson of the staff and went to inhabit a small estate on the outskirts of Edinburgh. When the first edition had been printed, Gordon Anderson and I sat in my room and went over it page by page, pondering how we might improve it — how stories could be further developed or others made more credible and all the small details with which, if you take pains, you can perhaps create a newspaper that people will want to read and talk about. When I finally packed up for the night about 11 pm, having been there for more than twelve hours, I would say to Gordon, referring to the later editions he was to produce, 'Surprise me'. I was down early at home in the mornings to receive the delivery of the paper, the final edition, through my letter-box, to discover whether there was indeed anything new and fresh.

I had long thought, as a reader of *The Scotsman*, that the most lively section of the paper was the page of letters from readers, some of these being so original and informative that I often, as editor of the *Daily Record* had lifted them to work up as news stories and to develop as campaigns. *The Scotsman* had a tremendous reputation for authoritative letters, everyone in the country, and a good many outside of it, who had something momentous to say about policy or politics, launching his notions in *The Scotsman*'s 'Letters to the Editor'. Apart from *The Times*, no other paper had anything like it. The *Glasgow Herald*, at that time, made nothing of their letters and they fell away to such an extent that James Holburn, who edited the paper for a period, once phoned me to ask if I thought it right that he should drop the *Herald*'s letters feature altogether, because he simply couldn't get any letters of quality. I told him as strenuously as possible that he would be mad to do this. The remedy was to give them prominence and space and to attend to the controversial aspect of his stories and features so that readers would be induced to respond with their own thoughts. The *Glasgow Herald* is now a very lively forum for the argumentative people of the West of Scotland.

Early in my days at *The Scotsman* I realised I had fallen heir to an endless controversy which was raging in the letters page. The subject was the fate of five trees in Lothian Road and the decision of the local authority to cut them down as they were unsafe, having rotted to such an extent that they might at any moment fall over and crush passers-by. Every adult in Edinburgh who hated change, and there seemed to be many of these, poured forth in white-hot letters a fierce protective concern for these specimens, saying that on no account should the environment be denuded of their picturesque presence. Some local authority supporters, including well-informed arboriculturists, it seemed, responded reasonably enough. All agreed that there was no doubt the trees were a positive danger. Still the controversy went bombarding on and as a new boy I did not feel sufficiently knowledgeable to suggest that the public might be getting a bit weary of it all. I went to David Terris, the chief reporter, and asked: 'How many trees are there in Edinburgh?' He didn't know. I told him to find out from the head of the City Parks Department, the Forestry Commission, the proprietors of semi-public squares and gardens, the Housing Department and anyone who might be able to take an intelligent guess roughly at the number of trees in the gardens of houses and blocks of flats. He came back in two days with an answer that was near enough; and it seemed that there were about two and a quarter trees within the boundaries of the city for every single inhabitant, from child to the elderly. That seemed to me to be enough to be going on with, and I told the people looking after the letters to let the controversy wither on its bough.

We were getting on. One of the questions that Roy Thomson had asked me in the early days, and to which he occasionally turned in my first few months, was the question of front page news. At that time *The Scotsman* had a full front page of small classified advertising, referring of course only to Edinburgh and the immediate environment in terms of business and properties for sale and services. I had said to him, 'We'll need to get news on the front page as soon as possible. It will never look like a national newspaper the way it is with these local ads.'

It had been the great battle with my worthy predecessor, Murray Watson, who for the ten years of his editorship had held so firmly to the pattern set by *his* predecessor, Sir George Waters, that when the Roy Thomson ownership took place, he even asked Waters to write the story for the editorial columns since he could not bring himself to put the announcement into words. He had quite refused to preside over any such change as the creation of a front page of news, banishing the local ads to the inside where they belong. He felt that the great contribution he could make was to go down defying this new proprietor and the whole onset of the twentieth century. He retired without striking his flag and sadly died very shortly afterwards.

I was gradually changing the main inside news page to what the front should eventually look like when we started it and in a very few months I was ready. I thought the best way of heralding the change was to clear a six-inch double column space on page one among the advertisements and to make an announcement from the editor that we would be carrying front page news, that they would all enjoy it, and this was the proper way for any newspaper with pretensions to style and quality to go about its business. I got a flood of readers' letters, balanced half and half between those who objected and those who welcomed the change; there were six from, I guessed, elderly men who were outraged and announced that they had cancelled the paper that very day. It happened that I instructed our circulation and marketing people to follow these readers up surreptitiously and they came to me months after the change to tell me that every one of the six had instructed his newsagent to restore his order. I was sympathetic with them. It was getting to be a troublesome post-war world and I found that the people who mainly objected to the change — and indeed any change in the paper — were the forty to fifty age group, mainly men, well set in their careers and battling with the difficulties of mortgages, school fees, high costs of living, price of holidays, clothes and everything else. They had enough instability and revolution to contend with anyway and they ached for something that simply never changed, like their granny in the chimney corner. When they wrote to me I used to tell them that I knew how they felt but that *The Scotsman* couldn't be an invariable factor in their lives, otherwise we would die along with our elderly readers and no new readers would come into our lists.

That first announcement was inserted in page one six weeks before we made the switch. I did another story on page one three weeks before the change and then on the day promised, or threatened, we came out with front page news. Most of the readers took it bravely and within a few weeks we had added some thousands of regular readers to our circulation numbers. What pleased me most, I think, and it became a good talking point when I was out addressing the people who asked me to talk to gatherings, was that many of the letters of commendation for the change came from very elderly ladies, often spinsters, of the type written about so warmly by Lord Cockburn in his *Memorials*; independent, self-contained, indomitable. And they wrote to tell me how very pleased they were with the new style, because as young girls they had often heard their fathers lamenting the change of *The Scotsman* from front page news to classified advertising on page one. This had taken place in the middle 1850s, so one was able to put forward the mitigation that we were merely reverting to the original style of *The Scotsman* in its more classical times. Other papers of our type followed us, but we were happy to be first, or at least among the first.

We also redesigned the logo on the masthead — that is, the title of the newspaper at the top of page one — which had been embedded in a thistle scroll since the very start of the paper. This appeared to me to have got a little out of date, and I got a good designer to do three separate drawings of the logo, edging it imperceptibly in stages from the old style to the one there at present, and few readers noticed the change. We also designed a new typeface. Or at least it was done by Casper Mitchell of Intertype. We got him to take the new typeface called 'Royal' designed by their art director, Edwin A. Shaar, and, being no laggards in the search for perfection, especially for a type which would have to stand up to high-speed printing and the various problems of ink and paper fluff which emerge there, we asked him to redesign some of the letters. He wrote an article at my request for *The Scotsman*, telling of his adventures with these new lower case and capital letters, including capital Q, 'a graceful adversary in whose lines lurk some devilish problems for the designer'. This was masterminded by our Joe Brown of the production staff in *The Scotsman*, who himself later went away to become the managing director of the Birmingham group of newspapers. In one of the less seemly traditions of newspapers, which consists of giving people advice on how to run their own business, I tried to persuade Intertype to let Casper Mitchell design a completely new type of his own, which they should call 'Casper'.

I brought in a large section of leader page articles where we could invite eminent interventionists or specialists, or better still our own excellent leader writers, to develop some theme at length of 1,200 words or more, and again this lifted the centre part of the paper. There was a familiar feature at the bottom of that page and I let it stay as it was, not only because it was written by a most able journalist and old friend, Wilfred Taylor, but because it had become a distinctive part of the paper for some years. It was written anonymously under the title of 'A Scotsman's Log' and Wilfred did it very well, mainly in short paragraphs which we gradually edged into a more rounded essay on a single subject. Everybody seemed to know it was written by Wilfred Taylor, and he used the editorial 'we', so that he spoke freely about 'our old school' or 'our wife', practices which lent themselves to sly allusions. I occasionally in my exuberance gave Wilfred valuable ideas on which to dilate in his column, but found that our relationship as working colleagues was somewhat different from our previous, and by no means diminished, friendly associations. In other words he was impossible to brief. He used to stand listening to me as I enthusiastically described some idea that had occurred to me and mentioned how he might give it his gifted interpretation. He would look at me, appearing to be listening, and over his eyeballs there would fall what appeared to be a curtain of icicles. None of these well-meaning suggestions of mine ever found its way into his column and I shortly gave up the attempt to add my decorative twopence worth. Wilfred writes what he must, or nothing.

There was a further difficulty in that he was obsessive about America and could not stop himself writing about it. Every second column seemed to have copious references to 'our colleague in the *New York Herald Tribune*' or 'our visitor from the news desk at the *Pasadena Journal*'. So I broke the news to him that I had decided to send him for a few weeks to the USA, there to rove about and file his column back to us. And also from that day it would bear his name, sometimes his photograph, and that 'our' was out. Off he went, nothing daunted, and in spite of the unexpected hazard that he arrived in America at the time of the Suez invasion, he handled the matter and the distorted news he was hearing very well indeed and was no doubt a splendid ambassador. I thought that the American experience, at long last, would help to get it to some degree out of his system; but this doesn't seem to have happened and as a mere reader of *The Scotsman* nowadays I see he is still at it. He well deserves a Congressional Medal.

It had been a lonely time, but after three or four months a great event took place. Seumas Adam, whose career in the *Evening Times* of Glasgow (he had left the *Daily Record* some time before the *Mirror* takeover) had been followed by Jim Coltart, was suddenly asked by Jim to come and edit the *Weekly Herald*, a splendid paper known world-wide, and subscribed to by Scots in every part of the globe. It was a paper of simple pretensions but it didn't miss anything of significance in the Scottish scene and the prospects for our country, especially under Seumas' direction. It was an amazing experience to stand with him in the window of my room in *The Scotsman* building on the day he started with the *Weekly*, and look towards the lights of Princes Street and the New Town, and think that here we were both together again, with a new inheritance.

After a time, not before the stated year was up, I decided on a change or two on my staff. Max McAuslane was willing to come and join me from Glasgow and I made him news editor, with David Terris remaining as chief reporter until he retired a few months later at the age limit. Max is the best news editor in the world and no one who worked under him at *The Scotsman* has much to learn anywhere else in his career. I found also that David Stephen's contributions to the *Daily Record* were dwindling. That paper was edging towards its present style with the poster-type headings and yelling that were mainly the *Mirror*'s invention in the early Cudlipp days. David came as a contributor and an ornament to the new weekend supplement which I had designed to be published with the Saturday paper. It was a novelty then, much copied since here and there, and it wasn't too bad right from the beginning, although I was disinclined to believe that it was immediately worth the description by Eric Mackenzie, the managing director of Crawfords, who was doing our publicity, as 'a work of transcendental genius'. He was a generous man and ingenious in the ways of publicity people. At one time we had a wonderful poster show through him all over London on the great hoardings, and the trade papers used to say that we must have had twenty to twenty-five sites in the City and West

End of London. We never had more than six at any time, but Eric and his young tigers moved the posters about across various choice sites. There was one which I had designed myself showing a chaotic abstract painting, all coloured whirls and sparks, with a calm announcement in the middle 'The Scotsman — an island of tranquillity in a sea of hysteria' which became something of a talking point. When Alec Guinness the actor came once to lunch with me, as he sat in the boardroom beside me he said, 'An island of tranquillity in a sea of hysteria'.

By this time I was receiving many invitations to go and speak to groups of people, in some cases many miles away from Edinburgh. I never refused any of these, because if I could not go myself I sent one or other of the leader writers, telling them that they would never have a better way of finding out what the public thought of their newspaper than to address a gathering and spend the next half hour in a question and answer session with them. As for me, for all the years I was editor of *The Scotsman* I never spoke to meetings less than forty times a year. It can be a humbling, but often an encouraging experience, and I consider it essential to anyone in the media.

Roy Thomson, contented now, was not taking long to discover new and feverish ambitions. The franchise was shortly to be available for a television station for west, south and central Scotland, to be based in Glasgow and he determined to go for it. We compiled the application documents in *The Scotsman* and he made his bid and won, so that almost overnight he and Jim Coltart disappeared for most of the week to Glasgow, supervising the building of studios and the transforming of the old Theatre Royal there into a television headquarters. Roy was unashamedly excited and frank about the expected fortune that would follow from this venture, and in the early days after its opening he used to summon me to his room when he turned up in Edinburgh to show me in a notebook he carried with him how the figures were developing into, it must be said, prodigious sums. I was doing somewhat better myself by this time, having been made a director of the firm with financial improvements, but I never understood then, nor can I think now, why Roy, who offered shares in STV at a tiny price to a number of people who had put little of their working lives into his Scottish newspaper ventures, never offered me the chance to invest. Those who did, putting in a modest £200 or £300, found themselves in a few years worth £100,000 or more. But I hardly minded then, nor now, since I was having the time of my life and there was something to show for it.

I went often to STV just for the interest of it, when they were getting near the opening time, and used to go scrambling with Jim Coltart over the scaffolding of the new studios, or would listen to him rehearsing amateur bands and skiffle groups, anxious for a break in the forthcoming programmes. After the STV venture had been running healthily for a year or two, Roy was looking for new worlds to conquer and an immense treasure was suddenly laid at his feet. This was the

Kemsley group of newspapers, in whose *Daily Record* I had slogged it out for, eventually, thankless years. Viscount Kemsley had come to realise that he was not equipped in staff or family to carry on the business, and modern technology and techniques were catching up with them. He phoned Roy one day to say that the whole business was on the market. Roy and Jim disappeared to London. The story has been told many times, but it was a miracle to those of us who saw it at close hand. It had been a night and day job lasting for long, with the two of them making occasional sorties into the streets of London to find a cheap café where they could obtain a low cost meal, this being Roy's prudent way of toning up for his destiny of becoming the largest newspaper owner in the UK. Eventually they had achieved, by putting STV into the pot, a reverse takeover arrangement so complicated that, when the news broke, only our Jim Vassie on *The Scotsman* was able to interpret it in a news story for our columns, with most of the other newspapers in Fleet Street and elsewhere fumbling to find out what the hell it all meant. They came back to Edinburgh to clear up and then set off, the pair of them, to London and the crock of gold, appointing me over their shoulder, as it were, to be managing director of *The Scotsman* Publications Limited as well as editor. I often said to Roy in later years that he had behaved like the last of the Stuart kings, crossing the border to London bearing all Scotland's hopes with him, and leaving all the problems behind.

We had a long struggle, for example, to persuade Roy and Jim Coltart to keep the *Weekly Scotsman* going. It was losing money every year, but not on a great scale and it carried the prestige more than any other newspaper we knew of into the far corners of the globe where Scots lived and worked and wanted news of home. We fended them off for years indeed, and when it was closed at last it was greatly missed by our scattered kinsfolk. Much later Jim Coltart told me how sad he was that it had ever been closed at all and that he now wished it had been kept going. Of course this was far too late. Seumas became general manager of *The Scotsman* and not a minute too soon, because we were running into a phase of trade union militancy, largely borrowed from Fleet Street. The shop stewards were able to invent points of principle and dramatise them to the extent of stopping the paper. I became the first editor ever in *The Scotsman*'s history to preside over a shut-down, for the paper had never closed even during the General Strike of 1926. Seumas became a skilled industrial relations operator, although no skill could compete with the bloody-mindedness which newspaper unions staged from time to time, and he needed these qualities when he was assigned to produce the new *Chester Chronicle* in that city and later to spend some years as managing director of our Middlesbrough newspaper. He did not return to Scotland to be at my side again until he reached retirement age, when he came back north and flourished.

Some old time *Scotsman* stalwarts were fading away. Two of them were notable heroes over a long lifetime. Bert Robertson was a kind of office and property manager who could do anything with a smile and a great spirit of willingness, and there was also Willie McMunagle, the production manager, who could cover everything from the engineering at the presses to picture reproduction and type. At that time *The Scotsman* was still reproducing half-tone newspaper prints at high speed better than any other newspaper in the world, and I continued the tradition of the great half-page black-and-white landscape photograph which was the envy of newspapers everywhere. The *New York Times* once asked us how we did it and, indicating a particular photograph, asked if they could get a print from us to see if there was some quality in the photography which they could not match, because they did not think that there was anything deficient in their printing on newsprint. We sent them a magnificent print, and in due course they sent us back a batch of papers, each one printed on a different press with a half-tone block made of our print, and not one, as they said, up to the printing quality in our original issue. They asked if they could send two of their press men, printers, to study our methods. We received these people and they were about six weeks with us, learning patiently from Willie McMunagle. Then they went back to New York, never quite achieving the quality we then had. Like all mechanical processes in the hands of men of skill, there is no one secret to good reproduction in newspapers. There are probably twenty or thirty secrets and to this day I cannot be sure that good Willie McMunagle revealed them all.

We produced *The Scotsman* coloured yearly calendar which you find hanging in the offices and homes of hundreds of thousands of exiles everywhere. It was Bill Thomson who took the pictures in the first years. He was a very old acquaintance of mine because we had been bank juniors together; later we worked together on the *Weekly Herald*; and here we were together again on the production of the coloured calendar. He had a great eye for landscape and I remember even when he was a youngster, slightly senior to me, when we both worked in the Burnside sub-office of the Commercial Bank, Rutherglen, he would often look out of our ground-floor window, up past the tenement roofs and say, 'The clouds are right, and so is the wind. There would be a great picture at 2 o'clock this afternoon at the Glenfinnan Viaduct.'

He had had some luck in his life. Just before the outbreak of war he had gone to set up a business in Orkney and almost immediately these islands became a restricted area so that every one of the inhabitants was required to have a passport photograph, which Bill took and charged for. He was very tough, with the heart of a lion and an iron digestion. When we went together to climb the hills or cover some story, he would not be bothered stopping for tea and sandwiches anywhere, but instead would swig from a bottle of ginger beer on the coldest day and then open a can of beans and scoff them cold. Few hardier men have ever taken to the winter roads and hills than Bill Thomson. Before he could afford a car he cycled everywhere in the hardest frost. Once as he was taking an accustomed short cut across the frozen surface of Loch Ard the ice gave way and he fell through into 10 feet of water, bike and all. He got himself out, sodden and icing up, but he was concerned for his bike and camera. He ran to a nearby farm, obtained a ladder and a long grapple on a rope, hooked up the bike, bore it to the shore, pitched his tent, set his stove going and sat there dismantling the lens of his camera and drying it out over the stove so that it could work again.

By this time I had got my new desk at last and had got Avril Gibb, calligrapher and good friend (now Lady Watson Stewart) to inscribe in letters of gold above the old fireplace on a panel this extract from the original prospectus of *The Scotsman* in 1817:

> The conductors pledge themselves for impartiality, firmness and independence . . . Their first desire is to be honest, the second is to be useful . . . The great requisites for the task are only good sense, courage and industry.

In 1967 we celebrated the 150 years of *The Scotsman*'s founding. One of the many ways I chose to mark the milestone was to create *The Scotsman* whisky. The firm of Mackinlay in Edinburgh gladly joined us in this venture and after some useful and painstaking whisky tasting sessions to get the blend right, we produced eventually the whisky bottled with a splendid label using the logo of *The Scotsman*; printed on the back of the label (you had to drink the whisky before you could read it) was a reproduction of the first-ever front page of *The Scotsman* on 25 January 1817. Its first paragraph read:

> Before proceeding to the ordinary business of our paper, we beg to observe, that we have not chosen the name of Scotsman to preserve an invidious distinction, but with the view of preserving it from the odium of servility.

As I mentioned to the glittering assembly on the royal occasion when we celebrated the birthday with a banquet, 'We're still working on this one.'

All the adult members of the staff and all the most notable of our friends and contacts received a bottle. The whisky was also installed in our boardroom to such effect that I went to Roy Thomson with a business idea I was sure would appeal to him. I told him that we had found the ideal boardroom whisky; that it had the world's best name and should be put on the open market by us with discreet advertising. It would undoubtedly sweep the business end of any modern city. Roy listened attentively to this proposition as I unfolded it, for he liked nothing better than a fast and profitable buck. Then he shook his head, saying, 'Alastair, it's not for me. I'm not going into the whisky business. I've seen too many good men ruined by liquor. Sure, you should go on and give it to your business friends and keep it in your boardroom, but we're not going to sell whisky.' Roy's father had been a drinker, and I think he spent all his life haunted by the fear of drunkenness and poverty.

At this time things were going pretty well with him, although some of the great ventures had not quite come off; but he was well into travel and holidays by this time and into book publishing and business magazines, expanding from his office in the *Sunday Times* in Gray's Inn Road. Like myself in the beginning, he hadn't made many internal changes. Apart from the disappearance of the Berry brothers, he had retained the entire former Kemsley board and brought them on to the board he created in London. This seemed to be far from a good idea. Seumas Adam reminds me of my remark to him when I first heard of these dispositions: 'In the name of God, these are the very people who went marching downhill with Kemsley!' I knew most of them and the only one who seemed to me qualified to redeem the group was Denis Hamilton, who had been the editorial director in the Kemsley time and who, it had always appeared to me as seen from as far away as the *Daily Record* in Glasgow, seemed to be the only one prepared to stand up and attempt to outpace the eccentricities of that regime.

On my London trips I used to rove through the rooms of the *Sunday Times* where I had a number of friends. Some of them had become half recluses, like Fellows of a distinguished college, dedicated to a scholarly life of leisure, without the need for great energy, like Cyril Connolly, who greatly deserved to be put to worthwhile writing in his superb essay style. The man I missed most of all was Ian Fleming, who had just started to write the James Bond books and, like me, did not think a great deal of them. He had been, for a number of years, the foreign editor of the *Sunday Times*, managing a world-wide chain of foreign correspondents. The stories they filed and which were used in the other Kemsley papers, apart from the *Sunday Times*, were of no great moment but Ian once showed me a dossier of memos which each one of them sent back every fortnight with off-the-record and behind the scenes political insights into the countries where they operated. This was a private service to Kemsley himself and they were so revealing, so much in many cases the very essence of foreign, political commentary, that I persuaded Ian to send out at least a weekly version of them to the papers, including my own *Daily Record*, so that we could use them and appear to be informed in an idiom rather more purposive than the commonplace stories. In return I showed him the report I had done about my Smith-Mundt American trip which had also been asked for by Lord Kemsley and which, as it happened, devoted some space and length to the style of *Time* magazine, not uncritically. This document was borne away to America by Ian, who stayed for a few days with Henry Luce, the owner. He told me how the two of them had discussed the paper and the proposed formula for its renewed success. Ian had also discovered how much I was being paid for editing the *Daily Record* and he insisted that I go to Lord Kemsley, our joint boss, to ask him for a rise amounting to double the present salary. I didn't do it in these terms but I was commissioned by His Lordship to write a weekly article on Scottish matters for the *Sunday Times*, and this went on for a year or two. I produced the articles in the small hours of Saturday morning after the Friday night paper had gone to press, and I was never paid for a single one. Years later, when we came to own the *Sunday Times*, that paper made a token retrospective payment, arranged by Denis Hamilton.

Ian Fleming wasn't the only one to be preoccupied with my salary conditions, although by the time of the 150th birthday of *The Scotsman* I was doing substantially better than when I had joined the paper. Looking over some old correspondence for material to be used in the history of the paper which we produced, I came across a letter written by the proprietors 100 years before and offering one of my predecessors the position of editor at a salary of £1,700 per annum. He accepted, as who wouldn't! At that time a handsome villa around Edinburgh, or down the coast, could be purchased for several hundred pounds; maids were £5 to £10 per annum, cooks perhaps a little more and there would have been little trouble about setting up a coachman with a carriage and two horses. The chief reporter would be lucky if he was getting £200 a year, and a desk reporter might be getting a third of that, or less. I was greatly taken with this Victorian example of 'differentials', a word much used among journalists, and I looked in to see David Snedden, who had recently joined us as our chief accountant. David was some time later to become managing director of *The Scotsman* and he is now chief executive of the Liverpool group of newspapers.

'Tell me, David,' I said to him. 'You know what Roy's paying me here. What should he be paying me to give me the standard of living, taking tax and present-day reductions into account, that this predecessor of mine enjoyed?' He thought it was a very interesting problem and set to work it out.

Half an hour later he rang me to say 'I've got the answer fairly roughly. They should be giving you at least £40,000 a year.'

Neither of us had much idea of how the deficiency could be remedied, but David didn't leave it there. I was hardly in my office the next morning when he rang me again. 'I was working at that problem again at home last night with the tax tables. There is no way, absolutely no way, you could be paid a salary today that would allow you to have the standard of living of that fellow.' The internal history records of *The Scotsman* show that my predecessor lived up richly to the lifestyle he considered appropriate for him.

For a number of years this £1,700-a-year man sat where I used to sit and was no doubt watched by the same searching and sceptical eyes. When people used to remind me of the gravity and humility which I ought to bring to my task — and in Scotland they very often did — I found some solace in the notion that some of the legends of our newspapers have been happily forgotten, especially the embarrassing ones. This editor's most distinguished public appearance happened in the House of Commons where he arrived once in the Speaker's Gallery during a debate and took an unexpected part in the proceedings. It couldn't be ignored. He said later that he had just spent a convivial hour or two with a statesman who later became Prime Minister, but that didn't do him much good at the time. Anyway, there he was sitting above all the oratory, pounding his stick on the floor and shouting, 'Rubbish!' and 'Utter bosh!' and other discouragements which our legislators permit to their political opponents but not to outsiders, and certainly not to journalists. One observer said of the interruptions: 'True enough, likely, but out of place.' All this was too much for the House and the editor was escorted outside by an official known as the Serjeant-at-Arms. I am sorry this wasn't the end of the affair. He had been a journalist long enough to know that most buildings which do business at night have plenty of back doors, so my quick-witted predecessor found one at Westminster in no time and there he was back at his heckling. Well, they got rid of him eventually. It so happened that some years later he turned the tables on them all by arriving at Westminster as a properly elected Member of Parliament, which shows that there are no limits to what a journalist can achieve once he has decided to better himself.

One of the great privileges of being an editor and perhaps any other kind of chief executive is that one can give opportunities, and I would have difficulty recalling anyone whom I promoted who didn't come through successfully. Opportunities abound in newspapers for people who can show something better than the others. I hadn't been there long before a figure started to be seen above the experienced sub-editors around Gordon Anderson. This was Eric Mackay, who was eventually to succeed me as editor of *The Scotsman*. He seemed to have what was needed for a job beyond the one that he had, with his ability to carry the ball further than the average. I took him from a junior rank one day and made him our London editor, where we badly needed some changes. He flourished there, doing well, and then came back to be my deputy, carrying rather more than a deputy's share of editorship because I had much extra work as managing director of the whole business as well.

I remember another case in a different department which has given me much pleasure since. During one summer when news was scarce we did an elaborate coverage of a ridiculous story which took the form of a walking race from John o' Groats to Land's End. Our reporters from the staff in Edinburgh were posted out along the route, each man filing stories covering three or four days of the great trek and having a free hand in their descriptions of the odd people taking part. I think it was round about the town of Dingwall that our daily stories developed a master touch of humour and urbanity. The copy was not named, but I read these stories for a few days and asked the news editor who was doing them. 'Albert Morris,' he said. I had not noticed Albert Morris particularly before then as a reporter, perhaps because he was getting routine stories to do; but there is always a special spirit that can be put into even routine stories without distorting the content nor puzzling the readers. He was a small, roundish, young man, with a ready wit that offended nobody since he was often the butt of his own jokes. In our staff canteen it was common to notice in a corner a table whose sole occupant could not be seen, but over whom huddled, like a giggling and heaving scrum, a group of the younger office girls, being greatly entertained. This was Albert Morris, eating and holding court with a commentary on matters of the day. So when he came back from his northern assignment I kept an eye on his material for a few days, then sent for him, telling him, as I had once told Cliff Hanley, that I was giving him a column immediately, with no instructions except to fill it with his own characteristic observations on everything or nothing. Far from expressing a seemly gratitude he was startled. He was indeed terrified. He begged me not to give him this task. He could never undertake it. It was simply beyond his powers. Where would he get the material? What would he write about? Every day, oh surely not! I tried to laugh his fears away, pointing out the opportunity it presented to a talent like his, and as he was still reluctant I suggested he think it over and we would meet again in a week.

When the time was up he came to see me, white-faced, and said it simply couldn't be done. He didn't dare tackle it. He was very grateful, but no thanks. If I insisted he would have to resign from the paper. It took another week or two to persuade him that it was all right and that he would get over the initial inhibitions in no time at all, and I was firm that he would start, say, the next Monday.

Well, he did. It was a fearful opening for everybody concerned, because we had kept a good space for him. But so determined was he to try to do the thing right that he forgot his own style and personality and for the first few days brought in — and we published — what were obviously stiff, unfunny, schoolboy essays which he had clearly worked on all through the previous night. Very soon, and almost with a click, he relaxed, and his column is prominent now and has a great following.

If I were to put flags in a map of the world where some of my old colleagues, who were young when I first knew them, are now plying their trade, it would be a busy sheet. I suppose there is nothing more arrogant and boring than the ageing pundit who talks heavily about 'my boys', as if this gives him a right to patronise them for ever more. We had much fun and adventure together and they never got as much from me as I got from them. I honour above all the people who stayed with me in *The Scotsman*, and the *Daily Record* in its day, some of them, like the fierce Alexander Macleod, went away for some years and then came back. Names which have been heard in far places include Cliff Hanley, David Watt, Neil Asherson, Richard Kershaw, John Forgie, Hugh MacIlvanney, Magnus Magnusson, Gus Macdonald, David Kemp, Arnold Kemp, Mike Gormley, Cuthbert Graham, Ken Peters, Bill Heeps, Joe Brown, David Snedden, Roger Nicolson, Elis Evans and Chris Maclehose.

I might have been dispersed myself. On three different occasions I was offered editorships in Fleet Street papers of significance, but I always felt that what I was doing in *The Scotsman* was more important. If I did anything it was to make *The Scotsman* speak for Scotland and as I used to tell my colleagues, 'If we don't speak for Scotland, nobody will.'

CHAPTER TEN
Royals

There was a summer Sunday in the 1970s when I was walking in mid-afternoon down the length of Grosvenor Place in London, on the way to Victoria Station. Late on Saturday, the day before, I had answered a telephone call from a nervous and urgent Occidental lawyer, calling from California, saying that he had a document which he was drafting, and could I meet him in London the next day and go over the clauses with him. I had flown down from Edinburgh and met my man in the Hilton Hotel. We had worked through the middle hours of the day, and I was heading for home by way of Gatwick airport.

There were cars and taxis and buses about, but I think I was the only pedestrian in the street. I was walking on the east pavement, alongside the wall of Buckingham Palace, which runs the whole length of Grosvenor Place. I noticed, lying in the dry gutter of the street, about thirty yards ahead of me, a tennis ball; and my heart warmed to it, for it was darkly coloured, a little worn, and had obviously not been used for tennis, but maybe some more strenuous game. As I approached the ball, I had a wistful pang; for it seemed like a small familiar. One time I had been an expert with a ball that size, manipulating it on concrete pavements and playgrounds, tapping it against walls and receiving it back with the man beaten, or standing on it to bring it round some lumbering opponent.

There was only one place it could have come from. There were no gardens for playing on the opposite side of the street, and probably all of the houses there were now offices. It must have come from over the wall. A children's plaything, and of course there were children in there. They had been kicking it, or throwing it, or bouncing it against the old bricks of the high wall. I knew what I should do, thinking at the same time that it was probably funny it should lie across the street from the Irish Embassy, where one or two policemen were standing at the entrance, hoping to look unobtrusive. I would walk to the ball, pick it up, and throw it gently back into the Palace grounds. Standing there, I would let the silence pass, until there might be a little voice saying 'Thank you'. I'd walk on well pleased.

I was six yards from the ball when the other consideration came to me, swamping my intentions. What would happen to a stranger who was to be seen stooping, and throwing a dark round object over the wall of Buckingham Palace. I could imagine the immediate alert; perhaps also the burst of firing from the Embassy roof and other adjacent vantage points. No risks taken by the guardians. We shall never know. But when I drew alongside the ball, I averted my eyes and kept walking down towards the station.

One way or the other, I have been many times inside Buckingham Palace, mainly in some official capacity. My first view of live royalty was 400 miles away, in Glasgow, during World War I. We had been told that the King and Queen were coming, and the schools were given a holiday so that the streets could be loyally lined. My mother took brother George and me to the corner of Dumbarton Road and Church Street, already crowded with massed ranks of people, mainly women, for the most part dressed in the fearful black uniform of mourning. Children were pushed to the front, but I do not remember a flag or a bright ribbon. We had long to wait, but they came at last, a long procession of cars travelling fast. The King and Queen were easily recognisable from the innumerable posters we saw daily in every shop and window. The crowd was deathly silent — not a cheer, not a greeting. No hands waved from their great square car. The King, a bowler hat in his hand, raised and lowered it slowly. It might be said that Queen Mary bowed slightly. It was over then, and we all went home. Royalty, I long remembered, was serious and grim.

I was a bank apprentice the next time, when the Duke and Duchess of York, not long married, came to Glasgow. This was a happy affair, great crowds bursting through the cordons and holding up the cars. She was unbelievably beautiful and pleasant, and I remember the glorious shining hair. I was on Renfield Street at the time they passed, because I was on my way to the head Glasgow office of the bank with a consignment of 3,000 dirty (to be consigned for burning) pound notes, and I nearly lost the bag in the stampede, for I had omitted to strap it to my wrist in the picturesque way of current security. At one point a youth was actually sitting on the bag, feet off the ground, as I was heaved forward with the crowd. I tipped him off and got my two arms round the bag, but stayed in the forefront until the royal couple were out of sight.

This was the lady who, perhaps more by sheer love and concern and personality, rather than by any contrivance, was to remake the battered image of the monarchy, which might well have gone down in the middle years of the 1930s, and which at that time survived perhaps only because our expectation was so much diminished that people settled for an appearance of stability in the background. She set to the fearsome task of sustaining a reluctant if noble monarch. When the war came she would not leave her home, and had it bombed like other homes; she stayed and shed tears along with the people, and went to see and speak to everybody, and lift their hearts, so that perhaps they lifted her heart

151

in return. So by kindness and courage she became the mother of her people, and then the grandmother of her people. To talk to her is to enjoy a raising of the spirit. Her family have all learned from her, but even now she does it better than any. There are the calm bright steady eyes, and the right questions and responses helping the talk along. Also the sparkle of fun and enjoyment of small things.

I am sorry to remember that I once fell foul of that conviction of our royalty that they know the right way to do things, and if there are formalities, they must be to a laid-down pattern. At one time in the war, during my stint at the Scottish Office I had sent to me, from a unit of young uniformed service women in some remote station, a picture of the Queen in one of the service uniforms she occasionally wore. They had bought this enlargement from some picture agency, and they asked if I could arrange to have the Queen autograph it, so that they might hang it up in their canteen. I sent off this modest request to the Palace, and in due course there came back a cold acknowledgment from a secretary, saying that the Queen was surprised to receive such a request from a departmental source, which was also apparently prepared to distribute the photograph 'at will'.

Naturally everyone senior to me stepped back from this involvement, and I was left to dispatch a penitent explanation, making the case incidentally that the girls had obtained the photograph in good faith and had hoped to honour their premises by giving it a favoured place. Shortly there came back from the Palace, not the original but a quite superb large copy of the famous Cecil Beaton picture, with the Queen in a wide foaming white gown, and wearing her courtly jewels and coronet. She had also signed it with a gracious style.

One day I was walking down Whitehall towards Dover House when I stopped to allow a large official car to slide out of the Admiralty entrance and into the main street. There was some traffic, and the car stopped for a few seconds eighteen inches from my nose. There were four admirals inside, all with the part braid and the ribbons that told of long service. One of them was the King. There was no police car, no detective escort. As I stood there, inevitably looking in at them as they talked, I was remembering that the night before I had seen a newsreel film of President Roosevelt in parade somewhere, with crowds lining the streets. It was an open car, but hefty men were clustered on the running board — an attachment not available nowadays — and a dozen or more heavy-footed men in canvas shoes loped alongside the slow-going vehicle as it went down the street.

One factor in the royal progress always interested me. Many times I was concerned in the wartime with royal factory and shipyard visits. There were no barriers as they went round, moving through the industrial scene, so that men and women workers, out of tremendous fervour and curiosity, generally downed tools and came along. There was always a huge knot of people gathered where the personage was. But the monarch was never jostled. However tight and heaving the throng, a small circle of space formed round him or the Queen, and they bore this vacuum along with them as they went. But the lord lieutenants and lords provost were thrust aside, and aides and ladies-in-waiting were engulfed. The royal people were hedged, as the true saying goes.

Another time I got into the doghouse when it became essential to dismiss from his office a certain lord lieutenant in Scotland. He had been somewhat less than satisfactory in his performance. This was a grave matter indeed, amounting to scandal, and I was told that the King took some respectful but strenuous persuasion that the man had to go. He agreed. I was not consulted as to the wording of the dismissal, but a press announcement was compiled and sent out through the department routine. I came back from some official duty to discover that the Scottish Office was in uproar, and there were thunder-clouds and lightning flashes coming from the Palace. In order not to draw undue attention to the disgrace, the responsible officials, skilled in parliamentary drafting, had compiled the announcement using a word of legal but ambiguous meaning. The paragraph read that HM the King had 'determined the appointment' of so-and-so as lord lieutenant of a certain area. In this context 'determined' means terminated. However, journalism is not a matter for ambiguities, and two of the most renowned newspapers had sub-edited the odd word to make their announcement read that the King had 'confirmed the appointment . . .'

The King read these statements at breakfast, and the ensuing tension spread and engulfed our bit of Whitehall, running back, of course, across the border and into the heart of the establishment. His Majesty was freely quoted as exclaiming, 'They finally made me sack this chap, and now I read that I have appointed him.' I found Sir Horace Hamilton, the Permanent Under Secretary of State, Sir David Milne, a chief of department, and others in a state of well-schooled panic. I was unanimously fingered as the frontline man. I took copies of the original document and headed for Fleet Street, where in personal confrontation with the editors of *The Times* and the *Daily Telegraph*, I described with suitable drama the scenes that their good intentions had caused; and persuaded them to print the original the next day. This was done, and we got on with the war.

Although it must be well known to most citizens that our royals meet and talk to many thousands of different people every year, I am always astonished at the readiness with which some of us expect to be remembered. Standing in a reception line once, I heard Prince Philip say to the man next to me, 'Haven't we met somewhere before? Where was that?' 'Inverness, of course' was the blithe response. 'Oh, yes . . .' the Prince struggled with this frail clue. 'Yes — and how are things going there?' 'Just the same as before, sir,' was the reply. HRH worked bravely on this bit of evidence, and passed on.

I don't think they cumber themselves with prior information about the people they are to meet, but generally start by asking what it is you do. They take it from there, and since, like super-journalists they know something about almost everything, they are able to sustain the short exchange. It has to be said too that it is gratifying to be remembered. Prince Philip is very good at this, and since when with the Queen, he is not the chief guest, he can break away and pick one out from the attendant mob. 'Nice to see you again,' he will say, on some oil occasion when the setting provides him with a hint as to whom I might be.

My first service for Prince Philip was when I was asked to entertain him to lunch in *The Scotsman* office, there to meet privately some of the Scottish daily newspaper editors. At such a time there are some formal preliminaries with someone turning up beforehand to advise on the procedures and protocol, which are rarely onerous. One of the points that I cleared was what the Prince might be expecting to drink at the meal, and also by way of an aperitif. I was told, 'No problem. Perfectly straightforward. Perhaps a glass of sherry, or even simply white wine.' It may have been that he imagined himself to have arrived in lavish company, but when asked, he stated an elaborate drink for which we had not made any detailed preparation. However, the undaunted Agnes Watt got it ready in a shake, and we were launched.

Since the Prince was not to make a speech of any kind to us, he was probably more relaxed than he might have been if under some constraint. It became a cheerful party. He asked us pressingly about the state of Scotland and the movement towards devolution, which was advancing at the time. There was a chance to give a full and, it must be said, an enthusiastic run-down on the whole scene, with his own questions much to the point and concerned with practicalities, as well as recognising the sentiments which lie behind all this topic in Scotland. 'Don't forget the Queen is also the Queen of Scotland,' he reminded, a statement I have heard him make on other occasions. It happens to be a statement which we do not much use ourselves. We prefer to call her Queen of Scots, a world people, and I feel sure she knows this, and I hope likes the idea.

The Prince brought with him that day his secretary, a lively young Australian called Bill Heseltine, who is now with the Queen and is a KCVO. There was an odd prologue to the visit. About the time the royal visitor was due to arrive I took up my stance on the front steps of *The Scotsman* building, to give the first greeting and escort the party inside. Any parked cars had been cleared away from the vicinity, and police stood around, with some spectators already gathering, although there had been no intimation. At this point an acquaintance stepped forward — he was one of those Edinburgh people devoted to ensuring that nobody else ever gets a swollen head — and said waggishly, 'Don't stand there looking so important, Alastair. The Queen isn't coming to visit you.'

I said, 'If you have three minutes to spare, just stand along the pavement behind that policeman, and see what you will see.'

Prince Philip is endlessly meticulous about the preparation of his set speeches. He wants to have notes beforehand, but not rhetoric, for he will compile his own speech. I remember that when he came to present awards at an industrial competition scheme, most of the lunch time was taken up by one or other of us being asked to come up to his chair during courses and filling him in on the many questions he wanted to ask. He was of course fitting all this into his own great knowledge of the industrial and commercial activity of the country. He has a unique range of knowledge and information at first hand, and much wisdom.

He is also ready-witted on the informal occasions, and can bring informality to times that might be heavy going. He flew out by helicopter with some of us of the Occidental group to inaugurate our huge ocean rescue ship *Tharos*, already at work beside the Piper platform in the North Sea. Red Adair had designed it, and he was aboard, ready to give HRH the patter. When the time came for the speeches, Prince Philip said, 'I don't know what I am supposed to be doing here. I can't very well launch it, for it's been afloat here for weeks on the job. How about me breaking a bottle of champagne over Red Adair's head. . .'

When Prince Charles was eighteen or nineteen, I was asked to organise a press gathering for him. Not quite a press conference, but it was agreed that with the help of the other editors I would gather in *The Scotsman* a group of young and promising journalists not much older than he. This was a great success, so that two more such gatherings were staged in Buckingham Palace later in the year and he could be regarded as fairly launched. From the start he was good at the informal conversation, following up with good questions himself, and with great cheerfulness. At one stage somebody bumped into him by accident in my crowded room, and the glass of orange juice he was carrying tipped on to his suit. Immediately Agnes Watt rushed at him with a small tablecloth, dabbing purposefully at the heir to the throne. 'That was clumsy of me,' he said. 'I always seem to be doing that.' I haven't seen any mishaps since, and it wasn't his fault at the time. On the way out he asked me again to thank Agnes for her busy plying of the cloth.

It has been satisfying to see him come swiftly to a kingly maturity. When he comes into his own, he will be good at it. His set speeches owe much to the style of his father: the disarming opening, the well-timed local or institutional allusion, and the inserting of the longer-term message; even the voice is the same, in intonation and inflection, with the light nasal at the top of the throat. He tends to remember the visit to *The Scotsman*, even although we are both long since away from that scene. There was a presentation in Edinburgh Castle, with the beautiful Lady Kirkhill, reading from notes, enumerating our modest achievements. When Prince Charles and she got to me, she embarked on her pronouncement, to be interrupted by the Prince saying jovially, 'I know this chap.'

He has a good sense of the realities, and may in time become a master of the timely minor indiscretion. We had him once for a day on the platform which extracts the oil from our Claymore oil field, where after seeing the machinery and gadgets he wandered among the roustabouts. When they told him how much they were earning in weekly wages, he said, 'That's not at all bad, it it?' 'Aye,' they said. 'But more than half of it goes in tax.' 'Bloody hell!' said Prince Charles, moving on.

There is an unmistakable divinity which hedges a monarch, and this makes a notable difference to the experience of being in his, or her, company. It is not so much a subtle matter of personality, although in our present monarch this is an abundant factor; it is more that these individuals have been set apart for a task of importance, perhaps no less significant now than it has ever been, since democracy is seen to have brought its own complications. The Queen has to remind and even to recommend, and by training and already by experience she knows more about the constitutional progress of the nation and the Commonwealth than any of the political figures whose duty it is to advise her.

During the wartime I was involved with the visits of the princesses to places of importance and production, generally in the company of their parents. Towards the end of the war, when she was still in her teens, the Princess Elizabeth generally wore the uniform of the services, and took her part in driving trucks and other vehicles. There was already a gravity about her, in contrast to the high spirits and maybe touches of rebellion from her lively sister. Much later a Palace man was to tell me of how they had both insisted on going out to the streets of London on the night of the war's ending and the Armistice, and how they enjoyed the crowding and the gaiety, unrecognised.

I first heard that Princess Elizabeth was Queen at the high dam in Loch Sloy. I had been, years before, at the cutting of the first sod there, marking the beginning of that whole great adventure. For months I had been trying to arrange a visit to see the whole thing in operation, already pouring its electricity into a network of lines running towards southern industry, and meant to bring a surge of prosperity back to the glens where the natural resource was based. So that this day of February, 1953, there were my deputy John Lees and good Tom Dawson, my London editor, and I alighting in the forecourt of the hydro station, which was humming and clean with the run of turbines. Out came the manager of the place, and before we got our greetings going he said, 'Have you heard that the King is dead?'

We stopped at the Tarbet Hotel to drink to the Queen's health and to telephone our office at the *Daily Record*, setting in train the elaborate systems that have to be rushed ahead on such a day. Most of the requirements were already moving. She was flying back from Africa. It was described later that her first official act was to preside over a Privy Council. One present told how she came into the room, in a dark dress, serene, and said, quietly, 'Please be seated, gentlemen.' She was 26.

She has a range of styles and attitudes, mainly dependent upon the occasion and the company. But there is always this supreme serenity, and calmness, and authority, since she can ask questions and make observations about anything, because she knows and has experienced so much more than most of the people she meets. There is a gravity, not a severity, but she can be amused. If the jest, whatever it is, has been successful, her face suddenly lights up in a blaze of pleasure, smiling with the relief of it. Her questions are searching, and when they are answered she ponders then, her brow intent as she thinks through the matter, and then asks again, and again, so probing to the heart of the matter. She gives time for the answers to come. She is a delight to entertain, and some of the concerts and dramas specially arranged for her in Edinburgh have been greatly successful. During the state visit to Scotland of King Olaf of Norway in the 1960s — he went on to England later, but informally — the whole court was in Edinburgh, and there was a performance of that old-fashioned and utterly outdated play *Rob Roy*, with hand-to-hand combats, gunfire, broadswords going like flails, red coats being routed, and all the rest, with the royals in the boxes cheering the action and choking, like the rest of us, on the fumes of primitive gunpowder.

I remember an unusual cocktail party, pre-lunch, in Holyroodhouse, with a few of us media people and our wives. The gathering could not have been less formal, with the Queen joining John Dundas and me, reminding John of an occasion he had organised in Oban during a trip round the isles on the royal yacht *Britannia*. The Queen pretended to blame John for the really horrible gale-force weather which must have been uncomfortable for the master of the ship in Oban Bay, and he had to take her some way down narrow Kerrara Sound to board the owner and her party. John recalled the time with good-humoured ruefulness, and I was able to mention that in Scotland we had never in any case expected to have fair-weather queens. John Dundas had become the Chief Press Officer in the Scottish Office, my own old job.

On a much more formal occasion the Queen asked what my job was. I replied that I had been editor of *The Scotsman* for a good many years and had then gone into industry, becoming chairman of our firm's North Sea oil interests. '. . . so you see ma'am, I'm a journalist who has come down in the world.' She smiled briefly and moved on. Then surprisingly came back to where I was, and said with a twinkle, 'A black mark for saying that North Sea oil means coming down in the world.'

Many citizens write to her, with suggestions but more often with problems, and much time goes to the answers, for any letter from the Queen is a matter of public interest and may be published by the recipient. Still, it is possible to offer modest advice, and it may be accepted.

157

There was a time when the City of Aberdeen, before the oil boom, was scourged in the early sixties by a plague of typhoid, needing drastic measures before it could be checked. It is a fair city, with a large tourist industry and many regular holiday-makers from far afield. There are not many places in all western Europe where there is more active as well as traditional medical knowledge. A formidable series of plans soon got on top of the devil that had visited them. But in the meantime the Fleet Street and foreign press had set out on their familiar panic trail. 'People are dying in the streets', was one headline, and American newspapers were filing stories 'from our reporter in typhoid-stricken Granite City'. From everywhere, and it was already June, terrified cancellations came, and ruin faced hotels and boarding houses. At this time the yacht *Britannia*, with the Queen aboard, was sailing round the Scottish coast, with visits scheduled for her to go ashore at various small places round the Moray Firth. It seemed to me obvious that she should go ashore somehow in Aberdeen (which she sees a good deal) now that the danger was over. It might stop and even reverse the fears. I sent a telegram from *The Scotsman* office, outlying the situation, and respectfully saying that a short spell of the gracious presence would set these fears aside and give comfort to her loyal citizens of Aberdeen. I followed this up with a telephone call to a man in the entourage, and he said there was no chance of the tour being changed. And sure enough, two days later I got a letter saying that the Queen greatly appreciated the concern I had shown, which she shared deeply, but that the arrangements for the tour had been carefully considered and could not now be altered.

But I had not waited for this. After my conversation with the man I had assumed would know, I felt it was time to do it in public. And that evening I wrote a leader to appear in the paper the next day. It was one of the few I was able to write myself in the last years with *The Scotsman*. It was published on the next morning, 25 June 1964.

ABERDEEN UNVISITED

The present Royal tour of the far north of Scotland follows a familiar style, and it is all the more welcome for that. Because of the metropolitan structure of modern Britain, these places suffer from official and social neglect, and the arrival of a most beloved Monarch is the best of all reminders that even the farthest inhabitant is entitled to, even if he does not always enjoy, a full citizenship. For these reasons the Queen will be received with gratitude as well as joy. She will be moving among people whose kin and forefolk have done more than most in service round the Commonwealth, and who deserve well of their fellow citizens everywhere.

The tour was doubtless fixed in detail some time ago. Nevertheless it should still leave room for the kindly opportunism of Queenship. Among all the northern communities one city by its ordeal and conduct demands a special form of attention. Aberdeen has been released at last from the medical barricades necessary for many weeks. At this moment the least demanding and the most deserving of all British communities, Aberdeen has raised its head again and is at once busy repairing the damage. A brief and informal call by the Queen to a city she knows so well would do more than any other single act to restore what Aberdeen has lost. Moreover, it would destroy at once the belief that the nature of Royal tour programmes rarely leaves room for the possibility of the great unexpected gesture of encouragement.

It will always be warmly remembered how, during the war, it was frequently the feature of a blitzed town's story that, within hours after the attack, the Queen's father and mother would arrive. There they would be, among the ruins, not to make speeches nor to receive presentations but simply to be there, silent and moved, sharing the agony, and by their presence reminding all that tomorrow would come and would be a better day. It is not to be believed that 20 years later, and in such different times, the arrangements for the monarchy are less flexible than they were then. Aberdeen has lost her holiday visitors. Through the odd impact of modern news, which can be made to convey a half-truth, they panicked and stayed away. How much heart it would give to that courageous city, and to people in trouble anywhere, if they could receive for an hour the most cherished visitor of all.

Before mid-morning of the next day, an excited telephone call came from Ken Peters, who was then managing director of Aberdeen Journals Ltd. (He had earlier been editor of both the evening and the morning papers in turn and I had given him his first job in newspapers.)

'You'll never believe this,' he shouted. 'The royal party came ashore half an hour ago at [some Moray port] and everyone in the cars — I mean everyone — was reading *The Scotsman*.'

He came on again at about 4 pm. 'It worked! It has just been announced from the Town House that the Queen will visit Aberdeen at 10 pm tomorrow night.'

She did too. It was the greatest Saturday night in the history of Aberdeen, with a hundred thousand people hoarsely greeting her in a frenzy of loyalty and love. The car in which she travelled had its panels pushed in, the detectives were swept aside, and as she stood on the balcony of the Town House she told the Lord Provost, as Ken Peters has since recorded, 'Now I know what it feels like to be a Beatle.'

We are fortunate above all people in having this unique family, brought together into our far from easy circumstances by a divine piece of casting. What they have to do, they do splendidly and with the greatest of courtesy and tolerance, and among them there is nothing they cannot compass. Some of them will tackle almost anything. Princess Alexandra is good-humoured and popular, and it is a study to hear the good-natured chaffing between herself and her husband. I imagine she enjoys being Mrs Ogilvie more than any other distinction. She came to our shore oil terminal in Orkney, at Flotta to visit us; and she was our distinguished visitor when we celebrated the 150th anniversary of *The Scotsman*, starting up the presses by setting off a button in the Assembly Rooms, half a mile away.

I introduced her by describing how the presses would leap to life with a roar, which we would hear by loudspeakers, at her pressure of the button, while the two resplendent pipers we had on parade would play a suitable tune or two, finishing with 'The Bonnie Hoose o' Airlie'. In the event, she pressed the button, and for many agonising seconds we waited in silence. The roar of the start-up came at last; I signalled the pipers, and they clicked and shouldered their drones, grunting and squealing at last into music. But the rascals played the first two simple parts of 'The Barren Rocks of Aden'. You can never trust pipers. They play what they like, especially if it's easy. Moreover, they have the ingenuous belief that nobody in the gathering knows anything about pipe tunes anyway. I had, as they say, a word with them afterwards.

Princess Margaret has been much criticised. It has become a habit. It has been shown for years how easy it is to do, and those who do it, by unsupported gossip or, what is even easier, mere invention, have lately come to realise that they may have been merely sharpening their teeth on her so as to limber up for the rending of her family. I am able only to have views as an observer of her public performance. When she undertakes to carry out a duty, she is there on time, wearing the proper outfit, uniform, or not; she is kind with questions, does not frighten the tongue-tied assembly, and she stays until the agreed time to go. This seems to be what she is expected to do. She will never have the satisfaction of a sovereign, in being able to touch the controls of state, even distantly, and having the force that comes from being the fountain of the law. Yet she is unceasingly hounded, with cameras peering out for the least indiscretion or pout.

Much the same has happened to Princess Anne, who opens things and unveils plaques and does these other chores so often that merely to smile must on some days be a creaking burden. Her fate has been, not only to like horse riding, but to be very good at it, indeed of international class. But the cameras are there not to see her riding smoothly, but to see her fall off; and if she stays on, no picture. From the earliest age she was intent, even in public, on learning as many useful skills as she could. As a young teenager she was seen by hundreds, when helping to take a small royal sailing boat round the west coast of Scotland, and especially through the Crinal Canal. There she was, doing as instructed, listening intently. Not many folk, publicly or in private, are so determined to do the dutiful right.

One would wish for all of them that it could be taken as almost sufficient that they perform their endless and repetitive tasks with the same continuing style — tasks that allow of no awkwardness, no pretension, no ambition. They, especially the Queen, have to know great numbers of public figures all over the world: politicians, cabinet members, privy councillors, bosses, leaders, services chiefs, prime ministers, ambassadors, people important to our state and to friendly states. This has to be done by getting the protocol subtly right without stiffness, and giving encouragement without patronage. If amid all this they succeed in building for themselves a personal life, all we should do is to see that they get the fragments of privacy which are all that they ever expect. We do wrong to seek exposure of their every second of time, their outbursts of freedom, their inward griefs. The burden they carry, all of them, is hard to sustain, but it might be lightened a while by a friendly averting of the public eye.

CHAPTER ELEVEN
North Sea Oil

It was an Ayrshire man, a friend of my brother George, who first told me about the oil in the Scottish North Sea. It happened in London about the year 1935, when my economy, like the country's, was starting a limping recovery. Old Armour, a geologist, had spent a lifetime in the coal industry, and he had some sort of headquarters job in London, where I used to meet him occasionally on one of my cheap-rate train sorties. We were at tea in the Thistle café in Tothill Street, with Tom Gibson, secretary of the Iron and Steel Federation, a tough Glasgow CA, my brother George and John Hunter of Greenock, an inventor, talking on the only topic we ever did, the future and perhaps even the prosperity of Scotland. Armour's story was that there would be oil long before the coal ran out. He drew on the tablecloth sketches of the sub-sea rock formations from south to north of the North Sea, showing how the structures ran in such a way as to favour the north rather than the south, and that when drilling techniques came to a certain pitch there was likely to be more oil off Scotland than off England.

This gratifying forecast, which at that time we stored away along with many another improbability, had to last us for thirty years. By the late 1960s it was all starting to be true. The Dutch had suddenly found great deposits of natural gas ashore on their land. Explorers rushed in to the waters whose sea bottoms had seismic affinities. Ships ran up and down sending off their small mysterious explosions. Gas finds crept north along the English coast. Then . . . we found Armour's oil. Immense deposits of good quality crude oil, lying there for all these hundreds of millions of years, started to be discovered, needing untold monies for their development and bringing ashore. By the early 1970s there were already four giant oil fields — a giant field is one with at least a billion barrels of recoverable oil — proven off the Scottish coast. At that time, in the whole of Texas and California, there were only two 'giant' fields.

We seized upon these successive items of information in *The Scotsman*, getting to know the American strangers who were making this possible, and setting forth, incorrigibly, to instruct the government, and especially the Scottish Office, as to how best to manage this gift of God.

162

In discussions with ministers, and in the leader columns, we explained how the country and its people, long since skilled in the innovation of technologies, could best be put into a posture to be prepared for the boom. An infrastructure of new roads, enlarged harbours and airfields, power-stations and public services, would be required. Technical courses must be set up in the universities and colleges. A programme of housing would be needed to accommodate those who rushed towards the boom. The Planning Acts would not be adequate to deal with the construction requirements onshore.

All this advice was freely and honestly given, and nobody took it. I was also moving among my former bank colleagues trying to persuade them to set up an oil department, a move which they took long to make, although it was the Bank of Scotland who made the first cautious move by installing an oil man at a desk in their head office on the Mound above the centre of Edinburgh.

Nothing is more likely to discountenance a self-appointed instructor and adviser than to be invited to join in and show how it should all be done. It happened on one of my newspaper visits to London. Bill Golding, then managing director of Thomson Regional newspapers, asked me to stay behind after our board meeting, saying, 'Roy asked me to speak to you. He has joined some American firms to invest in North Sea oil exploration, and he wants you to be president of his company.'

There was a shock of gratification. I had never been more eminent than chairman of my own newspaper group in Edinburgh, and the idea of a presidency seemed to match the immediate drama. Bill could not give me any further information, although he handed me a document which I suppose is our first consortium prospectus, dated January 1971. It was the forecast, by Oxy (Occidental) geologists, of what the North Sea could yield. I shortly knew this production off by heart, but I sped to fill in the missing essentials as they affected me.

Roy Thomson and Gordon Brunton, now executive head of International Thomson, had been acting in concert with Dr Armand Hammer of the Occidental Petroleum Corporation of the USA, a new and aggressive organisation which had prospered with oil development in Libya. Eventually our consortium or group — oil men don't much like the word 'partnership' — consisted of Occidental, or 'Oxy' as they like to be known; the Getty organisation; Allied Chemical of New Jersey, through their subsidiary Union Texas; and ourselves, with 20 per cent of the investment. We formed Thomson Scottish Petroleum Ltd, of which I was made chairman. Alas, not president!

There was a further disillusionment. It was felt politically wise that our firm should be based in Scotland, and I was on the spot. Moreover, since Roy Thomson dearly loved a bargain, I was to carry out the required duties in my spare time, unrewarded. Roy was not the first of my employers to discover that some of us are perhaps too much inclined to value the stimulus of new challenge more than money, an attitude which I have been accused more than once of trying to foster among my own staff. Ken Peters, whose first newspaper job was as a staff junior with me on the *Daily Record*, is among the foremost of these accusers.

Once, at the height of our newspaper success, when we were all working very hard, but profitably, for the firm, I had said to Roy in a burst of enthusiasm, 'You know, Roy, this means so much to Scotland, I'd be glad to do it for nothing.'

'Gees, Alastair, that's great!' he responded. 'Keep saying that!'

In due course we found so prolific a reservoir of oil, in the field that became Piper, said to be the most successful oil field in the world, that I had almost overnight to leave *The Scotsman* building and become a full-time oil man, this time for money. First we had one or two dry holes to overcome, in the bed of the North Sea, and some hurdles on land as well.

At the beginning, one's long dedication to a social conscience might well have seemed · naïve to oil men, who were believed to trample through frontier areas with heavy boots. But Armand Hammer's enthusiastic endorsement of our approach went far to set the pace for such recognition as we have had for looking to the natural and social environment. Also, the formidable men who started to appear, many of them with world reputations, were ready, mostly, to see the force of getting on good terms with the many groups — thirty-seven of them — through whom we had to steer the plans and their details before the whole shore construction was finished.

Close friendships were to grow with some of these oil men, new types entirely to us. One remembers Bob Teitsworth and Dick Vaughan of Oxy, founder members of the Hammer empire, which they ran from Bakersfield, California, where their oil and gas base was. There were John McCabe, Alan Wallace and Don Carlos of Getty's; Teverbaugh and Jess McCollum of Union Texas in Houston. We learned to set aside the jokey expectations of our British-based colleagues and not to expect these new partners to arrive in high boots and stetson hats. They were, on the contrary, dapper figures in douce dark suits, prone to take off their jackets when they arrived in your office; intensely numerate; given to wearing uproarious ties; to starting work in their offices by 8 am; endlessly patient and helpful and full of explanations to round the edges of our woeful ignorance.

The head of the Getty empire was in particular a special study. I came to know John Paul Getty well. A courteous and quiet man, his story was the whole modern history of the oil industry. It was something to have him as a partner. When we sat as a group, in the early days of our negotiating with the goverment for the concession of blocks, or as a consortium hearing some argument among geological specialists, he would be silent for most of the discussion. And then he would be gently moved to ask a question. And it would invariably be THE question.

He used to ask us for parties to Sutton Place, when we roamed through great salons, seeing there pictures whose reproductions we had been familiar with all our lives; only these were the originals. Or we would go there for periodic operating committee meetings, with the seismic sheets spread over the ancient refectory table, or pinned over the priceless tapestries. There were always groups of notable women in the house, some with famous names, although they were never very communicative with us, nor even among themselves. Paul's mother had been a MacPherson, and he once told me he had been brought up to be aware of his Scottish inheritance and the expectations which it implied. At a party which I gave for the consortium in the Caledonian Club to celebrate the inauguration of Piper field, I had the Queen's Piper along to play 'MacPherson's Rant' for Paul.

His last year or two found him sadly inadequate. His skin, blotched with age, was like a lizard's. He would nod off to sleep in the middle of our meetings. Once he awoke in time to take an important decision contrary to what his colleagues had undertaken in the pre-meeting lobbying; and as they were too fearful to put him right, I had the unhappy task of vetoing what he had just decided. Still, he was a memorable man, not to be forgotten. They flew him home to bury him in California, which for years he had longed to see, but in later life he could not overcome a fear of flying which had come upon him in his old age.

Gordon Brunton and I had our first meeting with Armand Hammer in that thrusting little gnome's suite in Claridge's, where we spoke business for a time before the giant circular table was wheeled in for dinner. We learned for the first time some of the fascinating truths of the oil business, and the jargon which explains them, as he took us patiently through the very elements of the scene in which he had himself not so many years ago been only a beginner too. Some of the basic facts of his life were already known. He was a medical doctor who had never practised. He had more than a nose for a deal. Every nerve end in his body was strained to that purpose. In the early years after the end of World War I he had set out to discover what it might be that the Russians needed, items they could not manufacture for themselves. He traded with them for years, becoming friendly with Lenin, and being a welcome figure to all the Russian regimes since the founder's day. It was common for one to visit him subsequently in that Claridge's living and office suite, and sit listening to him talking to someone by telephone, presumably in the Kremlin, in Russian. Later we were to have the closest of associations through his art exhibitions, and the displays of such a treasure as what is now known as the Codex Hammer, a medieval manuscript of untold beauty and, of course, value.

On that first time, however, he was sizing us up. It was clear that the Thomson input to the consortium's expectations was to be to steer a way through local and national government, and the planning and environmental tangle, and to know the local and national persons who would ensure that nothing would stand in the way of the urgent need to bring the oil ashore. In the event the Piper field was flowing ashore perhaps faster than anyone could have hoped for, but it all happened a long way from Claridge's.

I felt bound to mention to him that it was essential to make sure that the onshore oil operations, which would no doubt take place in rural and probably remote areas, must make the least disturbance to places of beauty and the way of life of the people there.

Armand Hammer responded to this with enthusiasm, and proceeded to tell us how he had been able to ingratiate himself with King Idris of Libya in the early days of his concession there. He discovered that the king had been born in a small parched oasis in the desert, where a meagre well sustained a tiny community and their stock. He sent two drilling wells up-country to that place, where, driving down far deeper than the original well, they found gushing supplies of artesian water which they controlled and brought flooding up, so that the desert, and especially the royal oasis, blossomed like the rose. No doubt the oasis is still there and flourishing, as is Armand Hammer: but where is the king?

Much earlier, when our consortium was shaping, there had come into the scene the splendid personality of Bob McAlister. An oil technician from the east of the USA, he had been appointed by Oxy, as operators, to run the whole North Sea operation for us. He was to make the most successful record in the North Sea. He too knew about his remote Scottish origins. It was familiar family history to him that the first American-born ancestor, arriving before the end of the eighteenth century, had been christened Washington McAlister.

I had a great friendship with Bob. He coloured nearly all that we in Thomson's did in oil, and although I may be no great credit to him, he taught me almost everything I came to know about the trade, and a good deal about the scientist's role in business as well. By the time he arrived in London where he set up an office, he had already commissioned a semi-submersible drill rig to start exploring in the blocks we must count on getting. He had negotiated the charter of this drilling rig, to be called *Ocean Victory*, which an American yard had only just started to build. This was the first of many revelations about the high-hearted American approach to venture risk. They had at that time, and mostly have still, all the available know-how; but how they put it to use! It was a study to sit in on a good-natured and highly technical discussion betwen Oxy's Jerry Williams and, say, Roger Stoneburner on where we ought to drill a well which would cost £1 million, whether there was oil there or not. (We always translated everything into dollars.) Under Bob McAlister's guidance we tried to avoid dramatic voting on major issues, even when something was in dispute. Usually we came to a consensus.

By this time Roy Thomson and Gordon Brunton were well abreast of the oil vocabulary, especially the words and phrases that added up to money. They grew accustomed to asking questions about pay sand, spudding, and reserve barrels, and neither was likely to forget any significant number which had once been rashly mentioned to him. Twice running I had to phone them later than midnight, following a call to me from Bob, to say that our first and then our second wells had turned out to be dry holes. It was early in December 1972 that I was able to tell them that our third well in block 15/17 had found good oil in plenty.

Block 15/17 had looked good from the beginning. Months earlier, on a London day of drenching rain, Bob McAlister and I had handed in our beautifully compiled application, in two volumes, for this and over fifty other blocks, along with a cheque for the first deposit. These handsome documents, probably now waiting for their thirty-year discovery, were received by Angus Beckett, a senior official in the Ministry of Fuel and Power, a quizzical bespectacled man who appeared to be the only British civil servant who knew anything about the oil business. He had been the petroleum attaché in the British Embassy in Washington, finding out about the business there and getting to know the major American oil figures; so that he was in a handy position in subsequent years to be blamed for anything which was thought to have gone wrong. By that time he had left and gone into industry.

Bob McAlister's confident application was based on the information thrown up in the seismic charts which he had bought on behalf of the group. These are underground maps of the rock structures that lie below the seabed. They do not show the presence of oil, but since oil tends always to float upwards to the surface, what the geologists are looking for is a 'cap' rock, very large and shaped like an overturned saucer, consisting of the hardest type of rock. In its endless migration upwards, the oil which teems in the heart of the earth might have been captured by this cap of rock, and is there for the taking; provided the cap rock has not been shattered by some prehistoric upheaval, in which case the oil will have escaped and landed on a forgotten shore, to puzzle and pollute the environment of extinct creatures almost as far off as the dead animals whose decayed bodies, crushed under the shaping world, had formed the oil.

We got six blocks in the fourth round of applications, giving undertakings that we would drill holes to probe their value, and lose no time in development should there be something there. The hand-out was made known at a mass meeting of the many interested parties who were eager to take part in what appeared to be the likeliest boom for many years, and the first in our scene. The drama was heightened by the decision, presumably by Angus Beckett, to set aside a number of the available blocks for open bidding in sealed envelopes, which were opened on the stage and the winners declared by the reading out of all the bids, the winners being those who had bid the most. The government raised over £40 million in this way, which proved also to a useful method of assessing the professional interest in the cla

Drilling started almost at once, first by means of a drill

then by the newly-built rig *Ocean Victory*, which made the actual discovery. The first guesses about how much oil might be recovered from down there were replaced by accurate measurements, while the financial experts in all the partnerships made ceaseless calculations about how much money would come ashore as well, an inoffensive obsession which still appears to go on almost daily, particularly among my Thomson colleagues. Other excitements were coming my way. In mid-January of 1973 I flew out with Bob McAlister in the helicopter to watch the 'flaring' of the oil from the drill pipe. We slept aboard, and were up at the late winter dawn to see it begin.

The flaring makes one of the truly boastful events in an offshore oil man's life. It is made necessary by the fact that oil having been found, it has welled up the drill pipe to the working surface, along a pipe which in our case stretched for a mile and a half below the bottom of the sea. The find having been completed, the drilling rig then goes away to another job — perhaps to drill another well to help evaluate the same field. A new platform apparatus is required to extract the oil from the discovered reservoir.

But what happens to the mile and a half of oil in the pipe? It cannot be extracted and put into barrels for sale. To spill it simply into the sea would mean immense pollution. The solution is to burn it off. In our case this took the whole day, with that gigantic flame, over 60 feet long and roaring with released energy, flying like a flag of triumph and streaming down wind from the rig, while water pumps drenched the hull and superstructure, and occasionally ourselves, to abate the fire risk. Helicopters sent out from our envious competitors in adjacent blocks flew over to note and photograph our gleeful flame. News travels fast, especially good news, and it was necessary to announce the find publicly almost at once, so that shareholders would have immediate access to the information. In those early days of wells and new finds we had some minor disagreements with our partners, since their requirements as laid down by the New York Stock Exchange Commission differed in some ways from the rules of intimations required by the London Stock Exchange. Thomson shares reacted strongly in each case, being volatile due to the relatively small number of shares available in the market. Even at the joyous time of the flaring it was possible to be a little preoccupied by the fiscal essentialities. These were, however, the problems of success, which tend to be more of a trouble, if less of a burden, than those of failure.

Doting meantime on the great flare and all that it might mean after our risk and hope, I was aware that occasionally a hiccup erupted into the clear flame, and a large puff of black smoke would interrupt the roaring of our flag of triumph. This was because a gout of liquid drilling mud had been trapped in the pipe, to be immolated in this way. Already there had been calling on me at my office some old friends greatly concerned about environmental risks which might accompany oil development: Frank Hamilton of the Royal Scottish Society for the

168

Protection of Birds, Morton Boyd of the Nature Conservancy, Sir Charles Connell of the Scottish Wildlife Trust, Jamie Stormonth-Darling of the National Trust for Scotland. I remember thinking about these dark puffs, 'I wonder what Frank and Morton and Jamie and the rest would say to that.' In each case, though, the menace passed swiftly. The black smoke, smaller than the billows that used to come from the funnels of wee Clyde steamers, would disperse down wind in less than a mile, while the prevailing breeze in any case was blowing them handily in the direction of Norway.

Later that day, flying in to Aberdeen in the helicopter, we crossed the shoreline north of Peterhead and flew down what was to become a familiar track over the bright farm fields of Buchan. It was a glorious winter day of sunshine gold, and looking down on the miraculous farms from no more than 800 feet you could see that from most of them came rising and drifting, wide clouds of thick grey-black smoke where the farmers were burning their heaps of straw and potato shaws and other yard rubbish. These thick wreaths of smoke lay and coiled heavily upon the fields, smothering near villages, and even the fashionable small resort of Cruden Bay was engulfed in a choking cloud, with the burghers no doubt coughing and blinded. Or maybe they were merely saying 'Ah, grand smell that! It'll soon be Spring.' Perhaps environmental dangers are seen only in what is new and strange, while ancient offences can be accepted as routine.

I narrated this contrast mildly at a meeting which I was asked to address to an audience of conservation and environmental specialists, to be greeted with cries of protest, as if I had contrived some unfair advantage, and somehow stolen their argument. By that time I had, by coincidence, noticed in an important daily newspaper a letter from a medical man pointing out the offence to the countryside involved in these stackyard fires, and claiming that their smoke was carcinogenic. This was an argument I have never used, nor even put down until now.

Bob McAlister named our first oil field Piper, and it is known wherever successful fields are mentioned. He asked me to name our second field discovery, some miles from Piper. I called it Claymore, after another gallant endeavour which meant much to me. I have a special souvenir from these times. Bob gave me a tiny jar which contained the first sample of crude oil from Piper, and I used to carry it about with me in a pocket showing it to the eager and the curious, and saying, of course, 'This cost a million pounds. It isn't worth a million pounds, but it cost a million pounds to get it out.' For many, it was the first North Sea oil they had ever seen. The jar had to be opened and noses pushed in to smell, while many a finger was thrust in, to cries of 'That's twenty thousand worth.' Jests tend to be repetitive. Roy Thomson wanted to have a similar jar, and when I got him one, he opened it eagerly and spilled the lot on his trousers.

Amid these frivolities, serious things had been afoot on my agenda for some time. I took what spare time was available to me to make

169

sorties into the counties of north Scotland, to find how they were facing the immense impact which would result from their nearness to large-scale oil activity. Some of the county convenors, and especially the planning and development officers, had been thinking of the future and what their council and communities might get out of the boom, if anything, if it came their way. The most satisfying of these visits was to Orkney, already a prosperous and well-run area, with good roads, a rich agriculture economy, fishing, tourism with good hotels, and a highly educated and urbane population, literate, musical, articulate.

The convenor of the county, that is, the chairman selected from among themselves by the elected councillors, was Donald Brown. Unusually tall even for an Orcadian, he had been a colonial civil servant for all of his career, and coming home on his professional retirement, had no wish to be idle, ran for public office, was elected for a ward, and here he was, seventy at least, running the whole thing most ably. At his side was a newcomer, the chief executive of the council, an Edinburgh lawyer called Graeme Lapsley, who had learned his trade through some years of service in the City Chamberlain's office in Edinburgh, and now had in his hands the control of that distant scattered group of islands, eighteen of them inhabited, with two small towns, two excellent secondary schools, and a total of less than 20,000 inhabitants. It happened that Graeme's Uncle John had been my mathematics teacher in the junior school of Hillhead High in Glasgow, and I always remembered the family characteristics now demonstrated by Graeme — witty, sardonic, needle-sharp, and utterly no-nonsense.

I proposed myself for a session with these two. When I arrived to meet them in Kirkwall, it was to find they had assembled half of the county council, people like George Marwick, George Stevenson and Edwin Eunson, and others who were to be important to us later. They had maps and data laid out. I told them of my interest that rural Scotland, which was bound in some areas to benefit from the oil developments, should be thinking of how it might get ready before the actual onslaught, and that it would be prudent at least to think beforehand of elements of infrastructure which might be required. They had the answers. Already they had commissioned an assessment of their group of islands, with areas designated for industrial purposes, and a measure taken of the services existing and which might be required.

At that time there was no question of our moving into Orkney. We had not even found oil. But I had the uplifting experience of a community, well led, and looking forward to the practicalities on their doorstep. All this was to be worth remembering.

Things were bustling along in the consortia, especially for the Thomson interest, and we had much to learn. The idea of the part-time chairmanship had become ridiculous. It was time for me to move. Early in 1973 I opted out of the editorship of *The Scotsman* in favour of the staunch Eric Mackay, who had been a good deputy for many years. I had hoped that Agnes Watt might come with me into oil. She had been my private secretary for all of my time at North Bridge, but now felt that she had better stay there. But I was to be lucky again. There now turned up in Edinburgh a girl called Rosemary Lobban, daughter of an Aberdonian doctor long since based in Cambridgeshire. She had no doubt hoped to follow her ladylike upbringing in the shires with a settled and genteel style of life in these calm parts, but a rangy fellow from Glasgow, called Walter Scott, snatched her away from her home and was preparing to marry her and settle in Edinburgh. He was a physics graduate from Glasgow who had taken a PhD in Cambridge, where he had become rowing captain in his college. This was seen by Ivory & Sime, the investment experts and fund managers of Charlotte Square, as proper toning up for joining their pension department, where he made some spectacular history until he went into business nearby for himself. Dorothy and I went to their wedding in the chapel of Trinity Hall, his college, an event of supreme Englishness, made notable by the presence of a guard of honour with club blazers and crossed oars.

Rosemary and I moved into a suite of offices, also in Charlotte Square, which I held to be the apt location for a new power in the oil business. For me it was a move of significance, being my first office location in the west end of any town. All my life I had worked in the east end of places, including when with *The Scotsman*, whose magnificent building is a feature of Edinburgh's East End. As a minor celebration of this translation I moved my personal bank account to the Bank of Scotland, West End branch.

Almost at once we were in the thick of it. I engaged the services of the best known oil and gas consultants. We were also learning fast ourselves, at least in the elements of procedures. It was obviously very complicated, and hair-raisingly risky. Some of the eminent advisers to the Thomson Organisation used to press me to persuade Roy to sell his whole interest in the consortium and get out. I never mentioned these advances to him, but more interesting was the frequent approach to Roy personally by Paul Getty. 'For someone who doesn't know the oil business, Roy,' Paul would say, 'you have far too big a stake. I'll give you a fair price for half of your exposure.' It was never easy to shake Roy away from his instincts, but he often said later, when the profits were running, that what finally convinced him he was on a winner were the efforts Getty used to make to buy him out.

Charlotte Square became a busy centre. We had frequent operation and exploration meetings round our boardroom table, where all these new Texan and Californian colleagues spoke of our new-found undersea mountains familiarly as if they were the Rockies. Enormous sums of money were casually mentioned, and disbursed. We once gave lunch in the boardroom to twenty-two people, a size of gathering which we had not anticipated when setting up house. Most of the arrivals had travel problems, requiring to board some different aircraft, or to hire one car and cancel another, or to phone or telex their distant offices, or even to make holiday bookings where they could catch salmon or shoot stags;

171

even to procure some unheard-of whisky to take home. Rosemary became famous throughout the oil world as a hostess and fixer. Later we took on to the staff Celia Boyle, who had been my junior secretary in *The Scotsman*, and it became clear she added to the attractions of the office. She's now in Vancouver, in the oil business.

There were also trips to arrange for me to all the oil cities of the United States, to sit in on similar meetings and give a schooled agreement to some monstrous cost. By this time interest was mounting as to where our shore terminal would be located. Once the oil is found and the area of the field delineated, there has to be installed a steel platform which stands on the sea bottom, with steadying piles driven in, and rises out of the water in a structure to accommodate machinery, installations, and living quarters. The exploration rig floats — it is usually called a semi-submersible — and when its job of merely finding the oil is done, it sails away. From the fixed platform which succeeds it, many wells are driven into the field, to extract the oil, put it through some elementary processes, and pump it by means of a pipeline laid along the sea bottom to some place ashore, where it will be further processed and loaded into the tankers which will take the crude oil away somewhere to be refined.

Piper and, when we found it later, Claymore were grouped in the North Sea about 100 miles almost due east of the town of Wick in Caithness. So our terminal had to be constructed anywhere suitable, and the nearer the cheaper, along any part of the Moray Firth shore, or some other near landfall. I knew these shores well. Bob Trainor, who would be responsible for the construction, had recently joined Oxy from the construction giants Bechtel. He and I set out to find the right place, while men with charts and shoreline sketches, weather data and tidal information, worked on the problem in Bakersfield. Sometimes by car, or in light aircraft, we covered all that coast. Early on it was clear that there was no great body of sheltered water on the mainland, so that tankers loading a few miles offshore from fixed mooring buoys would suffer, in an average year, an unacceptable number of days when they could not operate. One of the distant boffins in California came up with the theory that there seemed to be some mysterious change in the prevailing wind pattern somewhere between Brora and Helmsdale; and sure enough, I found on my Ordnance Survey map at that point a small headland whose ancient Gaelic name described 'the headland of the winds'. Sailormen had been there before.

Still, we had to find a haven for the shore installations, and these tankers. Mighty sums of money were being pledged to the building of the platform and all its assemblage of gear and plant; talks were going on about the placing of an order for the pipeline which was to lie along the bottom of the sea. How long would it have to be? Where was it going? Could we give the contract to British Steel? (No, we couldn't. British Steel asked to be excused from estimating.) Should we decide to make it 24-inch diameter, or 32-inch? Oxy's inspired guess was that we

172

spend the money and commission a 32-inch line, which the numerate will know at once contains twice the amount of oil as a 24-inch line. I found it useful in some situations to be able to talk learnedly about such scraps of technology. But all this wasn't getting us our terminal site.

Bob Trainor and I flew all over the north, and started to penetrate to the Orkney group of islands and beyond. Scapa Flow looked good, but we photographed Shapinsay and other prospects from the air. The picture, together with all the relevant data we could gather, plus Bob's wise commentaries, were despatched regularly to Bakersfield, to be pored over by the sub-sea experts.

They came up at last, not a moment too soon, with the decision that two sites in Scapa Flow were favourites, and it would be one of these. Scapa is the 50-mile-square enclosed sea within the southern group of the islands of Orkney; sheltered water, deep enough for the largest tankers, with good access to the open sea. I was at once alarmed, for both sites were frighteningly sensitive in sentimental or environmental terms. One would have involved the danger of disturbance to the wreck of the *Royal Oak*, sunk by German submarine commander Prien in a daring incursion into the Flow soon after the start of World War II; while the other, to the north-east, looked like encroaching into Waulkmill Bay, where, the RSSPB had already made clear to me, rare flocks of long-tailed ducks had their habitat.

The decision was about to be made in Houston, Texas, where we were to meet in the context of that year's Offshore Technology Conference, the oil man's great annual event. Bob and I flew out by different routes. On my flight I had a congenial companion in David Dunbar-Nasmyth. He had recently retired from being the Vice-Admiral and Flag Officer of the Royal Navy, based at Rosyth and covering the whole of British adjacent waters from somewhere about the Wash to the limit of NATO's territory in the north. His mission was to man the stall at the Houston exhibition of the Highlands and Islands Development Board, which had just taken him on. We had a drink or two while I told him about my recent sorties into the waters of his old command; and particularly of the difficulty that was about to break upon us on one or other of the Scapa Flow stations.

We got out my maps, so familiar to him. And he suddenly said, 'Why don't you go down to Flotta?'

Admiral David and I had been friends for years and had shared many a ploy together. One of the most memorable had been when, in his last year as the supreme admiral in northern waters, he had taken me with some other guests on a foray with a squadron of frigates into the North Sea. Things were going well when David came to me, took the glass out of my hand, laying it on a sideboard in the wardroom, and asked, 'How would you like to transfer to another ship?'

This was positively the first intimation. When we reached the deck it was to find another frigate racing close alongside at a simply hellish speed, the two ships, dead level, creating a foaming maelstrom between

173

them. A section of rail had been handily lifted away, and seamen were putting a loop of rope around me, under my arms and pulling it tight.

'It's all right,' said the admiral, 'you'll enjoy this. This will pull you on the deck of the other ship.'

'What do I do?' I asked, with a longshoreman's panic.

'Nothing really. Simply keep your hands down by your sides.' And they pushed me off the deck. I had a glimpse of a line of seamen tailing on a rope's end on the other deck, which now seemed a long distance off. Then there was this boiling flood below me. There had been nothing like it since the Dorus Mor.

Hands down by your sides! The old Army injunction is to keep the hands down the seam of the trousers. Never were seams so desperately pressed as mine. I dangled there for many a gale-swept second, until my feet got to the other deck and there I gripped with my shoe-soles. A patronising cheer went up, and I turned to the gap nonchalantly, to see the beaming admiral dangling across in his turn. I had not forgotten that I had been the guinea pig.

But when he said, '. . . go down to Flotta', I knew there might be something to be learned, though I had never, so far as I knew, heard of Flotta. David told me about this small somewhat barren island closing the south entrance of Scapa Flow towards the mainland of Caithness. In two world wars it had been the nearest landfall of the British fleet. One Sunday, early in the 1940s, 40,000 men had attended an open-air church service ashore there. There had been built the famous Garrison Theatre, where Vera Lynn and Tommy Handley had performed, once with the King and his admirals sitting laughing in the front row. As David told of these times, I realised that here I was with the senior sailor who probably, in terms of great ships, knew Scapa Flow better than any man alive; probably also the very last admiral to anchor the British Grand Fleet in Scapa Flow.

Before our journey was over, I had got him to agree to come and meet the oil men with whom I was to foregather the next day.

When our gathering came together on the next morning, with a main purpose of deciding on which of the two Scapa Flow sites we should choose, I started off by telling them about the meeting with the admiral, and suggested I should ask him to come and meet us. They agreed. David was with us within twenty minutes, able to answer all the questions about water depth, tides, underwater obstructions, bottom conditions — everything. He went cheerfully away in an hour or two, leaving us with the conviction that Flotta was the place.

We now had to get to know about Flotta. Before I got back to Scotland, surveyors and soil experts were already ashore, and had an area marked out, containing about six small farms. It was poor ground. Flotta was a dying island, with hardly seventy inhabitants, mainly old people, and no more than a dozen children in the village school. Bob Trainor was already roaming the place, seeing in his mind's eye the tanks and the structures that would rear there, and the places where the

174

pipe would come ashore, and where the treated oil would leave by pipe again to be loaded into the tankers.

I had to see that the people would not resist our coming. They had to be bought out of their long-established holdings, provided they felt that they were prepared to go, and to receive adequate compensation, to such an extent that if they never worked again they would live at ease for their lifetime. I simply went among them, calling at the houses; sitting at their firesides, drinking tea or the occasional dram, and finding out how they would face up to this amazing revolution in their lives. They were in no hurry to make a bargain, although we were, since we were now betting that we would make our terminal on Flotta, and the engineering and hardware was already the subject of firm contracts. We knew the length of the underwater pipe, the type of terrain for heavy construction, where the construction camp would be, and what would be required by way of extension to the existing pier. There was a great hustling to get items licensed, contracts drawn up with the local authority, planning regulations discussed and the applications in.

In the end we paid to these dispossessed farmers and crofters a land compensation of full industrial land charges per acre, and one or two of them, if not all, were paid a fortune. One farmer decided not to go, so the terminal was designed to by-pass his fields. The Orkney local authority, rightly looking to the long-term future of the territory, devised a series of imposts which they felt they could properly charge us for the rights to invade them on this scale. One was a royalty charge on each barrel of oil which came ashore. Another was to be the payment of a large outright sum which they called the Disturbance Fund. I tried several times to get them to refer to this sum as the Development Fund, the idea of 'Disturbance' carrying bleak and destructive connotations. I didn't win this one, and 'Disturbance' stayed in.

There were also others concerned about Disturbance. In Britain we have two important bodies who are charged with the statutory duty of advising the government about matters which touch on the environment and the integrity of the countryside: the Nature Conservancy and the Countryside Commission. These departments are staffed by a devoted band of people, well qualified, who keep a wary eye on all aspects of events which involve changes in the appearance of places and things. They were frequent visitors, asking to see plans, and requiring answers to lists of questions. Other environmental bodies emerged, not less fervent and curious, if not armed with the same authority. Many of these wanted formal and set-piece meetings, with minutes.

It was in the many talks and excursions involved in these procedures that Bob Trainor and I came to an unshakable understanding about the safeguards that would have to be built into the work, so that the eventual layout would be part of that peaceful flat landscape, leaving no unsightly scars and protuberances. Bob asked me to find the best landscape architect and designer, to work with him from the very beginning of the project.

I didn't know any such animal, but I went to the liveliest architect I knew, Alan Reiach, along with whom and a few others I had helped to produce the Department of Health's HMSO bestseller for the post-war market, 'Planning Our New Homes'. Alan knew the answer at once. The name he mentioned was Bill Cairns. W.J. Cairns, brought up in Moray, had studied architecture, taught it in an American university, was laden with qualifications, and had just set up in business for himself in Edinburgh. We met, and talked. I got Bob Trainor to meet him. This was the most important external association we made in all that time.

Bill Cairns was able to sit in with the engineers at the drawing-board, so that we appeared to get everything right at the start. He also embarked on a landscape assessment of the whole of Flotta and the surrounding shores, producing what must be a four-volume classic of preliminary investigation about the visual impact of the buildings and structures, and how, as shown by moving them in models in different layouts, they would help to conceal each other. We would build some low hills to divert the eye; study the blending colours in which these erections should be painted; find out what trees we should grow, what heaths and grasses, how high should be the buildings, what birds were on the land, what fish in the sea, how the tides and the winds behaved, what would happen to any oil spill with the winds in all the possible different directions. If we got all this right, so went the reasoning, we would not have to come back after the job was done, and, as with so many other construction sites, set about remedying what mistakes had been made.

After the land required had been bought I went often to Flotta to see the construction of the terminal. We put up a village of huts for the men who were to work there. The whole project had been driven on by the fierce urgency of Armand Hammer, who did everything at speediest. Immense bulldozers and earth-levelling machines were rushing about our acres of land. Some young highly-paid fellow was in the lofty cabin of each and the monstrous rubber tyres bounced these giants many feet off the ground as they roared about. I could not feel that these young tigers were deeply imbued with the spirit of conservation and necessity to protect the environment, which were to be the continuing factors that moved me. I conducted meetings on behalf of the consortium with all the environmental bodies, the Orkney Islands Council not being able to help much in this regard since they preferred to stand off and see, in neutrality, the arguments of both sides. In the event we satisfied everybody, in some cases building in clauses to the contract with the Council to safeguard the rights of animals, birds, fishes and flowers. Along with Graeme Lapsley I was giving a great deal of time and thought to the rights of those others of God's creatures, the people. By the time the whole project was complete and the terminal was running as a going concern, with everything tidied up and unobtrusive, we had won pretty nearly all the possible awards nationally and internationally for natural and social environmental care.

176

The Orkney Islands Council set up a Harbour Authority which they ran as their own concern, supplying tugboats to take the tankers in and out of the Flow. The consortium preserved some of the old buildings, including the remains of the Garrison Theatre. The island was already thickly strewn with the debris of two wars, with pillboxes and observation posts all around the shores, innumerable concrete foundations and bases, and some quite large buildings which had been command centres and map posts. Some of these we sorted away in the by-going.

In Thomson's, we had also to raise the money for all this and our share of it was very substantial, far beyond anything we could lay hands on at the time. I once went down to an office in the City of London and signed documents pledging to repay a loan of $220 million, thinking at the time that this was a potential default much beyond anything that I or my forefolk, however dubious, had previously undertaken. These were limited recourse loans, the collateral being the oil in the ground, a form of security lying handily between moveable and immovable property, in fiscal shallows that the Scottish banks at least had hitherto steered well to the north of. Indeed I was very content with the part that the Scottish banks had played in taking up a share of this high risk of provision of loans. A consortium of banks had been put together by the Republican Bank of Dallas, engineered by one of their staff called Ed Monteith, who has since joined us in partnership for onshore exploration for oil and gas in North America and who, as might be expected is a Monteith of Menteith.

It is often said that the UK, and especially Scotland, has failed to take advantage of the opportunities provided by the oil boom here. In Scotland we have more than our share of pessimistic pundits who see no good ever coming out of Nazareth. It has given me much pleasure to see at the great oil conference in Houston and similar events elsewhere, young enterprising citizens of our own, showing their wares, many of them inventive, and looking for orders. The United States of course had a great start in oil and we could not have got anywhere in the North Sea without American money and American knowhow. But they will not always lead the field, and I was happy to find young men, emerging from our overshadowed economy, come into the open and go for business.

All this time back in Orkney firm hands were taking control of their own destiny in this contest. It was fine to be able to help. In those early years we took every one of our new apprentices either from Stromness Academy or Kirkwall High School, sending them away to technical schools in the south where they seemed to have a gratifying habit of coming out on top of their classes each year. These tended to be boys who would otherwise have had to look for jobs in Aberdeen or London or Canada or Australia. Even from the early days I was able to promise that at least 50 per cent of the total permanent staff in Flotta and Kirkwall would be natives of Orkney. From the beginning, and even

177

now, more than 80 per cent of the staff is Orcadian.

It was getting to be a bit more than I and Gordon Brunton and Michael Brown, then our finance director, and our consultants could cope with and we started to bring in new people to be full-time devoted to oil. We took Rab Suttill, newly retired from Shell, for whom he had been the managing director of their Qatar development in the Gulf. Later there came Ian Clubb, a brisk Aberdonian accountant who had been for a number of years, the financial director of *The Times* newspapers and he took over from me as executive chairman of our oil interests. From the earliest days I had been chairman of the consortium's PEP Committee, a unique body as it turns out. The initials stand for Politics, Environment and Public Affairs and we looked after these matters with the stalwart help of people like Al Wallace of Getty's and Bob Stover of Allied and later their successors. Our own Thomson Oil board slipped into a lively going concern with new boffin faces appearing from time to time so that our present strength of nine members could probably challenge in low average age any board in the country deploying the sort of assets and returns. And this, even with the inclusion of such veterans as myself. I dare hardly list in this category the name of Ken Peters who had been for over twenty years managing director of the Aberdeen Journals Group of newspapers. I had picked him up in Glasgow as a young, newly demobilised Army officer at the end of the war. He did some good work, learning the routine jobs, and the day I offered him some significant promotion, he told me that he had been asked to go back to take up a senior appointment in his native Aberdeen. He became editor of the *Evening Express* there and then of the *Aberdeen Press and Journal*, becoming in due course, and pretty swiftly, the managing director of the group and with committee appointments to voluntary councils and institutions all over Scotland.

Towards the end of the 1970s, when the profits from our North Sea oil investments were starting to run healthily, we decided to invest in forestry in the UK on the grounds that since we were depleting a finite asset in the North Sea we ought to be spending some of the proceeds in developing a renewable asset. Martyn Baguley, an experienced forestry executive, joined us, becoming managing director of the Forestry Boards we set up. Our first purchase was Invertrossachs Estate, which Peter Tennant and his family had owned for many years, and this place remains our forestry flagship. We have planted something like a million and a quarter trees, made new roads and fences, and we have lately installed a deer farm on about 60 acres of good land which did not lend itself to our kind of forestry development. Environmentalists make much play of the 'serried ranks' of coniferous trees which form most forestry developments. I do not find these offensive to the eye, and since they give local employment and enrich the landscape in many ways they seem to justify their silent presence on what might otherwise be a wilderness. However, at Invertrossachs we have also created an arboretum and for a number of years we have taken about 100 school children from McLaren High School in Callander into the forest to plant trees there — not serried ranks at all, but ornamental and unusual hardwoods, so that in the years hereafter they can take their children and grandchildren to see these trees, for they will never be cut down and sent to the market.

Other changes were taking place. The last meeting of the three elderly men who had been mainly responsible for driving our oil venture to a successful conclusion came at Sutton Place, where some of us gathered for a meeting under the roof of John Paul Getty. There were of course Armand Hammer, Getty himself, and Roy Thomson, who had been for several years the first Baron Thomson of Fleet and North Bridge in the City of Edinburgh. After the business, we were invited by Paul Getty to visit his lions and we walked round the house to see two shabby lionesses in a large cage in the open air. The three senior partners, in black coats and hats, walked together, arm in arm, and in step, linked in respect if not quite affection, none of us guessing that they would never meet again. Two of them had greatly wanted wealth, power and fame, while for Getty wealth and power had been enough. I remember looking after them fondly, for they had all meant much to me. As they trundled along the path close-knit and going slow, they resembled an aged trio of skaters. Each, though, had his own dignity of achievement; each knew the value of things, but especially of time.

By the middle 1970s Roy Thomson was diminishing fast. My old friend, Harry Evans, who had been editor of the *Sunday Times* for a very successful chapter, asked me to do an obituary article about Roy to be kept in type against the eventual sad day. It was published in the *Sunday Times* issue of 8 August 1976, Roy having died a few days before, and I read it in my bed in Lamlash Hospital where I was lying stricken with a coronary seizure. I had much to say about Roy for I had known him better than most.

Man of our Times

The great fear of Roy H. Thomson — Lord Thomson of Fleet and North Bridge in the City of Edinburgh — was that he would not die at work, whether in London, Toronto, or some other base. In the later years all that he ever complained about were the small defeats that come with old age and made him cut his working week. But in spite of concessions there was always his spirited presence, driving on, questioning, speculating, demanding, expecting.

One hankered for a glimpse of what no one who worked for him recently had ever seen, and what eventually there was no one anywhere to remember — the man he had been 60 years before, if only to find out if that young fellow could possibly have been more vigorous. Perhaps it is merely success that people respect, more than energy or even the promise of genius. To be sure, there are memories of his early days, but no sure forecasting finger upon the motivating pulse.

For those who first knew him when he came to Scotland, he was already the set and elderly man, bustling along in a forward thrust, endlessly moving and asking. He was first off arriving aircraft, the first out of every board room, the short legs going, the tubby frame slanting towards the action, the head forward so that the pebbled glasses rode forward like headlamps. Even when his gait had diminished to a stooping toddle, the outline remained the same, focused as it were upon the glasses. They gave him his clear view of the near world, and in turn for the onlooker they made him at times grotesque, doubling his eyes as they split at the several levels of the lenses.

Since he had never known good eyesight all that he saw had always been from behind the glasses. They became the node not only of his vision but of his features, his personality. The folded face gathered up into shrewd lines towards the eyes, with so intent a projection that you forgot the eyes themselves were weak. The glasses revealed him. In one of the early British portraits of him, the renowned artist, seeking the man within, painted Roy not wearing the glasses but holding them in his hand. The result is meaningless. The features have fallen into a flabby unfamiliar mass upon which time has written nothing. The face, deprived of its permanent and familiar instrument of power, is unrecognisable, and it would even seem that the brain has retired, cut off from the communication of the glass.

His ability to concentrate was formidable. He would bend the better eye closely upon the sheets of some set of accounts, seven inches from his face, and peer into the heart of a business: generally one he contemplated buying. Figures and statistics were his main, but by no means his sole, guide to a business performance. A very nimble-witted Scottish accountant said that he had never met anyone who could sum a column of figures faster than he could himself until he met Roy. Moreover, he never forgot facts and figures. He seemed to know more about figures than accountants, just as he seemed to know more about law than lawyers.

Gossip writers and personality reporters used to talk about Roy 'beaming' behind his spectacles. Of course, he did not beam. He saw much more than could possibly be suggested by the Dickensian description of a benevolent buffer. To all that poured into the pin-holes of his narrowed vision there was to be added a verbal agility of wit and response. He was not one of your silent tycoons, hearing words and feeling no requirement to acknowledge them. Nobody ever spoke to him without getting not only an answer but a supplementary, a development of the theme, and perhaps some well-timed jocularity as well. . .

What is known about him is well known. His forefolk came from the village of Westerkirk, near Langholm in Dumfriesshire, and his loyal biographer of those remote days inserted the usual ritual anecdote indicating some fairly probable association with sheep-stealing ancestry which was always good for a gossip paragraph or two. More genuine and moving is the fine arched stone bridge which carries the Bentpath road across the Esk river at Westerkirk. It was built in 1730 and Roy's great-great-great-grandfather Andrew was one of the masons on the job.

A striking photograph dating from some years ago shows the peer and newspaper empire builder striding alone across the bridge, in a setting and style sufficient for a book of parables. He did this when in 1965 he spent a Sunday in Westerkirk for the dedication of the organ he presented to the village church. The tombstones of his own Thomsons were thick in the churchyard, for he could trace his ancestry in that village back to the 16th century, a span not likely to be matched by any other Fleet Street peer, far less one lately come from Canada . . .

The family emigrated to Canada in 1803, and for a handful of generations they made as little stir there as they had at home. When Roy Herbert Thomson was born in Toronto on June 5, 1894, it was into a home where the father was a barber and the formidable Aunt Sarah was at hand to usher the myopic teenager into the accounting of buying and selling the making of deals. It was not long before he had the feel of accomplishment and knew his own strengths, and then followed the long young years when he was to realise the gap that can exist between talent and success.

Clearly the first lesson was that he was not likely to attain wealth and power, the two things he sought, while he remained an employee. So the search developed, and almost failed, for the medium he could take into his hand and make distinctive with his genius for communication.

He was past middle life when he precariously bought his first newspaper, and at once was able to create for himself a setting in which he was to climb and tower. Thereafter one of his great compulsions remained the nightmare realisation that he had almost not made it. He was also to remain surprised at the ease with which success could follow a first success as if by an infallible formula, and astonished that so few people existed who cared to construct a simple pattern for their own success.

In this country the point of the story is bound to lie in the chapters of his adventures in Britain. Almost no one had heard of him when he arrived in Edinburgh to buy The Scotsman. Even then he would have been content with a modest shareholding of that paper. He learned fast, but the first year was rough for him and Edinburgh. After he had set himself up in London he used to make much rueful play about the remembered rebuffs of the North, and this was a theme to be taken up congenially by most of his biographers. To say that he was rejected by Edinburgh society is to talk nonsense. As Roy himself came to know, there was probably no place in the world which ultimately regarded him with more real affection nor more desired to welcome him back . . .

Many vigorous things have happened to British newspapers since he first arrived here, but it has to be remembered that he came when Fleet Street at least was running down, almost without ever having examined itself and determined its role. The Kemsley newspapers, bought in a complicated financial shuffle, when incidentally he matched the financial experts in mental agility, had reached the point of dispersal. Their future road seemed to be milestoned with the selling off of one provincial paper after another. Roy Thomson brought in the idea of effective and tidy management, and the conviction, which he passed on to newspaper staffs all too eager to accept — who wants to work for a proprietor who is content not to be making a profit? — that the pretentious mysteries of the newspaper world were susceptible to some new disciplines which would better arm them for their job without robbing them of their rights, whatever these might be.

The turnabout in the Kemsley chain was to become a memorable demonstration of this belief. Overnight he appointed managing directors to all the group centres, and it was perhaps merely an incidental that in more than half of the cases the new managing directors of today had been the editors of yesterday. There were two brutal logics here, worth remembering because this is not the chain of affairs now. In the first place there was little existing trained management anywhere in the newspaper world. And, secondly, editors are managers anyway, even the Olympian ones, and as they carry out the main burden of their tasks long after every other chief executive has gone home, they tend to develop a habit of solving the left-over problems.

He thought, therefore, that the job of management was to find the sales and advertising revenue in sufficient quantity to make the paper viable. 'There's nothing wrong with any newspaper that two more pages of advertising won't cure,' he used to say, thereby no doubt giving more fuel to those who believed he meant this and other such statements in terms of profits only.

Here comes in the other great and lasting contribution he made to our newspaper scene. He set editors and journalists free to pursue their tasks.

It is often said of him that he inaugurated this and that detailed improvement or change in various of his papers. He didn't. He introduced people, and expected them to do the innovating. The story of his change of The Scotsman to front page news has been told as if he sat these long nights over a design board laying out trial pages, rejecting, projecting. Nothing like that at all. I started with The Scotsman on the basis that we agreed to change to front page news, and he never saw the whole result until it came off the presses that first night. But his endless support was there all the time, as well as the unerring feel he had for public reaction to a new move. Our main and most interesting discussions on The Scotsman were on the theme of the probable reaction of most of our existing readers to some of the principles we might develop in edging the paper towards an up-to-date version of itself, and his response in these areas grew more true and interested.

It was in the large areas that he excelled. An idea such as The Sunday Times Magazine, applied to a British newspaper at enormous cost and risk, was a typical joust for him. Equally the bid for the licence to set up Scottish Television, which he drove through when friends and associates were begging him not to. In such decisions what spoke to him was primarily his own instinct about what a suitable majority of the potential public would expect.

Year after year his actions and of course his talk proclaimed that the printed word was flourishing and had a future. For most of his first years in the full national scene nobody spoke this with such conviction nor spent so heavily in investing for a long future of the British newspaper.

One of the legends about him which was most eagerly grasped had to do with the belief that he influenced or perhaps even wrote the editorial opinions and articles on matters of great public interest. Of course he was at pains to deny this whenever the matter was put to him, and although his denials were familiar, the question was one which was put most often to his associates. Wherever one went people asked if it were true that Roy Thomson left this freedom to his editors. There was a reluctance to believe it or perhaps even a sad acceptance of the other kind of arrangement and an assumption that it was inevitable.

Not only did he make no effort whatsoever to influence or direct editorial opinion; he did not even try to have material inserted which affected his own interests even in a minor way. Not that he took no interest. He was of course interested in the editorial views and often in conflict with them.

Once I was writing in The Scotsman something under my own name — a measure occasionally resorted to by editors — and had to mention in the development of the theme something about the Thomson financial interests. I stated that what I had to say would perhaps not be pleasing to my proprietor, and went on: 'But then he is not the editor of The Scotsman. I am.' This, I think, appeared to both of us the right relationship.

It was a relationship which had many benefits. It was possible to discuss with him, in a context which gave one the last word, editorial ideas and novelties where he had a prolific flow of originality, and because of his readiness to understand the mass public mind, he was often the ideal person on whom to try out certain new notions. 'That would go well,' he would say, and this could be a timely endorsement because he had superb journalistic instincts.

He was in disagreement with most or all of his papers in political orthodoxy, in racial and industrial relations matters. But these were the views reached by teams of journalists whom he had engaged personally or caused to be engaged, and they had their job while he had his. Few people outside understood or even believed this, and they might not feel any more inclined to believe it now. It was one of the great privileges of working with him, and none the less for being casually implied . . .

It says much for Roy that at his height he would accept a rebuke from his staff. Anyway his interest was in learning more and more about newspapers and in enlarging his certainty that they had a future, and above all that the quality paper had a future. He believed and he developed in all of us a mounting belief that the good newspaper was an information and marketing service that people positively wanted.

At the beginning of his experience with The Times this was in some ways overstated, but the roles were soon adjusted. So by sheer dedication and some old-fashioned style of leadership he demonstrated that the journalistic task was an expanding adventure, and that the papers we run could respond to sensible management on the spot. He talked freely about this, making no secret of it, but like the basics of his money-making life style, he remained astonished that so few went and did it that way.

There was probably only one matter that could truly offend him, and that was any reflection on his honesty. I never knew him to break his word . . .

As his British years went on and the sum of papers grew he could not stay so close to the individuals he had known earlier. Until the end he remained on friendly and familiar terms with all The Scotsman staff he had known in the earlier years, giving the impression he respected them like old comrades of the first battles. By this time he was a world figure of business and industry, familiar in investment and enterprise in half a dozen centres as well as in North America and Britain.

He was a happy man. Even a serious business meeting with losses to discuss, could suddenly find itself borne along on a jocular tide of stories and leg-pulling. He liked to tell stories — jokes. One of his favourites was about the Salvation Army officer, the one with the pay-off line: 'Keep driving the blighter south.' As the years went by the word 'blighter' changed gradually back, according to the company, to the original, until he would deploy it even in formal gatherings, such as a Royal banquet. It pleased him also occasionally to call for a well-worn story from one of us who might be present and who had probably revealed the story to him in the first place. 'Tell them the one about . . .' he would say, calling us in as if we were repertory players.

183

When he spoke in public he was at his best in his own vein and with no notes prepared. Many a time his impromptu intervention has rescued a stolid gathering. When he spoke unprepared, it was like his conversation — bright, unexpected, altogether satisfying.

In business he overflowed with enthusiasm. He could always find time, in the midst of heavy preoccupations and crises, to consider lesser topics and to switch his mind to an altogether different perspective.

When the going was hard, as in the endless murk of the union troubles, or in times of slump, he had stores of resource within himself that reminded one of Will Ogilvy's Border moss troopers, from whom, of course, he himself had come:

> Girth-deep moss and clinging mire,
> Taught them patience in desire;
> Pikes that thrust and thrust again,
> Steeled their hearts and made them men.

. . . Only a big scale can measure his vast achievement — not just the fortune but the practical performance: the making of his own personality. He redirected the whole British newspaper industry and the people within it, giving them a future of privilege and opportunity they hardly thought they possessed. To be sure there were faults, not of much account in the full picture, and his critics will be among lesser people, including those who owe him much. Nothing can take away the thought of the indomitable heart of him, a strange and adventurous man from nowhere, ennobled by these great virtues of courage and integrity and faithfulness.

The last sentence of that last paragraph has attained an odd sort of immortality since it is engraved on the memorial to Roy in the crypt of St Paul's in London.

Much will still be written about the British offshore oil industry, for great developments and adventures are still to come. It is to be hoped that the British government will make better than its pretty paltry use of the amazing results. For me it represented one of the two eras of high adventure which I had never hoped to deserve; the other was in the world of newspapers. Each of these had been a cherished privilege; and each had happened in my own country, which long before I had vowed to serve and never to abandon.

CHAPTER TWELVE
Contemporaries

In the 1930s, when it seemed as if he had been permanently discarded from political life, Winston Churchill took to laying bricks, painting pictures and writing books. One of the books was *Great Contemporaries*, and this is exactly what he meant, for from his earliest days he had thirsted for association with people distinguished in social and public life and he wanted to note how he had been influenced by some of them. These were not ordinary people, and indeed ordinary people play little part in this or any other of his books, yet while his writing style and noble phrase-making endowed them to a prodigal extent with grace and wisdom and intellectual ability of a high order, what was memorable was that they were all motivated by his own greedy demand for fame and recognition. Not many of them had names which have since gone ringing on down the years, so that it is possible to look back and realise that most of them were all too contemporary. No doubt they all ranked among the sort of people whom the editor of a responsible newspaper must get to know and even to understand, but that editor has perhaps a wider selection from which to choose his friendships. I was never disposed to go seeking for attention from eminent politicians who were also the dispersers of patronage. They have a dull life for the most part, among equally dull people who are mostly on the make, and even nowadays not many of their new recruits appear to be feverishly motivated by the need to covet honour. My great fortune has been to have, for friends, many people who were enormously more interesting than the apparently great. The happiest of my days have been spent in the company of friendly, generous and wise people, open-hearted and full of wit, not looking for favours and not pretending to be able to give them.

Because it was my proper job so to do, I have known seven British Prime Ministers and at least one of these was a friend before he got to 10 Downing Street, and after. They were a mixed lot, skilled in political machinery but not in most cases noted for great human qualities, and some with failings only too easily observed. I do not include in this list of seven Churchill and Clement Attlee, although I was often in their company. Occasionally Winston Churchill would come to Scotland and make some great speech during the wartime, and in his preparation for this he would get me to look out for him the full poem in all its verses of Charles Murray's 'Auld Scotland Counts for Something Still', a remotely pawky piece which 'Hamewith' — the pen-name of Charles Murray — no doubt wanted to repudiate in his later years, but which Churchill clearly felt fed and flattered the pathetic Scottish requirement for nostalgia and forgotten triumphs. I also often saw him perform in the House of Commons, and when it was bombed, the Central Methodist Hall in Westminster, and thereafter when the Commons sat in the House of Lords. Of course I was not in on the great secret speeches, but his accounts to the House of current battles and successes were powerful in the extreme. Towards the end of the war he had ceased to be a robust figure, but in speech and gait, and no doubt thinking, he went at his own pace, clearly enjoying the ruthlessness demanded of a war leader. Some mantle of special authority had fallen upon him, since he was clearly the last hope of a generation that had almost failed in its destiny. I remember once, when he emerged from a House of Commons performance — for of course he did not sit through the whole proceedings — he brought with him almost his entire government and most of his Conservative supporters, this horde moving across the lobby, with himself in the middle like a queen bee, glowing with satisfaction, his curious toddle making him revolve gradually in the midst of this mêlée. It was a study in sycophancy as about 150 men, some of them renowned for their vanity and tiny talents, crowded in, shouting prepared phrases of acclamation and striving as it were to touch the hem of his garment.

When Clem Attlee succeeded he brought with him a shock of coolness and detachment, and peacetime Britain became a business again. The last time I saw him was when he had been dragged to some government reception and, since he was unbelievably frail, had been placed into a seat against the wall. He was the oldest looking man I have ever seen. His head, like the worst of the caricatures that had been frequently done of him in his active time, was not even a skull, but a shapeless formation with the withered parchment of his skin drawn untidily across it. He had achieved much in his lifetime, but now he was far away, his last straw being to appear as the skeleton at a political feast.

The only drawback to the recollection of Harold Wilson as the most effective of 'my' Prime Ministers was the merciless way in which he paraded his efficiency. His great gimmick, and it was no more than that, even at the best, was to recall in public or private conversation every useless detail of the footnotes '. . . you will find that in my speech in the House of Commons on . . . Hansard page XXX column YYY . . .' and other tricks which are no better than party games even when well done but which, it is greatly to be feared, impress political parties. Harold Wilson seemed to me a decent man. He had a good home life, he kept his party together, and he was very loyal to his supporters, which is perhaps the least reprehensible of political virtues. James Callaghan was again a very good party man and had kindness and humanity in abundance. Before he became Prime Minister he had made a mission on behalf of the Labour government to Northern Ireland in the early days of the Troubles, and he seemed to understand that situation almost better than any other politician I have heard on the subject. It was particularly memorable that he had spoken to Bernadette McAliskey, and had not only treated her like a daughter, but had appreciated exactly how and why she felt as she did.

Harold Macmillan had brought to the premiership a lifetime of political ingenuity and original thought as well as a large style of scholarship and business achievement. His grandfather, who had founded the business, was the son of a modest crofter in the north of the island of Arran in the Firth of Clyde, the ruins of his birthplace hamlet being there to this day. But Harold Macmillan will not thank you for calling him a Highlander. He was certainly the best all-rounder of the people I knew in Number 10, where I once saw him at a small lunch party give a hilarious demonstration of how he had lately seen a Japanese musician playing a nose-flute. The first time he invited me to 10 Downing Street, shortly after I had become editor of *The Scotsman*, and when he was newly Prime Minister, he took me aside and said curiously, 'Tell me, are you really editor of *The Scotsman*?' and when I admitted it he said, 'My God!' as if to say to himself, 'I think I've got problems but here's a chap with real trouble.'

In my terms, if it does not sound presumptuous, Sir Alex Douglas-Home was the most notable of these Prime Ministers, if only because he had for long been a hero and a legend in my part of the country; and also for such virtues as described by Margaret Thatcher when she said of him, 'He is the wisest man I have ever met.' Other qualities are there. I once went in to have a drink with him in Number 10 and as we spoke I asked him, 'What would you say your main worry is just now?' He talked immediately about the predicament of a remote African tribe called the Watutsis, who were threatened with genocide by a neighbouring African state. It seemed to me significant and not without a hint of benevolent imperialism that the head of the British government should have at the top of his current priorities a concern for an African tribe who presumably had very little to contribute to the current world predicament. Some of us in Scotland had looked to him for a long overdue attention and solution to the Scottish situation. No doubt he had been too long under the British political harrows to be able to turn aside at short notice and set our wrongs to rights. There's no doubt that the long history of his own forefolk had conditioned him in many ways to get a proper perspective to be the British Prime Minister. I used to give myself the pleasure, when introducing him to public gatherings, in my role of chairman or such, to tell the audience how, if a man has lived for 700 years within a mile of the English border, he tends to have a powerful sense of survival.

187

The first time I met Mrs Thatcher she was a junior minister in the Conservative government and came to one of my dinner parties in the House of Commons, along with more senior members of the cabinet and the Tory establishment. There were a few of us there from *The Scotsman*, for we had a prominent responsibility in the political scene, and inevitably there came up in the conversation the usual patronising and irritating phrase (I shall not quote from whom) 'I love your Scotch b-r-r.' This led of course to a discussion of accents, carried on with good humour although with a hint of mild needling of the lady guest by some of her senior colleagues in the government. I remember how Margaret Thatcher drew herself up coldly and declared, 'Of course, I have no accent', an assertion which was unhappily greeted with laughter by her fellow Tories and in which the Scots among us did not join, perhaps for the reason that it appears we have problems of our own.

Apart from Prime Ministers, there were of course other characters in the House of Commons whom I may remember with even more affection. Ernest Brown was the National Liberal MP for Leith and had been the first wartime Secretary of State for Scotland, a man who had survived into many cabinets although he had no visible means of political support. He was the absolute in egocentricity, believing that he was universally well-known and indeed popular. It was a study to walk with him through his constituency of Leith, when he would pause every now and again to wave enthusiastically to some woman working at the kitchen sink, three storeys above, and she would stare down at him in ignorance of who this forward stranger might be. He was even more dangerous to accompany on the streets of London. He would sally, with one or two of us as his entourage, out from the front door of Dover House, the Scottish Office in Whitehall, and walk smartly across the road heedless of the rushing traffic. Buses and taxis would squeal to a halt with drivers screaming personal curses at him. 'They all know me,' he would say contentedly, continuing on his way.

After Tom Johnston came Arthur Woodburn, Secretary of State for Scotland under Attlee. He had been imprisoned in Calton Jail in Edinburgh as a conscientious objector during World War I and had studied politics there as well as teaching himself shorthand. Also there was Joe Westwood, a wary little politician who had been a miner and trade union leader and who once told me, 'I would do absolutely anything in the world to stop mining — to stop a man having to go underground and dig coal with a pick at a face. My father was killed in the mines and my grandfather was killed in the mines, and I had an uncle whose bits were brought home in a sack.'

The last minister I worked closely with before I left the Scottish Office was George Buchanan, one of the so-called Red Clydeside MPs of Glasgow, who said that he had been offered the Ministry of Health by Clement Attlee but had opted for a job in the Scottish Office, and became an Under-Secretary of State in charge of housing. He thought if the housing problem were to be solved it would solve the rest of

Scotland's problems. It is still unsolved but George Buchanan made a vigorous assault on the scene and was thwarted on all sides. He fretted greatly at Civil Service procedures. I once heard him saying to the head of a department, 'We musnae be laskadainical.' He was a devoted Socialist with no time for the niceties. One day I heard him in the House of Commons, where I was sitting in the official box, challenge a Tory who had claimed that the matter under discussion was non-political, with 'Whenever I hear anybody say he's got nae politics, I know he's gonna vote against me.'

Wartime brought some interesting new characters into politics, including such a man as Sir John Anderson who became Lord Waverley. As Home Secretary he visited us in Clydebank where the town had endured two days of fierce *Luftwaffe* blitz. Much had gone wrong in the administration there because the children had come home from the first evacuation and they had to be gathered up again after the first night of the assault and sent by buses to destinations which no central body knew about, and parents were desperate to trace them. The bombing had missed the shipyards but the factories were out of commission and of the 6,000 houses in Clydebank only six had escaped damage. Many of course were utterly demolished, and there was to be further devastation on the succeeding night. I commandeered a truck from somewhere and took one or two people up to Singer's factory where we walked into the deserted building and purloined ten typewriters from the desks of the typing pool along with masses of stationery and copying paper. Returning to the centre of the burgh to the more or less intact town hall, I sent a runner out to find volunteer typists and these girls sat at desks and typed out lists of children which were coming in from the evacuation centres, often written badly on paper stained with rain. These sheets were posted up all round the town giving the names of the children, their home addresses and the new address where they could be written to. The morale was good in that town. For example, cigarettes were already short, but on several successive days I passed a tobacconist's shop which had been blown apart with hundreds of packs of cigarettes spilled out on to the pavements and I never saw from day to day any indication that even one had been lifted. All this happened shortly after Coventry was badly blitzed and I put to John Anderson the idea that if he would make a statement to the Press saying that in his view, Clydebank had been worse hit than Coventry, it would do Clydebank a world of good. He agreed at once because this was his view anyway, and women went about the streets for the next day or two saying to each other with great satisfaction, 'They gien us worse than they gien Coventry.' Anderson was a pedantic fellow, and one of his senior officials told me that at a later stage in the war, when he was sitting at his desk as Home Secretary, news was brought to him that a courier carrying papers to some other ministry had been mugged and his briefcase stolen. Anderson folded his hands severely and instead of saying, 'Have they

189

caught the fellow?' he boomed, 'Has the miscreant been apprehended?'

In the Scottish Office Public Relations Department we picked up all the work of the Ministry of Information north of the border, and many another amateur diplomatic venture as well. Some of the countries who might come under the German influence in the early days of the war sent missions to this country to see what truth there was in the Nazi story that the British industrial output and economic war effort were in ruins. One of the nearest successes in this chapter concerned the Bulgarians whose government sent a mission of two men and a woman to see the war effort in Scotland and to come to conclusions as to whether Britain might conceivably win the war. It was their bad luck that they persisted in comparing the prowess of Bulgaria in all fields with what might be seen in Scotland. This was before we started out on our tour, when by way of preliminary they were assuring me that the shipbuilding and war effort of Bulgaria was unmatched by any other country of like size. I took them down the River Clyde where a whole new British fleet was building. 'Ah well, perhaps this is much better than we can do,' they said, but they impressed upon me that their agriculture was unsurpassed and more bountiful than that of any nation on earth. So I took them to the fertile plains of Lothian and the great plain of the Forth where in that autumn of 1940 a bountiful harvest was neatly gathered and loading the ground. They had never seen anything like this, nor indeed had anyone else, but they fell back on their ace card which was that the vineyards — ah, the vineyards of Bulgaria — nowhere was anything more fruitful than the vines of Bulgaria. 'Would you like,' I asked them, 'to see the biggest vine in the world?' Yes, they would, and where was it? I said, 'It's here.' At that very moment we were driving through the Stirlingshire village of Kippen where the famous undercover vine, twice the size of the one at Hampton Court, was hanging in great clusters that needed separate supports or they would have broken away from the branches.

That night we dined with General Sir Ian Hamilton, the British Commander at Gallipoli, and as it happened, one of the only British generals who had ever been any kind of a hero to the Bulgarian people. They sent off their dispatches recommending that Bulgaria stay neutral or come in with the West but it was too late, and they were already being over-run.

There was also a somewhat more purposeful mission from Turkey which I remember well, not least because one of them was wearing a MacTavish tartan tie, which is my tartan. We gave them the same treatment and Turkey remained neutral and, I may say, impressed. All this activity was briefly described by a Clydeside colleague of mine at the time as 'Wee jobs for the Foreign Office'. He himself was an ingenious worker in the cause and for some months he ran a political discussion group on the war aims in a men's public lavatory in a working-class district, on the grounds that it was cheaper to assemble in this all-weather gathering place than in any of the nearby pubs, who were running out of supplies.

Presiding over the Scottish Office activities at this time was the senior civil servant in Scotland, a tiny figure called Sir Horace P. Hamilton who, during World War I, had been as a young man plucked from obscurity in some Civil Service backwater to become Private Secretary to Lloyd George, who had already broken the spirit of four orthodox private secretaries. Hamilton was with him as Chancellor of the Exchequer, and later Prime Minister, and had become a KCB in his early thirties. His main contribution to the bureaucratic World War II effort was an exhaustive knowledge of rights and protocol. He addressed his equals in letters as 'my dear so and so', his immediate and not too distant juniors as 'dear so and so', and executives of considerable junior rank below him as 'dear Mr so and so'.

As heads of department, or almost so, were such figures as the convivial and extremely cautious Sir David Milne; Sir Charles Cunningham, who became in due course the head civil servant in the Home Office in London; Sir Douglas Haddow, a special friend for many years who was later chairman of the North of Scotland Hydro-Electric Board; Sir William Murrie; James McGuinness; Jock Aglen; and Matthew Dobie, whose spare time was spent in reading French classics in the original tongue, and, indeed, in the original volumes. Jim McGuinness was the leading light in founding the Scottish Baroque Ensemble and getting the Queen's Hall restored as a concert hall created out of an old church. All this he did in his retirement. Jock Aglen, as Private Secretary to Tom Johnston, played an enormous part in helping to pilot through the Hydro-Electric Bill. John Mack from Glasgow University had been the Snell Exhibitioner at Oxford, and became our Intelligence Officer. There was also, as a close colleague, Forsyth Hardy, the historian of the documentary film movement.

During the wartime I turned up several times in Dublin, where some matters could safely be pursued, although at diplomatic arm's length. It was astounding to go there and walk the streets, which blazed with light and were crowded with young men not in uniform. I once walked down O'Connell Street, immediately on arrival, with a large ice-cream in each hand, licking them alternately. I was never one for great steaks of meat but I did not stint my intake of eggs and sausages, because they were real. Several times I visited John Betjeman who was attached to the British Embassy as Press Attaché, and who performed an entertaining role, especially in the time of severe petrol shortage in Ireland. The British Embassy used to have an official allocation and John, ever buoyant, used to drive along the main streets and hail some of his friends with, 'Can I give you a lift on English petrol?'

John had been a frequent visitor to us in St Andrew's House, the headquarters of the Secretary of State, and although it was many years before he reached the full flower of his eccentricity, he was always engagingly outspoken. The first time he came to us I met him at the station and escorted him up Waterloo Bridge, in the middle of which he started to declaim, pointing to the recessed niches in the side walls, 'Now that's the *real way* to use a blank wall.'

Once in the Secretary of State's absence I showed John into the less than dignified ministerial room with its tawdry concealed lighting in the corners of the ceilings. 'My God!' roared John. 'The people who invented cornices — and look at the blasphemy that has been committed here.'

On a Dublin visit he took me out to an enormous mansion house which he occupied a few miles from Dublin, where he assured me there was only one cold water tap and no significant domestic supply for other purposes. This last claim did not, as it happens, have to be investigated, because at a certain point in the evening after we had drunk a little Guinness, John tapped me on the knee and said, 'Follow me, Dunnett.' And he led the way through the french windows into the long garden. I paced obediently after him until we came to a dead end at a final brick wall covered with roses. 'This is one of the great pleasures of my life here,' John told me, 'when I perform this ritual every night.' And he unbuttoned himself and demonstrated the ritual, in which out of courtesy I took part.

John Betjeman had a splendid post-war run, becoming Poet Laureate and gaining other honours and recognition. In health though, he seemed to have fallen upon evil days, and I was much grieved lately to see him in a wheelchair and slurred of speech, paraded like some oracle whose mumblings, even, are to be treasured. It was not a worthy thing to do to a man who has enjoyed better days.

There was a time when I got official agreement to find someone to install, in the British Embassy in Dublin, to counter the very effective work being carried out by men in the German Embassy who had learned Irish Gaelic and would speak it in the pubs as well as going to the ceilidh dances and getting in touch with a section of the Irish people. I had in mind a very able young professor, John Watson, whose father had occupied the same chair of Celtic languages in Glasgow University. He would have done a magnificent job for he was young, athletic, a great mixer and ceilidh man, and a scholar already moving towards a European reputation. He would have greatly liked to do the Dublin job, but he felt he ought not to take it since he wanted to serve in the armed forces. He joined the Navy as an ordinary seaman and within months had been drowned in a destroyer which went down with all hands in a North Sea engagement with the enemy.

In St Andrew's House I started a weekly Friday morning conference to try to supply weekend stories to the press, mainly built round various wartime personalities who happened to be in Scotland around that time. This gave one an extraordinarily interesting perspective on the whole war scene. We got some of the generals and the Navy and air people, and there were uniformed strangers of every kind and most of the western nationalities to draw upon as well as the civilians that we were using to give lectures around the country. I used to chair this meeting every Friday morning, and I remember particularly in the early days a senior Norwegian officer describing the retreat from his country which finished with an action in a fjord at Andalsnes. He described how this mixed allied unit had hung out for a day or two. He paid a great tribute to the courage of a small Polish mortar team in the adjacent hills which had held a large German contingent at bay for many hours until all their ammunition had been spent and they had taken, he thought, to the boats. During this description two Polish officers, sitting at the other end of the table and due to give some account of something or other, became agitated and spoke to each other feverishly in Polish, interrupting the Norwegian's discourse so much that I had to call the thing to attention. They then told us that they had been the officers in charge of the very same Polish mortar squad. Another participant in this conference was the poet, T.S. Eliot, whose spare-time war effort was touring the country at odd times to lecture to groups on modern poetry. When I announced him he informed the gathering that he really had nothing to say to them. He had only come because he had never before been at a press conference and wanted to see what one was like.

Once the press conference took the form of what we called a porridge party. It was at the time when Tom Johnston, the Secretary of State, was pressing the claims of porridge and milk as the best all-round breakfast food which would sustain anybody through a long working day, so I introduced him and some of his officials to the press. He knew all of them anyway, and after Tom had given a spirited account of the virtues of porridge, a button was pressed, the partition between the rooms dropped down, and there was a chef ready to dish up plates of porridge from a steaming pot. Tom was a genuine porridge-lover and when we made our sorties into the country he had porridge in all the hotels every morning. He was scathing about people who sprinkled sugar on porridge, unrealising that Mrs Johnston preferred her porridge with sugar; but being a discreet wife and help-mate she generally contrived, especially in her own home, she told me, to sprinkle the sugar on the plate before the porridge was dished out on top of it.

I also held meetings for the Editors of the Scottish daily, evening, and national Sunday papers to meet Tom and be told of his activities in Scotland and how Scotland would face the post-war years. He generally brought along a foreign secretary or some other cabinet minister whose writ ran over the whole of Britain, because of course Tom was the Scottish Minister of Agriculture and Fisheries, of Education, of Home Affairs, Police, Health and Housing and many another portfolio.

Ralph Law was a rare character in those Civil Service days, and one to whom I had a warm attachment. He should have gone far but in the post-war years, when he came safely home from the Army, he died too soon to inherit the renown that was his due. In the early years of the war he was Private Secretary to the Secretary of State and we used to foregather in the sleeper train once or twice a week at London's King's Cross Station, having a nightly ceilidh after we had got our Secretary of

State safely bedded down. Joining the train one night I found him on the platform taking the last of the fairly fresh air, but, unusually, hugging his briefcase to his breast instead of throwing it on to his bunk and leaving it there until he was ready to turn in.

'What's that?' I asked him. 'What's all the security?'

'That,' he told me, 'is the Crown Jewels.'

When we got aboard the train he asked me to come to his cabin to show me what he had in the briefcase. It was a dazzling collection of jewelled artefacts wrapped in wadding and tissue paper which he was conveying over the border into Scotland under such conditions that they would never return. It seemed that some very elderly Scottish noble lady, nearly associated with royalty, had inherited these objects, the prize among them being a badge of the Garter Order with the enamelled saint surrounded by a blaze of glorious diamonds. The law officers of the Crown had been busy on this horde, which had been bequeathed by the lady as a personal treasure to the British monarch. However, at the time of her death, that king happened to be the recently abdicated King Edward VIII, and some legal powers had been secretly involved at the highest level to prevent the priceless items passing out of the ownership of our royal family so it had been decided that the best way of laying a regal hand upon them in an interim way was to get them into Scotland under such protection as our body of law would be able to afford. You can now see these items under lights and resting forever modestly among the Crown Jewels and the Honours Three of Scotland in the Crown Room in Edinburgh Castle, but that evening they were far from being safely there. As Ralph spread them enthusiastically on his berth in the train bunk we doted upon them and indeed toasted their continued integrity in a dram or two until at some point in the evening Ralph discovered he had lost one — none other than the George Badge. We scrambled among his bedclothes, gathering up the other items, but the badge had gone in our patriotic fumbling. In a fever of guilt we stripped his bed throwing the mattresses aside and at last found the item fallen down the back among the unswept carpet dust of many a journey. Even now I go occasionally to pay my tribute to it.

I remember, too, the day we unwrapped the Scottish Crown Jewels from the swathings and the lockfast iron chests where they had been concealed against the bombing. The few of us present touched and handled the Crown, the Sceptre and the Sword with a kind of grieving reverence, and although we had one or two normal jokesters among us, I remember being particularly struck by the circumstance that it never occurred to any one of the six of us even to contemplate to put that abandoned Crown, jocularly, upon his head.

Among the treasures concealed against possible wartime damage were many priceless records of our realm. Some of them were in Borthwick Castle and I went there once with a splendid man and companion, J.G. Kyd, who was then the Registrar General for Scotland. He was a great hill man and patriot, who occasionally put out treatises on the names given year after year to Scottish infant boys and girls. Master of names that he was, he was the one who gave to the other Alastair Dunnett, also a journalist, and me the names of Red Dunnett and Black Dunnett. I was the black one. We went up that day to walk the causeyed ramparts of the castle and he took me by the shoulder and named every peak and small ben top of the Pentlands. Years after, his eyes clouded with cataracts, so that although his legs could still take him up his hills, they were grey with the mist of decrepitude. At last he was given a miraculously successful operation, and I walked the streets of the New Town with him soon after he came out of hospital. With his arm in mine he would exclaim his delight at every north-looking crossing to see the blue of the river Forth and the colour subtlety of the hills of Fife which the surgeon had given back to him.

J.G. Kyd was succeeded as Registrar General by a long-winded character called Edmond Hogan who had been one of our liaison team in London for the Department of Health. Ralph Law once told me how Edmond had taken to the telephone in London to clear two small points with the head of his division in St Andrew's House in Edinburgh. He spoke, not listening much, for forty minutes to deal with the first item; and then he said, 'Now, Harold, don't let's make two bites of the cherry. As to the other matter, I wished to propose to you . . .'

Another of this small group, also full of character and eccentricity, was a doctor called Macfarlane, a Highlander who had worked with the oil companies in the Middle East in the 1930s and who had played his bagpipes while walking round the ramparts of Baghdad. He was less imaginative than most Highlanders, having inherited some practical genes from somewhere. We sat together once in a cinema in London to watch a film whose star was a younger passion of mine, Loretta Young. At one point the camera zoomed close up to her so that I was able nearly to swoon at the sight of those glorious eyes of hers, faintly protuberant and lit with some fictional passion. Macfarlane was busy nudging me diagnostically and saying, 'Old boy, exophthalmic goitre.'

I also remember with some affection Jack Herbertson, who occupied an obscure clerical post and had one of the liveliest and wittiest minds in that whole gang. We used to play feverish games of table tennis in the basement of the temporary wartime Scottish Office, Fielden House in Great College Street, London. Walking once across Parliament Square with Willie Mackinlay we met Jack, and I stopped to introduce him and pass the time of day. When we moved on Willie Mackinlay said, 'What does he do?' I mentioned the modest task to which Herbertson had been assigned and Willie Mackinlay blurted tersely, 'I could have guessed that. He's too bloody intelligent to be a senior civil servant.'

When the blitz was on and the bombs were falling on London, we were all at pains to demonstrate our sangfroid, knowing that as grown men and reasonably fit in wartime, we should probably have been elsewhere. I had a basement room in Fielden House with a bed in it where I slept, and even a small kitchen off where I cooked meals for Douglas Haddow and me from our short statutory ration. It was thrilling to get out in the early morning when the 'all-clear' had gone, passing through the small streets in the Westminster neighbourhood. The main sound was the tinkling of glass as the courageous small shopkeepers swept up the damage and got on with business. In that time one learned to whom London really belonged, for there were none left but natives, all the incomers and idlers and rentiers having gone to safer places. Some of the Londoners of course found it difficult to take, and older people, especially mothers with young children, holed up for a year or two in the underground stations where bunks had been erected, and these citizens slept through the night with late trains running only a few feet from their noses — trains seeming brighter lit and more reliable than they are now. For some Londoners this tinker life went on long after the bombing had stopped, and indeed by the end of the war in Europe it had become difficult to decant them back to wherever they had come from, if that still existed. Walking the streets late at night under the blitz I used to take great comfort from a brass plate inserted into the paving stones on the pavement opposite the Home Office. It read, 'Aberdeen Adamant'.

I can honestly say I enjoyed my time in the Civil Service, coming to admire many of the men one found there, for they were moved by a genuine vocation of service, if not of reform. The top grade ones among them wielded enormous power but tended to use it wisely. They had also given themselves in many cases the title of 'permanent' on the ground that ministers come and go but the Civil Service is self-perpetuating. Innovation was something to be avoided and this went with a habit of caution which turned some of them into frightened men. It was very good to get back to newspapers, especially as an editor, who must meet simply everybody but has the precious opportunity of choosing some of the attractive ones to be his personal friends, provided that they also feel so disposed. There can't be many editors who have received a positive fan letter which ends up:

Ever fondly,
Lillian Gish,

just as I may well be the only editor who ever took part in a television entertainment programme on the same bill as the Beatles.

The actor Laurence Harvey, who died still young and splendid, came visiting to our home a great deal. I got him to pose for a series of pictures showing the primitive conditions backstage in the Assembly Hall, the Church of Scotland gathering place where great plays are put on during the Edinburgh Festival. There was sometimes Joan Cohn with him wearing much jewellery, and they both agreed jocularly that his practice was, on receiving some enormous sum for appearing in a film, to buy costly ear-rings and things and hang them on her by way of a floating reserve. Once at dinner I could not keep my eyes away from a large ring which she was wearing with a stone, apparently of crystal, not sparkling like a diamond, but at least an inch across, and I said to her naïvely, 'If that stone wasn't so big, Joan, I'd say it was a diamond.' She took it off and threw it across the table to me, saying, 'Do I look the kind of girl who would wear anything but diamonds?'

One of the most memorable of the literary figures was surely Compton Mackenzie — Monty — perhaps because he was certainly the most picturesque. Very early in his life he had invented a character and a style for himself, upon which he elaborated as his long years went by. Most of us in Edinburgh had an affectionate regard for him, although he bored some, and his posing was sometimes trying. I knew him longer than most of those who came about his home in Drummond Place in Edinburgh, for I had been with him often in the Highlands and in the strange house he had built for himself above the sands at Eoligarry in Barra.

Whatever gathering he was in, he had to be the central personality. He loved to perform, telling his own tales and playing all the parts in character. Like his early infant memories, which he came to believe went back to the time when he was only a few months old, his adult adventures lost nothing in accumulated detail, and he was always the heroic figure. He kept late sessions at his home, holding court in his high armchair, at which he expected that all distinguished visitors in town should be presented. When you arrived late, it was to be seized at once into the listening circle. As the sessions stretched into the early morning hours, some drooping and exhausted victim of the show would excuse himself and leave, thinking possibly of an early morning start the next day. As soon as he was gone Monty would say, in a voice of tolerant contempt, 'He can't hold his sleep.'

Some of us, driven on by the tireless and determined Fanny MacTaggart, the Norwegian wife of the genial Sir Willie MacTaggart, President of the Royal Scottish Academy, tried very hard to have him nominated as the winner of the Nobel prize of literature, compiling a great dossier of his undoubted innovations in forms of the novel, although by that time he had lost what had been a huge flair, and he was doing not much more than hack work. We lost this campaign, although I cannot remember who won that year. You met in that house also from time to time the frail figure of his beautiful actress sister Fay Compton, whom my mother had seen in London at the opening night of *Mary Rose*, passages from the name part of which, for years, my mother would movingly repeat. To the end Monty kept it up, even his remorseless name-dropping, which peppered his conversation with personal tales of such as Willie Maugham, Oscar, Noel, Dickie and Edwina, Ivor, and Don Roberto.

That last was Robert B. Cunninghame Graham, on whom I imagine Monty had modelled some part of his image. He was a Scoto-Spanish cavalier, familiar with the ranches and the horses of South

197

America, and he could write briefly and memorably of what he had experienced. As a Presbyterian and a Calvinist myself, I have long treasured, by way of mortification, the description that the Don once gave of some grim and graceless church figures of the Upper Ward of Lanarkshire: 'For they worshipped a jealous God, and it would ill become them to be more gracious than He'. Cunninghame Graham was a hero of our youth, for being a laird and also a Socialist as well as a Scottish Nationalist, he had gone to prison for some remote and spirited defiance of orthodox laws. I have never experienced a better nor more kindly chairman of a meeting. If one was to speak under his auspices, there would be a generous introduction, then he would sit gazing at the speaker, chuckling and nodding in agreement at the points, however feeble, and bearing you along with good-hearted encouragement. One of us, in a group at his feet somewhere, once asked him: 'When, do you think, will Scotland have a Parliament of her own?' He pondered this, and said, 'Not in the lifetime of anyone here. Not in the lifetime of the children of anyone here. Perhaps in the lifetime of the grandchildren of some here.'

I have a rich memory of William Soutar the poet, who wrote those beautiful children's verses and bairn rhymes which Seumas Adam and I had doted on for some time before I came to know poet Will in the 1930s. It was a lifting experience to visit him in that bedroom of his home in Perth. A World War I disability had paralysed him from the waist down, but it had not touched his sweet spirit, although it was to keep him to one bed until he died. In the subdued panelled room which was his world there was a window where he sometimes could not bear to look. He sat up there among his pillows wearing a dark jacket, a white shirt and a bow tie, looking not unlike Maurice Lindsay, one of our later poets. He had a gentle fine Scots voice, and he liked discussion and mild argument; always seeking to know about Scotland outside, which he was not to see again for the many more years he lived. At Christmas time he always sent me a new poem written in his own hand, and also became a generous fan of my radio short stories, looking out for them, and listening so that he could send me a kind analysis. I wonder what he would have thought if he had been with me the night that Bob Grieve, asked to 'do' something Scottish, recited grandly Soutar's poem 'The Tryst' ('O luly luly cam' she in . . .') after a dinner which had been put on for Bob and me in a certain club in Boston, USA.

An altogether gloomier literary pilgrim of those times was James Barke, whom we often got to write truculent feature articles for us in the *Weekly Herald*. James was a hard case who had started his career by writing a few self-consciously coarse books about modern life in the West of Scotland, and lamented that he had escaped the full recognition which he believed he deserved. He once confessed to Willie Ballantine that Mrs Barke had advised a woman neighbour not to read her husband's books — 'I don't think you would like them. They're not really very nice.' Later Barke became greatly attracted to Burns, and wrote a series of fictional volumes covering the whole of Burns' short life. These drew much attention, although forgotten now, and we have not yet seen any sign of a Barke revival among the new generation of Scots publishers. James identified himself fiercely with these publications, which must have required much industry and research. A basically humourless person, he believed that he was uniquely endowed to match our great poet in wit and repartee; and as he told me more than once, if there was to be an after-life, it would be James Barke who would be most eagerly sought out above all others by Robert Burns, to bear him company.

It may be necessary that some writers who consider themselves renowned, should make much of these claims in public. This was the case with Hugh MacDiarmid, whose real name was Christopher Grieve, and who was called Chris by all his friends. However, he was a real poet, and such an innovator in terms of phrase and language that he almost single-handed invented the Scottish Renaissance. He worked tirelessly at the task of promoting his kind of output. When the whole body of his works comes to be sorted out, scrapping the plentiful doggerel, there will abide some lyric fancies which are permanent, perhaps of divine inspiration. Chris also believed that society at all levels owed a living to the poet. He was once asked to be a guest at an international congress of PEN to be held in Glasgow. At this time he was living on the remote island of Whalsay in Shetland, and some guarded undertaking was made that his travelling and some other modest expenses would be paid. Chris arrived days before the start of proceedings, booked himself into the Central Hotel in Glasgow on the account of PEN, had the expensive suite stocked up with liquor, and ran a continuous series of parties for his cronies. It was not long before somebody referred these events to Peter McCallum Smith, an impulsive, red-faced journalist who much later was a reporter on my *Record* staff, and who at that time was acting as unpaid treasurer of PEN. He rushed to the Central Hotel, closed the account, and announced to the international poet: 'That's the end of that, Grieve. Bed and breakfast for you from now on.'

I discovered when I reached *The Scotsman* that Grieve had a feud with the paper which had lasted for many years. According to John Buchanan, this had started when Grieve, in a book he had published as the author, had lifted a whole article from *The Scotsman*, written by somebody else, and had printed it as a complete chapter, without reference nor acknowledgement. The paper had remonstrated with him, to be abused on grounds of unfair discrimination, and Grieve apparently denounced our paper thereafter for many a day. I never became part of this warfare, and we had many a further meeting, although I found his philosophies had not much advanced from earlier simplicities. When he died I realised that I had known him for over fifty years.

I have mentioned another Grieve, Bob, to whom I grew close and who, in my terms, did much more for Scotland. Scotland owes much to him. He became Professor Sir Robert Grieve, our leading planner, who left his professional chair and his advisory work for several Secretaries of State to become chairman of the Highlands and Islands Development Board. He gave that body more purpose than most of the incumbents. It had always been a strange puzzle to me why our paths crossed so late as they did, for we were of an age; had been brought up in working-class Glasgow; had suffered unemployment in the depression years of the late 1920s; but, more importantly, had taken to the hills at about the same time, until each of us knew every corner of Scotland. Yet we never met at that time, and the only hills I have ever climbed with him are in Norway. My hill climbing had been more hill walking, while Bob became one of our most renowned alpinists. On the day his grand-daughter was born he led two severe first-time climbs in the Black Mount. By the attractive convention of organised cliff men he was invited to name the two climbs, and he called one Grand-daughter's Gully; the other after himself as a grandfather. He went to Norway to learn their form of cross-country ski-ing, still not much practised in this country.

Bob Grieve came with us on some of the cruises run round the West Coast by the National Trust for Scotland. I, along with Dorothy, led these cruises for many years, first as deputy to the unforgettable Jim Robertson, the shipping man, and later on my own. We were all the willing slaves of the driving genius of the Trust's director, (Sir) Jamie Stormonth-Darling, who took great financial risks in the setting up of these famous cruises. They were enormous adventures. What with them and our family sailing, I have landed on practically every one of the inhabited islands of Scotland, and many of the uninhabited ones. There came with us, especially in the Norwegian ship *Meteor*, great ornithologists and archaeologists, like James Fisher (the only man I have known personally who has landed on Rockall), James Richardson, with the great title of HM Inspector of Ancient Monuments, George Waterston, Chris Milne, Bob Cumming, Joe Eggeling and Seton Gordon. On the small islands it was sufficient to put the people ashore and let them roam about, but sometimes we made treks across parts of the far mainland, and there must be some still around who remember being led down some track at the end of a hill day, by David Wemyss — the Earl of Wemyss and March, president of our National Trust — playing bagpipe tunes on a mouth organ.

Since we are so far away at this point from douce orthodoxy, I must remember the name of my kinsman Malcolm Campbell, with whom I used to fraternise in Berlin on my visits there in holiday time, and where he worked as a correspondent for an American news agency. He seemed to be far from a brisk news-getter, being more concerned with the Celtic remnants in European settlements where they had left their names as bits of the geography. He was a student of such soldiers of fortune as Field-Marshall Keith, whom the Germans think is one of theirs, even to the pronunciation. Malcolm himself, in his slightly vague way, had seen the making of some history. He knew the early Hitler in the years soon after World War I. Germany was in chaos, with roving bands and no thread of government. Malcolm had obtained from some source a smart British officer's dress tunic, with wide lapels, and cut in to the waist, and as he wore it about the streets this youngish revolutionary agitator, who was calling himself Adolf Hitler, began to pester Malcolm to sell the tunic to him. Malcolm fobbed him off for some time, and the price went up, so to get rid of him he sold it to the fellow, and Hitler strutted off with it, adopting an even more precise style of militarism. It amused Malcolm to note that, always after that, Hitler wore a jacket of exactly that same cut. Trust a Campbell to be in on the start of some movement! Not only that, but Malcolm had had a hair-raising encounter with Mussolini, although he was not able so accurately to document this one. During one of the early street shoot-ups in post-World War I Berlin he had fled from the street along with some other passers-by and taken refuge in a deserted office room above the fighting. Another refugee was a short thick-set Italian who was so curious about the events of the revolution that he kept fearlessly hanging out of the window to see the fighting. The room was dark, but Malcolm remained certain that this was in fact Mussolini, learning how to exploit civic unrest.

We called once in Berlin upon an old Scoto-German warrior called Campbell-Jäger, who had been a colonel in the Prussian army. He was elderly, and looked exactly like a stage Prussian; but Scotland meant much to him, and he often visited Argyll. He was outspokenly anti-Nazi; but once told us that the men had been to mend his telephone. This meant of course that they had installed a listening tap, so conversation had to proceed with many a finger to lips, and lifted eyebrows.

When war eventually broke out Malcolm got home to Argyll by way of Sweden. I tried to persuade him to write of his adventures with the dictators, for he had often after these first encounters interviewed each of them. But he was on another tack. He set to and wrote an enormous semi-fictional book, fey and full of Celtic mysticism, apparently about the resurgence of our old gods, who according to him dwelt, awaiting the call, under the island of Arran in the Firth of Clyde. No publisher wanted to touch it.

My visits to Germany, holiday or official and especially to Berlin, were also useful in allowing me to report to Neil Gunn on how his books were selling there. The big book shops in Unter den Linden often had full window displays devoted to Neil Gunn, whose stories were mainly concerned with the hardships of dispossessed Highlanders in their own land. Gentle Neil imagined that his success in Germany was due to the fact that the Nazi regime accepted the books as anti-English establishment; but I like to think their other merits were clear, even in

Nazi Germany. Anyway, great sums in royalties piled up for Gunn in Germany, and since their treasury regime would not allow the export of funds, he and his wife went occasionally to Berlin and lived it up on the proceeds in some sumptuous hotel.

One of my modest contributions to the arts was to be a governor of Pitlochry Festival Theatre for well over twenty years. A fellow governor was another friend from Edinburgh called Lord Clyde, who was Lord President of the Council, which meant that he was the senior judge in Scotland. There was a unique family tradition there because he had been dux of Edinburgh Academy, a qualified lawyer and Member of Parliament, Lord Advocate and eventually, Lord President of the Council. His father had followed exactly the same course and had held all these honours also in his day. Clyde had fascinating stories to tell about such personalities as F.E. Smith, who as Lord Birkenhead came to address the students of Oxford at some meeting when Clyde was president of a students' gathering, possibly the Union. With one or two fellow students he met the great man and escorted him to the hall, becoming aware that he was far gone in alcohol. Birkenhead noted their suspicions and said, 'Don't worry, it's only my legs. When you've introduced me as the speaker I want two of you to take an elbow on each side and lift me forward and rest me on the lectern. I'll be all right then.' So he was and the speech was brilliant.

Clyde's father had had a similar tale. As Lord Advocate for Scotland he had to brief the young F.E. Smith to support him in making the government case for some Scottish Bill. The briefing took place in a room in the House of Commons in which Smith had already installed some bottles of champagne, which he poured into glasses and perched here and there about the bookshelves, the window ledges, the desks and even the chairs; with that earlier Lord Clyde presenting the case Smith listened and questioned, all the time swooping about the room snatching up a glass and draining it until the drinks were done, by which time he had mastered the brief. The Lord Clyde I knew had a large house in the country in the topmost floor of which he had installed a huge toy railway, handsomely landscaped with tunnels and hills, most of which, he told me gleefully, had been made out of pulped copies of *The Scotsman*.

Much closer to me and entirely endearing was Harald Leslie, later Lord Birsay, who became chairman of the Scottish Land Court with the full rank of a judge. He had been the sheriff of no fewer than seven Scottish counties and had been in everything — in every good cause — chairman of this and that and greatly concerned with homeless boys, national savings, the Scottish National Dictionary, the RAF cadets, and above all concerned with the cause of Scotland. He was the most memorable Scottish orator of my time, with a great booming sonorous voice that no one who heard it will ever forget. Moreover he loved a ploy and a dram with it. The Birsays had a home in Orkney and Harald used to lapse back most readily into Orcadian speech. I called once on him in mid-morning at that house looking down over the lands and the Brough of Birsay, and in no time at all he and I were installed on either side of a great peat fire with a large glass of Highland Park in our hands, while he was announcing: 'My, Ally-ster — me is richt blythe to see thee.'

Also in the law was the 100-year-old Sheriff Wilton, who used to call on me in *The Scotsman* office to promote the cause which he had flogged at for over fifty years. The sheriff had been retired for far longer than he had ever worked at the law and he had devoted these years to an attempt to get a Civil List pension for the two spinster daughters of the man who he claimed had invented finger-printing as a means of identification; whereas Scotland Yard, supported by the Home Office, steadfastly maintained that the system had been invented by some Japanese. He used to tell me stories about how he had dangled the little girls on his knee when they were babies. But they were now elderly and enfeebled and when they died he died too, and I never heard what came of his campaign. He was a brusque, bearded little man with a good eye and a firm handshake; coming to my office up and down the steps, of which there were plenty inside *The Scotsman* building, he was generally accompanied by his seventy-four-year-old son, who was a done old man.

For the last dozen years of his life I had a good friendship with Harry Lauder, 'the grand old minstrel of Scottish song' as Winston Churchill used to call him in a burst of unoriginality. As a young Scot I had gone through the usual reaction of repugnance at everything Harry Lauder did and stood for, believing that he carried round the world a vision of Scotland dripping with meanness, nostalgia, false history and bogus bonhomie. However, he carried into the nearest he ever got to retirement some mysterious quality, not only of the great entertainer but the great philosopher, friend and reminder of past virtues. Whenever Churchill visited Scotland for some public occasion the grand old minstrel had to be there for a private meeting and often for a stage appearance when he would sing 'Keep Right On to the End of the Road'. John Winant, US ambassador to Britain, once asked me if I could help to persuade the British government to get Harry Lauder sent to Washington as the British Ambassador in the USA.

He proved to be a marvellous staging post for foreign visitors of some distinction who had to be conducted on various prestige tours round the British war effort. There was many a memorable scene in his big house in Strathhaven when we would sit down to an evening meal — not a dinner but a high tea, as Harry would explain — and no sooner had we sat down than he would have us all rise up while he sang a blessing over the food. In that house there was a great wall covered not with stags' heads, but with comic curly sticks which he had wielded on many a lyrical occasion on the stages of the world. With Americans he would select one of the party and lead him to this wall, cut a stick free from where it hung on ragged string and hand it to him solemnly, saying,

'Laddie, hae this frae me. That's the stick I used when I sang "I Love a Lassie" in Butte, Montana'. After the high tea we would all sit round the fire and Harry would give us his philosophy and sing many a song, for his voice kept up until the end. I once met a man in Glasgow whose father, an eminent throat specialist, had told him that Harry Lauder's throat was the finest he had ever seen for singing. He was very good at summing up people, as had always been his secret with audiences, and he knew whose leg to pull and whom to treat straight. We were sitting there one night with Arthur Christianson, then the eminent editor of the *Daily Express*, which he had been for many years, and Chris was pressing the old man with sceptical questions with Harry patiently replying and explaining. At last Harry turned to me and said, shaking his head, for I had brought Chris, 'Oh laddie, it's an awfu' job educatin' the English.'

At one of these nightly ceilidhs I once had the extraordinarily embarrassing experience of prompting Harry's memory in one of his own songs. To keep the conversation going I had asked him, 'Harry, of all the songs you have ever sung, which is your own favourite?' The old man was much too shrewd to give a direct answer to any such question and he said to me in reply, 'What's your favourite, laddie?' and I immediately said, 'The Lass of Killiecrankie.' Thereupon he started to sing it:

In days of old I used to be
the smartest lad that you could see.
The King he even wanted me
  to go and join the army . . .

and at that point he stopped, dried up completely. He had forgotten the words. There flashed wildly through my head an agonising decision. Should I prompt him? Would that be too embarrassing? How could I cover him up? Should I just resume the conversation, or lead a little polite applause? I suppose a second or two passed before I made my move. I started singing offhandedly as if I had been singing with him all along:

Now I'm growin' auld and frail . . .

'Naw, naw,' said Harry, butting in, 'naw, naw. . .' but I was of course right. The old master frowned to himself for a second or two, nudging at his brain and then his face suddenly cleared and away he went, the old minstrel:

Now I'm growin' auld and frail
like a dug withoot a tail
ower the heid o' Jean McPhail
the Lass o' Killiecrankie.

and we were away again.

Harry had a lot of pedantic opposition from serious Scots for most of his lifetime, but his own gallant story carried the day and I suppose some of us came to realise that it wasn't because he was the great clown who had suddenly become a great prototype of Scotland. It was simply because we hadn't enough famous men of other kinds around.

It was a wartime event on the fringes of the arts that gave me my first contact with Sir Iain Moncrieff of that Ilk, whom I was to come to know, and for that matter be his chairman at many a laughter-filled meeting as he addressed National Trust and other gatherings on the subjects of heraldry, history and pretty nearly anything else that came to his mind at the time, especially his ancestors of whom he seemed to have more than most of us, and all with labels of some distinction. Somebody had decided to make a patriotic wartime film called 'We'll Meet Again' starring Vera Lynn, and I was asked if I could arrange to produce a part of the British Army into which the hero of this film could be fictionally deployed. By the usual routes, as they say, I got us a few days shooting with the 5th Battalion of the Scots Guards at Chelsea Barracks, to discover that Iain was the adjutant of this body of men. The highlight of this epic was a far from military scene when Vera Lynn, seated on a bench, sang, 'Gin a Body, Meet a Body, Comin' through the Rye' while five Scots Guard pipers, ringed round her, played the tune on the bagpipes. No concert soprano has been able to shout down five Scots Guards pipers, but the whole scene was shot with Vera mouthing away, to do it again in some studio without the pipes so that it could be dubbed in.

The greatest man I have ever known and worked with in terms of influence and inspiration was the late Tom Johnston whose chief press officer I was for all the wartime years, first when he was Regional Commissioner for Civil Defence and then when he was Secretary of State for Scotland. His name is far from forgotten, but there are fewer people about who knew him, or remember the time when his name rang round Scotland for years on end as the one man to whom we could look for our vision of what Scotland might become. To be sure he was never well known outside of Scotland although he had held high political office in the British scene. He was the first politician of top rank and quality in ten generations who had devoted himself utterly and exclusively to Scotland.

He was at it earlier than most. At the age of twenty-one he was elected to the School Board of Kirkintilloch, and to keep him out of mischief they side-tracked him on to the convenership of the Evening Classes Committee. In the by-going he pioneered school meals for the local children, simply because many of them were too hungry to be able to learn in class. The evening classes were a different matter, being attended by a few reluctant conscripts. Since there were official grants going for teaching, he invented the notion that a dancing class would bring the mobs in, and so it did, the qualification for attendance being a ticket of enrolment at some more pedantic course of study. Soon he got a boxing class going on the same basis, and this proved to be a pack-out as well. Indeed, it was too successful, and the wave of denunciation started up on the grounds that the young councillor and his colleagues were teaching licence and bloodshed. They stopped him.

This sort of experience was a good apprenticeship. There were scenes in a wider context when as a junior minister at the Scottish Office he became chairman of the Marketing Committee of the old Empire Marketing Board just at a time when the Scottish farmers in the north-east were unable to find markets for their splendid Aberdeen-Angus beef. In no time at all Tom Johnston had launched the powerful marketing apparatus of the Board into the sale of Scotch beef in the South of England, on the very reasonable grounds that Scotland was a part, indeed a substantial and founding part, of the British Empire. The hoardings filled up with succulent posters, and sales started to boom under the influence of a selling apparatus designed to promote British demand for New Zealand lamb, Canadian cheese, and other desirable commodities which many Scots thought were more worthily and desirably supplied around our own door. He next embarked on a scheme to swap Scotch herrings (also having lean times commercially) for Jamaican citrus fruits, and was having a splendid time in this area also until the Treasury managed finally to get him stopped.

However he was proving more difficult to stop, and was fast learning the techniques of respectable circumvention. He was also pretty adroit at putting his case. Much of this stemmed from the pamphleteering and propaganda work which he learned in a hard school of journalism on the newspaper *Forward*, founded, needless to say, by himself. This early socialist weekly differed from all its dim contemporaries in the fact that it used the popular newspaper devices in a good-humoured way to put over its message. There were comic strips, fiction serials, hilarious footnotes, mickey-taking interviews, gossip columns, reports in depth. In this school also Tom learned or developed his great flair for getting the facts. Nobody who dealt with him in later years ever risked taking a half-baked story or proposition to him and he was often able to overcome even ingenious opposition by simply a dogged production of facts that refuted flamboyant and emptier claims.

Everything he did, however, was a mere toning-up in preparation for what he was to do when he became Secretary of State for Scotland. The appointment was remarkable in any case, because Tom Johnston had really declared his intention to retire from political life. I don't think he was in any way an enthusiastic politician. He saw politics as a useful instrument with all sorts of devices and aids which could be prised loose by a resourceful hand and applied to practical ends. I think he saw that by accepting the senior political appointment in Scotland he could suddenly command a situation in which he might be able to work off a lengthy agenda of items which were in his mind essential to the long-term health of the country, and this is what he set out to do.

There existed in Scotland certain local or domestic government departments which had a surprisingly large amount of autonomy and which provided a setting within which apt consideration could be given to the problems that would exist for our country as soon as the war finished. Tom Johnston made it known and demonstrated that he was going to devote himself to these considerations. He started by gathering all the MPs of every party in two or three meetings and telling them something of his vision of the future and the difficulties that would be waiting for us on such a scale that we would pretty soon be doubting if we had really won the war, which of course we intended to do in the meantime.

He started to develop the theme of common agreement. Our national characteristic and hobby was argument, and he went about telling people that it might be a better idea if they all met and decided what it was we agreed on, not what we disagreed on; and having found certain points in common we should go strongly for these. He got Winston Churchill to agree that he set up what he called a Council of State — a name with constitutional pitfalls which experts were swift to point out. This body consisted of all the active former Secretaries of State for Scotland, some of whom were still in substantial office in the government or public life. They agreed with Tom that if there was any subject on which they were united for the benefit of Scotland the Prime Minister and the cabinet would be bound to accept it and let us go ahead. Immediately he had immense political leverage right through from the roots to the treetops, and he started to use it. It was this Council of State that unitedly endorsed his idea that the water power possibilities of Highland rains and rivers should be harnessed to create hydro-electric power which would in turn feed electricity into the paraffin-lit homes of the north and west, and the surplus power would be sold to benefit these neglected regions who in the whole world of energy had only this one asset. The profitable schemes would pay for uneconomic schemes. The cabinet took the whole idea and approved it. The time was found for debates and a major bill went through both Houses of Parliament without a division.

The thing started on the side of Loch Lomond with the head-waters coming from a dam at Loch Sloy, a lost glen lying below the western ridge which had once been the headquarters of the Macfarlane clan and where no living soul now dwelt. We had a great party the day the first sod of the Loch Sloy scheme was cut. There was no trifling with an inscribed silver spade. At the appropriate moment Mrs Johnston climbed aboard the biggest bulldozer that could be found, put it into gear and swept forward, slicing up an immense carpet of turf. This was in 1945, and most of what has happened in the years since to provide very substantial up-grading to the remote parts of Scotland has stemmed from that moment and the social responsibility that was implied in the act. Later, Tom Johnston became chairman of the board

207

and kept it on course as he saw it for years of his dynamic retirement.

The same vigour went into his decision that tourism was going to form a large part of our post-war endeavours and provide a lot of the overseas income we were going to need. Again the Council of State gave its unanimous nod. A committee of enquiry was set up and all was ready to make an immediate post-war start. Preliminary to this, however, was a typical characteristic touch of practicality. To clinch the assets that lay within the usual vague supposition of many visitors that they have remote Scottish ancestral connections, Tom set up the Scots Ancestry Research Council, which will in practical terms find you a granny or two. He got the money by asking the late Earl of Rosebery to hand over for the public good his race winnings gained when his horse Blue Peter won the Derby.

There were his famous wartime endeavours to develop in Scottish schools the art of cookery and housekeeping on a really substantial scale, much opposed by the pedants. He set afoot the celebrated nationwide competitions for the best recipes for cooking herrings and potatoes. He saw that the great new emergency hospitals that had been built at the beginning of the war to accommodate the enormous number of air raid casualties were standing idle, because the air raids had not turned out that way, so he started pushing into them all the waiting list patients who had accumulated in depressed civilian ranks during most of the 1930s. And for these people, wartime proved to be a more benevolent social scene than the stricken days of peace. No one ever excelled him at getting to the real root of any problem. Sir Horace Hamilton, who had known all the notable politicians and public men in government in his distinguished career once told me that the only person he had ever known who could match Tom Johnston at getting to the real heart of a situation was Lloyd George.

It is pleasant to remember also what he was really like. To look at his photographs now you will see a face which could be given the description of dour. He was very far from dour. If you look closely at the photographs you will see the good humour in the eyes and the explosive laughter about to come seething from the thin-looking lips. In fact, he laughed a great deal, and to travel with him about Scotland by one precarious means of transport or another was to move in a good humoured ceilidh with plenty of jokes and mimicry and anecdotes, and a great deal of fun. He gave speeches and private talks and off-the-record discussions with local authorities and gatherings all over Scotland, even in the most remote parts, and there was never one of these discourses which did not include a glimpse of a good and prosperous, if hard-working, post-war future for Scotland. He was, of course, a political nationalist, but far more important, he was determined that the immediate task should always be to get on with improving the place as you found it, and not to wait for some millennium arising out of a political majority.

Often he used to tell some of us in late night discussions that this

208

remained the most important task. 'Unless we get things going in Scotland now and develop our own resources,' he would say, 'you chaps will inherit a poors' house' — as if we were a kind of embryo Scottish cabinet. Sometimes it wasn't only a poors' house but a graveyard, but the message was clear. Do what lay at one's hand and the political solutions would be that much easier. Eventually he went to cabinet meetings and the House of Commons and the Scottish Office in London with a lot of reluctance, and only because he could there effect some benefit for the northern land. This he did with implacable ingenuity. I remember him once telling some of us of a cabinet meeting he attended when he had said, 'Gentlemen, if I don't get this for Scotland, I am going to tell the 51st Division when they come home from the war to bring their bloody bayonets with them!'

Even in the remote Highlands people recognised him as someone who spoke for all Scotland and was devoted to them, Lowlander as he was. He had a feeling for the Scottish destiny and in return Scotland gave him a loyalty and renown that no other Scot of our time has received or deserved.

It is true that certainly nowadays he is not much known beyond Scotland, but this would not have worried him. Indeed, it would have confirmed his long-held view that Scotland needed to create her own standards in dignity. In the end he refused all power and pomp, and was able to write for himself an epilogue like this:

In the comparative obscurity and quietude of common citizenship in this realm, may it be counted to me for something of wisdom and in expiation of my manifold follies and ineptitudes, that the message I was able to give my countrymen was that in co-operation and mutual aid and not in fratricidal strife can we win through to material plenty for all, and to a spiritual and cultural development and greatness for each of us.

I do not know anything that more aptly expresses the modest nobility of a true Scottish aspiration. It was because he carried it out better than anyone before or since that Scotland and Scots keep him in our hearts, as he had done with us.

CHAPTER THIRTEEN
The Most Vulnerable Profession

The more I see of the world the more I realise that the whole affair could do with some tidy editing. It is probably the case that this assumption, however arrogant, is the one which leads newspaper men into other aspects of business life, and if you think of it, it is astonishing how many journalists you find turning up in business. This profitable deviation is one which draws contempt from your dedicated journalist. I remember how my marvellous George McCarthy, whom I rescued from the foundering *Daily Herald* to make him London financial editor of *The Scotsman*, practically repudiated me when he realised I was leaving newspapers to go into business in the form of the oil industry. He behaved like a dedicated believer to one who had betrayed the faith of his fathers and become converted for money, wrongly as it turned out, to some more glamorous and picturesque religion. I am afraid I never had this purist dedication, believing in ends rather than means.

As it happens I had a more comprehensive introduction to the trade than most of my mentors. I was myself a weekly newspaper man, trained in the tradition and recognising it as not inferior to any other. The greatest virtue of any newspaper is its involvement with its readership and the weekly newspaper has this quality to a supreme degree. All that I knew best in principle, practice and even in techniques was learned in weekly newspapers, and anything done later and perhaps in a larger setting was maybe writ larger, but not necessarily sounder. Editorship is of course an aspect of management, and when I came to that stage and abided in it for most of my time I had already behind me so much in detail of production and technique and general know-how, because I had covered it all, that I knew better than most of the high-grade specialists whom I had to manage how to do almost anything in the way of newspaper production. It reminded me of a conversation I once had with the man who became General Sir Horatio Murray, at one time General Officer Commanding the Army in Scotland as well as Governor of Edinburgh Castle, who later became the Deputy Commander of the whole of NATO forces. He asked me once to accompany him on a tour of inspection of some of his command outposts throughout Scotland, divisions and battalions being posted here and there north and west of Edinburgh. Chatting with him one night I asked how he was able so accurately to put his finger on the deficiencies and potential gaps in performance of these remoter units, and he said, 'Alastair, I was an Army lieutenant for thirteen years and they can't kid me.' He had slogged it out in a desperately run-down defence establishment and, like the rest of us, had learned the hard way.

It is possible to write with contrived self-righteousness about the independence of the press, and how nobly editors have, in their day, held to this against all odds. I was more fortunate than most, especially when I got to *The Scotsman*, when Roy Thomson did in fact take no part in forming the editorial policy and direction of any of his newspapers. His idea was simply to make money from them, but he did it in the sense of providing the community with the sort of papers they wanted and deserved, and it was always a great puzzle to him why some of his so-called regional newspapers, in districts which were largely industrial and in the old radical tradition, did not support the Socialist cause; but that he felt was up to his editors. Newspaper editors in their memoirs or reminiscences make fairly large claims to have sustained the great moralities of independence. However, most of them are there because proprietors tend to select as editors people more or less like-minded with themselves.

Otherwise it is a solitary job, and when the heat comes on it is amazing how many colleagues step back imperceptibly from the discomfort. Thinking of General Murray and the many predecessors of his, and those who succeeded him, all of whom I have known well, I have come to the belief that, of all the professions, the one nearest to being an editor is that of a general in the British Army. He lives in the same world of day-to-day opportunism and decision, with the need to motivate large and disparate groups of men, and the privilege of coming to a part of his decision by the consensus of first-rate professional juniors; knowing that, at the crunch, he is on his own. Lawyers and doctors and accountants do not have this interesting predicament. They have things tied up professionally among them and when things go wrong they close ranks.

There is a tendency which is becoming very clear in this country and which gives me much concern. This is the fact of a growing distrust of the press in general. We have few friends. Everybody has a story against the press. Everybody has been offended at some time in some way by a newspaper story. I used to tell my colleagues: 'Every sentence in *The Scotsman* offends someone. Even if it's true. Especially if it's true. There is someone who didn't want that published.' I used to illustrate this editorial predicament in a parable, which has become something of a legend, called 'The Banks of Allan Water'.

This fancy arose out of a trip I made to Bridge of Allan in the early days as editor of *The Scotsman*. I had been asked to go and address some gathering of people about newspapers and as I sat alone in a railway carriage, pondering what I might say, there came into my head the

211

words of that sentimental and rather tragic old Scots ballad 'The Banks of Allan Water'. I found myself singing it, being in good voice at the time. The words go something like this:

On the banks of Allan Water
When the sweet spring time did fall
Was the miller's lovely daughter,
Fairest of them all.
For his bride a soldier sought her
And a winning tongue had he.
On the banks of Allan Water,
None so gay as she.

On the banks of Allan Water
Where brown autumn spread its store
Was the miller's lovely daughter
But she smiled no more.
For the summer grief had brought her
And the soldier false was he.
On the banks of Allan Water,
None so sad as she.

The third and last verse then goes on to describe the girl being abandoned by her lover, dying of a broken heart and the disgrace; and there she is lying dead beside the Allan Water with the winter blasts blowing and the snow falling heavily. A very sad tale indeed.

It struck me that this little human story might at one time have been true and it occurred to me to ponder what might happen if in fact it were absolutely true and *The Scotsman* had decided to publish it. So there it is in the paper and the story illustrates the pitfalls of newspaper editorship.

The first thing that would happen would be that the editor would get a call the next morning from the public relations officer of the Scottish Association of Master Millers saying that the President's attention had been drawn — their attention is always drawn, they've never read it themselves — to the story in *The Scotsman* which reflected severely upon the morals of the families of master millers. It was well known that millers were exemplary husbands and fathers and their children were models of rectitude. He would expect us to publish a full apology withdrawing the allegations in the next morning's paper, giving it, of course, a space equal to that occupied by the offensive story in the original.

There would then be a friendly call from one of the bosses of a Scottish bank saying, 'We're all men of the world; we know how these things are readily misunderstood' — he was speaking in his capacity of chairman of the Committee of Joint Stock Bank General Managers — he understood quite well how things were but some of their older customers had been very disturbed and, as it happened, all the major

Scottish banks had a branch office in Bridge of Allan where the story was set. Would we mind putting in a statement saying that the reference to the Banks of Allan Water had nothing to do with the Scottish branch banks who were represented there. And then of course there would be a call from Mr Waters who lived at Bridge of Allan and Mr Allan who lived at Bridge of Allan, and even a Mr Allan Waters, no doubt demanding public apologies and making it clear that they weren't the Allan or the Waters or the Allan Waters referred to in this libellous story.

We're only beginning, because almost immediately, a spokesman would be on the telephone from the Scottish Tourist Board saying that the chairman was furious about this wintry scene depicted in Allan Water which was a famed tourist resort. Did *The Scotsman* not know that the sunshine record in the Isle of Tiree was higher than the sunshine record in the Isle of Wight? Then there would be the Scottish chairman of the British Legion on, saying he repudiated the whole story about this soldier and in any case, *The Scotsman* had been too cowardly to print the name of the soldier and were we perfectly sure it wasn't a sailor? Then a nice young fellow would come in great trouble to the front counter of the newspaper saying that all his friends in the factory were laughing at him because they knew his girlfriend lived in Bridge of Allan and her name was Miller, and everyone was saying, 'Is that true about your girl, she's gay!' And many other interventions, like the chief executive of the Stirling District Council saying that ever since their council made an arrangement with the Central Region for the joint use of the new mortuary building in Stirling, dead people just didn't lie around in Bridge of Allan any longer. And there's no end to it, it goes on and on, with over the ensuing weeks lots of telephone calls and letters from other ladies all over Britain saying they had read this story and it was very like something that had happened to a friend of theirs and could we give them the name and address of the soldier.

It all underlines the fact that an editor lives in the constant nightmare of knowing perfectly well that it's very dangerous to print the exact truth. The truth, in other words, is not enough.

Newspaper men do not even try to explain to the citizens what our job is and how we do it; and how we do it in their name. We have tasks to perform in newspapers which are not much understood by the public and which are all too well understood and not much liked by the politicians. When I was a member of the Council of the Commonwealth Press Union I tried to persuade my colleagues to float the idea of a world Newspaper Day, when we in newspapers would take it upon ourselves to explain our task to the public in whose name we were exercising the various freedoms that we had. We would publish articles, speak to bodies like the Rotary Clubs, and Publicity Clubs and Chambers of Commerce; celebrate people in other countries who were suffering for defying censorship; and in general make it clear that whatever our virtues, and our excesses and even our abuses, these were exercised in the name of the public because the rights belong to them and the excesses and the abuses were being nurtured by them if they supported the wrong kind of prints. I tried to convince the CPU that when the freedom of the press and of the printed word was being fought for and won, not many ordinary citizens complained about our excesses, for they were excesses of principle and non-conformity, and I believe that in the times of these early struggles the people of what were about to become the Western democracies recognised that we were struggling to gain a right in their name and that people died for it.

Nothing happened, and the good people of the CPU still take part in their genteel international conferences while the lights go out in so many countries in the world where the word is printed. Journalists, and those who care about what we do, seem to talk about the freedom of print as being one of the freedoms we have won forever. But it may turn out to be one of the freedoms that man has taken into his hands for a short time and then lost, because we didn't care about it enough. Today even in our own country we have to consider a whole area of debasement in our own profession — great organs of circulation masquerading as newspapers and periodicals exploiting one of the hardest won of all human freedoms, turning our personal adventure into a pander's gold mine.

There are a many great public individual voices raised from time to time in favour of the principle of the freedom of the press and I find it difficult to trust any one of them. You cannot expect local or national politicians, involved with the thrust for power as the main goal, to see as clearly as we do the balance of a local or national question. It is no time to be bashful about this aspect of modern journalism. I for one have never been prepared, and I have declared this in public many times, to concede to even a democratically elected parliament or assembly (some of whom seem to be giving away our liberties) the sole right to judge what is best in the interests of the community or the state. This matter of the 'public interest' must remain largely in the hands of the newspapers. I believe in that description of our profession given by Carlyle and Macaulay — 'the fourth estate'. That is what we are, an estate of the realm. If we do not speak for some causes, nobody else will. It was common for me as editor of *The Scotsman* to have Establishment friends mention some leader or article to me privately and say, 'That needed saying' or 'I have been saying that for years'. But not one of these informants was likely to write a letter in support, or say a public word.

I have found American newspapers to be much more valiant, if only because their country believes that patriotism is not a naïve quality to be dealt with by urbane cynicism. I once spent three months touring the United States and found, in remote corners, small towns where the focus of the place was the local newspaper. I remember a small, southern town which had fallen into grievous hardship in the depression years and even the zest for leadership had died out. The editor of the local paper, in almost a one-man effort, rallied the whole town. He organised meetings, he raised funds, he listed and printed the assets of the place, the technical and educational achievements and possibilities, the roads and rail and other communications, the water and power resources. They printed an expensive booklet about this, burst their budget to find a highly-paid salesman and sent him to the north to sell some businessmen the idea of starting up a branch factory in their town. And he did. He got several. One led to another. And my friend the editor was like a cheerful schoolboy as he showed me round his flourishing town, especially in and out of the classrooms of a new high school they had built for themselves.

There was another town I wanted to visit in another state where I hoped to meet the mayor and the local Tennessee Valley Authority representative, and the agricultural adviser, and the banker, and somebody to do with education. I phoned ahead to the editor of the local paper and asked him if he would be good enough to try to arrange for me to see some of these people, mentioning the time when I hoped to arrive. When I got off the bus there was somebody waiting to take me to the newspaper office. There all the officials I had mentioned had been gathered together ready to be asked my questions. That newspaper office too had become the central meeting point, the powerhouse of the town's ideas and forward movement. This is involvement, this is identification. These papers had become the official organ of all the development potential in their circulation areas and they reflected in a way I had never seen, or thought possible, the interests of the citizens.

It seemed to me also that they had kept their independence, and this is important, for if you find yourself always in full accord with the interests of the majority of citizens, it is time to look at your editorial commitments. One of the best editors I ever knew, who died at the age of ninety-two, once told me, 'A journalist should never join anything.' It is a severe injunction, but he meant that if you abandon your objective authority and start supporting a cause which is not in the general interest you may find that your judgement is distorted every time the cause becomes news. It is probably this aspect of newspaper life that leads politicians to dislike the press. They tend to see cases and causes either very light or very dark, one extreme or the other, and that is their job, but journalists and the rest of us know that the truth generally lies somewhere in the middle half-tones.

Publishing a paper outside of London has many difficulties. Overmanning has never been a problem with us, but just as the main problem of Scotland is England, so the main problem of non-London newspapers is Fleet Street. The Fleet Street newspapers have made our whole British newspaper scene entirely lopsided for they spend money, as Roy Thomson used to say, like drunken sailors. They are not busy enough personally and they have invented for themselves the phrase 'the national press' with the aim of making the rest of us, if we were so disposed, feel like remote provincials. However, Fleet Street has ceased to be the Mecca of good, young journalists and there is far better writing and research and the essential community involvement going on away from Fleet Street than there will ever be in it now. I look at some of the productions that once had great names and marvel at how the people who run them and produce them think they can possibly commend them to any kind of public, even one with little expectation. A paper itself has to be a personality in its own right. It has to speak with a distinctive accent and must not become the vehicle of one or two distinguished named journalists or personalities. There must be an editorial theme, distinctive and recognisable, running through pretty nearly everything, and even if some of the items run athwart that theme, they should be at a recognisable tangent to it. I see newspapers nowadays, for I am only a newspaper reader, which are like the Speaker's Corner in Hyde Park, filled occasionally with people who put up their soapboxes and lay about them with no editorial perspective whatever in mind. It is clear that most of them are owned by people with more money than sense, and if they think their ownership has given them some kind of power they cannot even be reading their own newspapers. It has all become a part of the great British deception, which most people in these islands have now rumbled, that London is the centre of everything. Moreover, in their incessant sales and resales and reversed takeovers and swaps they have robbed good journalists, the historians of the day, of honest continuity. These practices are not new in newspapers but they have lately spread far afield. I have in my time as a journalist been in seven takeovers, shut-downs or amalgamations. That's enough for anybody. Nor should journalists ever be deceived by thinking that when there are difficulties, the public will rush to their aid. They will not. They dislike us and rejoice in our difficulties. We have failed to explain to our readers that we are the custodians of one of their own limited liberties and that however badly we do it, we do it in their name.

Newspapers and journalists have no special privileges. We have no rights beyond the rights possessed by every individual citizen of this land. To be sure we have more facilities and if you go around asking questions with plenty of gear and electronics and have behind you the backup of a regular printed sheet, you appear to have authority. Journalists sometimes turn up even in one's own tail who are led to exercise this false authority with pressure for which there is no warrant. In the many years I was an editor there was much to forgive because of the occasional lost story and bungle, but what I never forgave the representative of a paper of mine was any kind of bullying and harassment of a decent citizen caught up in some human predicament. In British newspapers, however self-important some of them may aim to be, there is much still to do in demonstrating genuine involvement with the community they seek to serve.

The community, and especially the business and professional community, has become absurdly apprehensive about having any sort

216

of contact with the press. They have not been told how to use the press in their own interests. I once compiled a sort of Ten Commandments for people to have in mind when dealing with the media, using this in talks to gatherings of various sorts, when often the meetings' secretaries would ask me for copies and distribute them. They were merely simple suggestions and rules, like this:

The best relationship with newspapers is to be achieved in normal times when there is no critical situation afoot. However, the time comes when management is being pressed personally, or on the telephone, for information about something important that has happened. The heat is on, and some response must be made. Here are 'Ten Commandments' — points of guidance which may be useful.

1 Don't say 'No comment'. Nobody is asking you for comment — what we want are the facts — what happened? The phrase was used by President Roosevelt in important wartime conferences and it has become a pretentious way of saying nothing.

2 If possible tell the facts — all the facts. There is less harm in the truth than nothing. The press will get a story from somewhere. By the time they come on to you they have probably got one anyway. If you don't make a statement your case may go by default and you may appear to accept the facts as stated from other sources.

3. Try not to tell anything 'off the record'. Journalists don't want to hear things off the record. They want to know only what they can print. Very occasionally it may be necessary to give a confidential background to do justice to the story but don't try to make this an excuse for censoring out the topical element in what has happened.

4 Don't be interviewed by a reporter whose name you don't know. Ask him his name. He knows yours. Have him declare he is a staff reporter. All sorts of reasons for this, most of them obvious.

5 If telephoned and you want time — say so. Tell the reporter to ring back in x minutes and you will have a statement ready. Read it out and get the reporter to read it back to you.

6 If there is confusion and a lot of calls are made before you can say anything official, tell *all* the enquirers that there will be a statement at a certain time and that nothing official will be released beforehand. So long as this is not obviously a delaying tactic they will probably accept. What makes a reporter mad is the fear that his competitor may be getting something.

7 Never ask a newspaper to give you publicity. You don't buy the paper to read publicity. You buy it to read news. If you don't think it has got news come in and tell the newspaper about it and they

may find a news point. That is their job.

8 Always remember you are being interviewed. Information you give a newspaper man is for publication. He is not asking questions to gratify personal interest; and remember he is a professional.

9 If you have a relationship of trust with your local newspaper and there is a speech being made which they may not have time to cover, this might work: write out two or three paragraphs containing the main points to be made and hand it in to the newspaper guaranteeing that it will be included in the speech. Even under conditions of staff shortage they may, if they trust you, use something on that basis.

10 About public relations officials: journalists regard PROs as officials who make arrangements and facilities and they don't regard them as spokesmen. They want to speak to the people who make the decisions and who can deal with supplementary questions.

Not only are newspapers the most perishable commodity in the world, they are also the most vulnerable. We are the only profession which puts, day after day, its entire contents into the shop window, to be picked over and denounced by the public. We have no cover-up, no traditional device for fending off criticism and attack. All that we have is there for everyone to see, and this puts us into the hands of jovial or ill-natured critics who in their own fields can count on better protection. I remember a well-known surgeon who was to be seen occasionally in the club dining-room where Clem Livingstone, Hugh Gillespie and I often went for lunch. He would sit in the lounge, plentifully supplied with aperitifs, and amuse himself by marking in red ink the literal errors in the first edition of our evening paper. Now, every newspaper man well knows how unsatisfactory is his first edition. It is not that we do not know how to spell the words. It is not that we do not want to correct the spelling mistakes. Indeed by the time the paper is on the streets the typographical corrections are already in type waiting to be inserted. It is simply that there are two choices in the time available: either you put the paper away, rough as it is, and catch the trains, the buses, the vans and the vendors to take it to the sales points; or you hold it up, make the corrections, and miss the first edition sales. We do the first, as one can see, and even at that the paper is a miracle of high-speed co-ordination, production, and logistic techniques.

Our surgeon friend used to sit there, drinking and inking his copy, so that when we arrived he used to greet us with: 'Better than yesterday, Clem. Only eleven mistakes today', or 'Not so good, boys. I make it seventeen', and he would hold up the paper so that the other drinkers could share the jest.

Newspapers can readily overestimate the amount of influence they have on the thinking of the day and the aspirations of their readership.

One of the most heartening messages I ever had on becoming editor of *The Scotsman* happened the very morning Dorothy and I left for Edinburgh with our furniture in a van. Although it was early in the morning when I was about to leave the house in Glasgow Street, the telephone rang. It was Tom Johnston who had just read the item in *The Scotsman* saying that I had been appointed editor and he told me 'I want to say congratulations to you, to *The Scotsman* and to Scotland.' I spoke to him many times after that, in the years that were left to him, about campaigns that I felt were important and where his advice was always worth while. Some of these skirmishes with authority we won and others we only half won. Journalists should never display medals for the campaigns which they have often overdramatised, but it is a zestful side of the business and it gratifies the reformist ambitions which one may have had on entering a profession at all. I have never, for example, believed in any kind of censorship whatever, and one of the items which solaced one in *The Scotsman* was that for many years I honestly believed that our aim towards quality of style and thinking and even writing would prevail in the end, since there would be a gradual upgrading of taste and people would come to see how they were being deceived and would repudiate the other thing in the other kind of newspapers. It may be happening, but it is happening very slowly, and one generation may easily lose the ground a former generation has painfully won.

One of my young reporters in the *Daily Record* once brought to me a selection of horror comics which were selling for a few pennies to children of any age. They were printed and published in America and had been imported by some of the newsagents in the British cities. They were of so repellent a character that it was unbelievable they could be sold in public and to children under ten years old who bought them with ghastly fascination. These were not sex comics. Necrophilia was a common theme. Dead mothers, their faces eaten away into a half skull by the corruption of the grave, would rise in their shrouds and haunt their own young children. We did not even need a very long printed campaign nor did we try to spin it out. A few of the new, post-war Members of Parliament joined us as we denounced the whole thing and the House of Commons quickly banned the import and sale of these horror comics. I see that something of the same is going on today with the revelations that horror video tapes are available to quite young children.

A healthier campaign we ran also in the *Daily Record* was centred round the brilliant work done by an extraordinary Anglo-American character from Sussex called Joe Hobbs, who had made a fortune as a rum-runner during the prohibition days in America. He had a big, powerful yacht offshore in California and, being a skilled navigator (he was skilful at nearly everything, including what the Canadians call 'shooting the bull'), had no difficulties in getting supplies ashore. He would talk freely about these ploys, including the occasional times when he was asked to take to sea for an ostensible fishing trip some cuckolded husband whose wife was engaged in dalliance. Even now the names he mentioned freely had better not be spoken, but when Joe had made his pile he came to Scotland and bought Inverlochy Castle as a gentleman's retreat. He then discovered there were one or two ailing crofts and farms on this fine stretch of land in the Great Glen and he set out to bring the Great Glen to life, giving well-paid employment to the crofters, opening lime quarries and liming the land heavily, building great shelters, and in a year or two he had the Great Glen cattle ranch running, which it seems to be doing still although he is long since gone. Seumas Adam and I used to go to stay with him in Inverlochy and discuss the campaign which we were running for the improvement of hill cattle conditions in Scotland. The first time we went there I had just bought a new car and along with it a new boiler suit for wearing while crawling under the car. Since we were going to stay only overnight I had nothing in my bag but the boiler suit, a pair of pyjamas and a toilet bag. The valet unpacked my bag in the splendid bedroom at Inverlochy and I entered the room later to discover my pyjamas laid out on the bed and the boiler suit solemnly hanging up, the only inhabitant of the immense wardrobe. We had often campaigned for improved land conditions and an official belief in the productivity of the Scottish uplands, given capital to spend on improvements, but Joe Hobbs' cattle ranch in the Great Glen was a visible proof that this could actually happen, so we worked our way towards a situation where eventually the subsidies available for the breeding of hill cattle in Scotland were much improved. There were ditching, drainage and fencing subsidies and the whole new chapter of the black cattle's return to the hills was opened up. I don't see the *Daily Record* doing much of this nowadays.

Soon after I became editor of the *Daily Record* I decided to take action about some part of my obsession that newspapers were gravely out of touch with their readers and with the real sources of news, especially when there was no crisis. So I set up, early on Friday afternoons, a meeting which could be attended by all the editorial staff, if they felt attracted to it; not only the specialist writers and the reporters, but also the sub-editors and the backroom boys who never had an opportunity to interview the makers of news. This meeting was addressed by leading figures of industry, by heads of government departments, chairmen of infant quangos, trade union chiefs, people in the arts, and indeed anyone who had come through with some significant new idea. This ran for some time before I discovered that my old friend, Bobbie Clough, editor of the *Newcastle Journal*, whose managing director he was eventually to be, was also working along the same lines. Our thoughts came together, and spread into the well-meaning if impracticable headquarters of the Kemsley Newspaper organisation, to whom we belonged. They took up some such scheme which ran, with no great urgency, until the Thomson takeover. After a time the whole thing became systematic, with a firm training scheme and awards, under the direction of Jack Bryers, whom I brought into newspapers from industry to be the training and personnel man for *The Scotsman* Publications, Ltd. It was to be an appointment which none of us was to regret.

So far as I know, there is no newspaper group which has followed the Thomson pattern of training, although some of them wait eagerly to grasp the products as they emerge. The most reprehensible area of neglect lies, as with so many other deficiencies, with the Fleet Street newspapers, who in my time at least refused to take in juniors or to do training of any kind, preferring to snatch the finished products from the non-London papers, baiting their offers with such large salary sums as these juniors will never honestly earn. I came to regret this habit not so much from a resentment at commercial opportunism, but because it cuts out from our profession the talent lying at the Fleet Street doors. Who am I to make claims for them, but it is a fact that the young Cockney boy and girl are among the liveliest youngsters in our islands; and you cannot find them in newspapers. Fleet Street will not give them a chance. The last time I found myself arguing this case with a Fleet Street editor I said to him, 'If a young and gifted Charles Dickens turned up, you would not give him a job.'

When I contemplate now what kind of an editor I was I wonder if from time to time I didn't display signs of personal weakness. I always believed in the consensus way of running newspapers. One would make a decision and see if anybody ventured to oppose it or suggest some amendment and it was always useful to have the ensuing discussion, although naturally one could always get one's own way. It depended on the wisdom of the other fellow, and perhaps on his determination. I remember when we were all set up on the eve of the Queen's Coronation in 1953. The night before, when preparing the paper for the morning of the Coronation itself, I had a huge centre spread with an axonometric picture of central London with the Coronation route. Denis Hamilton had commissioned it specially at my request and it was intended to allow citizens who were following the procession by radio and the very few who would see it on television, to move with the carriages, as it were, from street to street. And we had other tricks throughout the paper.

It was very shortly before press time when we got a flash saying that Hillary and Tensing had climbed Everest. In a moment it had been decided that that would be the lead story. I was in no doubt whatever at all about it and we flung our resources here and there, clearing the front page, deciding on one or two feature items, struggling for extra pictures and I wrote the banner heading for page one myself. It went:

EVEREST — BRIGHT NEW
JEWEL IN HER CROWN

I stayed with the teams for a time on the editorial floor and in the case room enjoying the brisk, ordered panic that so lifts the editorial heart at a time like that, and then I went into my room to contemplate one or two other things when there was a tap at the door. It was John Lees, my deputy, a tall, thin, Lesmahagow-born Glasgow University graduate who was so staunch and friendly a helper. He was saying diffidently that there was a fundamental error in my heading because Everest was not on British Commonwealth soil at all. It was part of the kingdom of Nepal, an independent state. Well, I knew all this and I just laughed, saying something to the effect that Everest itself was the triumph for these British people; their efforts had laid it at the feet of the Queen for her Coronation day. Of course we all knew Nepal was an independent and separate kingdom but Everest was a possession of honour for that magic time. And off he went.

But, he came back again on two separate occasions, pointing out that there might be diplomatic repercussions and that it would be too clumsy to have to explain to our readers that Everest was not in fact a British possession and that by merely climbing it for the first time ever our fellow countrymen had not by that act captured it as a possession of the British Crown. I was unmoved by his distress, on the grounds that the *Daily Record* was unlikely to be the centre of a diplomatic incident and that those among our readers who cared about who owned Everest were not likely to lie awake feeling they had been cheated. If poets could use poetic licence our headings could be allowed a little licence too. John went off unsatisfied and turned up again with the same story. I found myself thinking: 'Who am I to cause this decent man such distress?' and I told him to cancel the heading and get something else done. So the *Daily Record* went to press with some footling bald statement with no spirit nor colour to it.

I tried something once in *The Scotsman* of a longer-term character and it equally failed. I had been there for a few years when I realised I was becoming uneasy about the whole coverage of the House of Commons and the House of Lords and the business of Parliament in its committees, gallery and lobby work and all the rest. We had a very solid and in many ways an attractive team, ably sketching the day's work and missing nothing of importance. But every time I visited them I was becoming uncomfortable about the easy system they and their colleagues on other newspapers had constructed for themselves. The usual phrase was to describe Parliament as 'the finest club in the world' and it had become this for the journalists, whatever it had done for the Members of Parliament and peers. It was a study to walk through the corridors with one's lobby correspondent and hear him greet eminent statesmen and Prime Ministers on all sides with 'How's it going, Ted?' or 'Busy questions today, Harold?' and other amiable greetings. So it became clear to me that the parliamentary teams looked on themselves as a permanent element at Westminster. Prime Ministers and senior Secretaries of State came and went, but the recorders of the action were always there. So I proposed a scheme by which top-grade reporters and first-class writers, preferably younger than the average, would go on a rota to cover these parliamentary jobs for about three years at a time, and the whole team would be switched round and not become cosily dug in. The scheme was greeted with horror naturally by the Westminster team, but also, to my great surprise, by most of the senior team in Edinburgh at our head office. The general belief was that you needed to spend about twenty years at Westminster before you began to understand what it was all about. I knew that this was daft and a good reporter could get the hang of it in six months. And certainly if he had the talent and the independence he could steer clear of any easy-going manipulation of himself long before that time; but there was a great outcry of hurt feelings and wounded professional pride; of what-will-the-House-think pleas; you-can-have-my-resignation poutings. I realised I could not afford to drive it through since I was still on my own and there were hard competitive times ahead, so that I could not afford to deal with a running mutiny. Looking back I am sorry that the move didn't come off. It would have freshened up parliamentary reporting considerably and done the House of Commons, as well as my paper, a great deal of good.

As a newspaper man at heart I remain greatly grieved that we have failed to tell the public what we do and what we conceive our duty to be. Our job is to find out the facts and to print them. Most of the people we come in contact with are concerned to prevent us from learning the facts at all. Among these people are some whose forefathers died to win the freedom that we now exercise in their name. It is a freedom that affects us all and frankly it is too important to hand over to a few embattled and unsupported journalists. People always used to be talking to me about the responsibility of the press to the public and I used to say in reply that I was conscious of this great burden, which made me want to talk to them about the responsibility of the public to the press. These people we strived to serve, however inadequately, as they pass our lit windows tonight and every night, what do they know of our dim battles, with conscience and the law? What do they know of our search for truth?

CHAPTER FOURTEEN
Scotland

I have a covenant with Scotland. This is a theme which has sustained me since my youth and I had hoped to see some modest aims come to fruition in my time; it has given me great physical and spiritual rewards and adventures, although it cannot be said that Scotland got very much in return. Perhaps as I get older I find the theme ever a little more elusive, but I must try to sum it up.

I believe in Britain. I believe in a United Kingdom that is a *united* kingdom. This is very far from being what we have now. Nobody but us ever uses the word British. If you ever hear anyone else talk of Britain he is either a politician who has to watch out for the votes, or a businessman who has to mollify the workers in his Scottish branch factory. Or he is a Scot, for we use the word doggedly in the belief that our neighbours will catch on. We are the only ones who are trying to make the British idea work. No Englishman in his right mind ever refers to Britain when the word England will do, and the average Englishman thinks that somewhere along the line in his nation's long and not ignoble history they took over Scotland as some sort of subject province. In a way this is in fact what it has turned out to be. The Act of Union is nearly 300 years old. It was intended to set up a joint Parliament of England and Scotland, but in no time at all it had become an incorporating union, with Westminster continuing as the English Parliament plus a proportion of elected Scots representatives who won't get very far unless they appear to endorse specifically and implicitly the centralising theories that hold that body together. Outside of Scotland and in the rest of the world there is no Britain whatever. The name of Scotland has disappeared. This is an inexplicable thing to have happened to a country which was a nation longer than most; which was the basis of our present monarchy; where there were first spoken in all history words about freedom, democracy, independence, equality, the rights of people, and the dignity of man made in the image of God and other matters of interest and importance to the human race; which is a founder member of Great Britain and a mother country of the Commonwealth; and which in its time has made, out of all proportion to its size and population, significant contributions to all the sciences, all the arts, all the philosophies, most of the sports, many of the innovations, and even a few of the decencies.

'I am quite unable to account for this,' Neil Gunn once said. 'I know that it exists as part of that age-long, and now nearly successful, drive to annihilate all vestiges of the Celt. Any effort on the part of any section — such as Ireland or Wales or Scotland — of the Celtic fringe to form itself into a nation is not merely opposed but bitterly resented as if it were something in the nature of a betrayal of human progress.'

This is the stage of thought that has been now reached by many Scots, it seems. This is what we have come to. Dr Samuel Johnson, no great friend of the Scots, on his tour of the Hebrides had seen this danger and told one of the Macdonald chiefs: 'Your sons will be tamed into insignificance by an English education.' Unlike the sons of other nations who will not accept a serf status, the Scot abroad is not of much use to us except to subscribe to inoffensive causes. I once calculated for Tom Johnston that there were over 20 million people who were Scots or of Scottish descent in the whole of North America alone, but neither in Canada nor in America is there a Scottish vote nor a Scottish pressure group nor any minority wedge elbowing for some privilege for the old country. When the Scot goes abroad he tends to merge into the life of the country where he finds himself, and he often discovers there that by the grace of God he can put a hand to the shaping of political and industrial events, which is more than he can readily effect in his own country. I think we at home, whose mere continuing survival gives perspective to the whole world brotherhood of Scots, would prefer it that way. What needs to be done we can do at home ourselves.

My idea, ever since I was able to reach the conclusion in my remote younger days, was to reconstruct the whole method by which Britain is run. I do not say *Great* Britain, imagining that to be an arrogant and bumptious assertion. There are all kinds of ways of governing a country and of setting up its structure of political administration, and the one prevailing in Britain just now is about the worst that could possibly be contrived. If a group of the very best management consultants were set to the task of contriving a method of running Britain there might be some novel ideas and even differences of opinion, but not one of them would plump for the method we now have. My idea is a federal one. Members of the Establishment laugh outright when this is mentioned. It is a method which seems to work in the United States of America, in Canada, in Australia, and in most of Western Europe, and it is difficult to discover in what detail it would fall down in Britain. The ideal would be to have it set afoot simultaneously with a Scottish, Welsh and Northern Ireland Parliament for each of these countries; one for England unless they wanted to split it further; with an imperial Parliament in some central spot dealing with matters where there was an undoubted common interest. In my early simplicity I used to think this was an uncomplicated change and I believed at one time that a structure of this character would even attract the Irish Republic into

225

membership. They would have been quite welcome to come in as a Republic, not requiring to accept the Crown. But for weel or woe they belong to our group and they have shared many of our griefs and sorrows already. This will have to wait, as will some of the other elements. Wales has given up altogether for our lifetime, and Northern Ireland may now be beyond redemption, but Scotland could well and healthily go first and show how to make a go of a system that everybody adheres to except Westminster. There are great cries from official sources about the impossibility of 'setting up another layer of government', but this comes badly from a regime prepared, at a stroke, to eliminate the Greater London Council and other metropolitan boroughs simply because they have become troublesome to the centre.

As I travel round the world I hear no ready animosity expressed about Scotland in any of the countries of Europe nor elsewhere. Nothing in the long sacrifice of our pioneering generations seems to have stored up ill will or given us the name of unreliable or dishonest; and it may well be that with all these Scots already in place about the world we could establish a fifth column of goodwill here at home to carry the flag and give a new meaning to the name of the Commonwealth.

I have to assert the idea that on sheer grounds of efficiency something of this sort must be attempted soon. Britain is a badly run place, needing the decks cleared, and as I have said almost any system would be better than the one we have now. It has to be recognised that sentiments like this are popularly described, and dismissed, as nationalism. I occasionally meet a Scot who will tell me that nationalism is dangerous, leading to wars and strife and the deterioration of good relations between people; while he is himself an internationalist. When a man like that tells me he is an internationalist I know he is searching for an excuse for having done nothing for Scotland. These internationalists might do well to have a close look at the international situation which exists on their own border. Almost the only Scottish problem is England.

The English are truly a remarkable people. They are the supreme nationalists and their nationalism is of the most dangerous character because they do not come to it by any intellectual nor patriotic conclusion. It is already there instinctively in their bloodstream. Everything that is English is right, and anything that deviates from that canon is a foreign aberration, one of God's blunders, to be treated with amused tolerance or˙implacable hostility. Fate deals with them in a kindly way. If there is any luck going they have it. They have put about the notion that they are the masters of compromise. But if anything ever comes up that they have decided is their right, they will not yield. One of the great attitudes of mind, which has prevented Scotland for 1,000 years from being utterly engulfed by their flood is this — that the Scots are the only people in the world who have never underrated the English. In any proper system of government in the small British Islands, they would be natural and friendly allies and we could do great things together. But when the Act of Union comes at last to be rewritten it will have to be a cautious and safeguarded partnership, for they take their own world with them wherever they go and their own set of rules which they want to have adhered to, whatever has gone before. This must greatly have puzzled Edward Heath who negotiated our entry into the Common Market in the first abortive attempt, when in *The Scotsman* we pushed hard for a European presence in the EEC, campaigning to have Britain in at the time the Treaty of Rome was being written. When eventually Britain decided to join they thought the rules should be changed to accommodate them, although the thing was already a going concern. Heath also in discussion with some of us formulated the idea of a separate legislative and parliamentary Assembly for Scotland which his party adopted and then mutilated. Edward Heath seems to have sulked out of British politics, but his considerable contribution as our only major constitutional reformer of the twentieth century is still to be assessed.

The two major British political parties of the last fifty years have each blithely accepted the principle of some separate Scottish Assembly at least as a beginning. As soon as one or the other comes to power, however, the promise is laid aside. You will find it difficult to discover any kind of Scot in his own country who comes to any sort of accepted public eminence unless he conforms to the modish centralist and unionist theme, and yet these respecters of persons, for example in Parliament, invariably vote in favour of a new constitutional set-up for Scotland. My own experience is that I find it almost impossible to discover in Scotland any adult of whatever station who will claim that the present arrangement is the best that can be achieved, and who does not long for a new deal which would make the significant decision-taking for Scotland be taken in Scotland and not 400 miles away. Most of the people at Westminster, however concerned they are at the predicaments of the world, think nothing of Scotland and will give no time to our concerns. Once, sitting in the official box in the House of Commons during the passage of an important Scottish bill, I heard this dialogue from two English members as they herded to the division lobby:

'What's this?'

'Oh, some Scotch thing.'

For myself I thought for many years that this would have been settled in my own lifetime and that I should at least have been a witness, if not a participant, in a Scotland engaged in a new and rich partnership, on equal terms again, doing the best things for ourselves here at home and setting free the abounding talents and the spirit of the Scot in his own place. Even if this is not to be in my time I am certain that before long it will prevail, because I cannot believe that my kinsmen, for all they have done, for all the beliefs and dogmas they have shaken, will be content to dwindle into a provisional destiny; and even, like the eunuchs and racial slaves of ancient Greece, to accept a name that is not their own, and to deny their own fathers.

In my personal destiny, whatever it may be, I find much still to hearten me. I have changed, but the hills have not changed. If they cannot now restore my one-time agility, they restore my soul. And when I go on them I go sometimes with my two sons, who came to a love of them without any inducement from me. From their youngest days I tried not to bore them with any long-winded tales of beauty and prowess and the pleasures of simply being in country places where their heritage lies. They came to it themselves. Ninian was scarcely seventeen when he too, not prompted by me, took to the hills and the far places with a small tent and a sleeping bag and went away alone for weeks at a time. Mungo, who has been more with me, found it all for himself and is able to see me safely up some hills where I used to bound, going ahead of me and steering me round the difficult places as if I didn't know them already, although I seem to have ceased to stride so freely across the rough parts. When the three of us go together into the far Highlands my role is to take the first steps with them and then come back and get the picnic ready while they go to the high ridges and come back to me. If, as some clever people say, this is the only immortality we shall ever know, it has been a great reward to be going on with: and there has been a lot of fun in the by-going, among friends.

INDEX

230